The Wondering Brain

Thinking about Religion with and beyond Cognitive Neuroscience

Kelly Bulkeley

Routledge
New York • London

Published in 2005 by
Routledge
Taylor & Francis Group
270 Madison Avenue
New York, NY 10016
www.routledge-ny.com

Published in Great Britain by
Routledge
Taylor & Francis Group
2 Park Square
Milton Park, Abingdon
Oxon OX14 4RN
www.routledge.co.uk

Printed in the United States of America on acid-free paper.

10 9 8 7 6 5 4 3 2 1

Library of Congress Cataloging-in-Publication Data is available from the Library of Congress.

ISBN 0-415-93840-6 (hc: alk. paper)
ISBN 0-415-93841-4 (pb: alk. paper)

"This sense of wonder is the mark of the philosopher. Philosophy indeed has no other origin, and he was a good genealogist who made Iris the daughter of Thaumas."

Socrates, *Theaetetus*

"O, wonder! How many goodly creatures are there here! How beauteous mankind is! O brave new world that has such people in't!"

Miranda, *The Tempest*

"Man is the animal whose nature has not yet been fixed."

Friedrich Nietzsche, *Beyond Good and Evil*

For Conor, Maya, and Dylan

Acknowledgments

Many people have contributed support and guidance in the writing of this book, so many indeed that I can hardly find adequate words to express my appreciation. Sarah White of Franklin and Marshall College sparked an early interest in the subject of this book with her question about Socrates, dreams, and "philosophical wonder." Nick Street was the first editor at Routledge to encourage my efforts in writing about wonder, and after him Damian Treffs and William Germano helped shape and refine my manuscript, with the able assistance of Gilad Foss. Luis Galvez could not have been more friendly and accommodating in helping create the book's illustrations. I had the opportunity to present my ideas to several different audiences and receive valuable feedback from them, and for that I thank the following: The International Association for the Study of Dreams; The Center for Theology and the Natural Sciences; the steering committees of the Person, Culture, and Religion Group and the Religion and the Social Sciences Section of the American Academy of Religion; and the students and faculty of the Graduate Theological Union, John F. Kennedy University, Santa Clara University, Harvard Divinity School, and St. Lawrence University. I owe special gratitude to the many friends and colleagues who offered their generous counsel as I developed the book, including David Kahn, G. William Domhoff, Marcia Hermansen, Tom Traub, Steven Bauman, Lewis Rambo, Franz Metcalf, James Jones, Roger Lohmann, Kelley Raab, Kimberley Patton, Don Browning, Diane Jonte-Pace, William Parsons, Jeffrey Kripal, Lee Irwin, Ed Pace-Schott, Nina Azari, Jonathon Feit, Dolores Nice-Siegenthaler, Lewis Rambo, Obadiah Harris, Jeremy Taylor, Tracey Kahan, John McDargh, Pamela Cooper-White, and G. William Barnard. And, to Hilary, Dylan, Maya, and Conor, words will never be enough to say how much I love and appreciate you all.

Table of Contents

Introduction

Introduction

I. Spheres of Wonder

This is a book about wonder. Specifically, it is a book that seeks a deeper understanding of wonder by means of a new integration of religious studies (RS) and cognitive neuroscience (CN). Pursuing such an integration might seem a quixotic quest given the long history of antagonism between religion and science, a bitter history that continues right into the present day. Particularly in the United States, where many religious communities are hostile to evolutionary theory and many scientists are scornful of spiritual belief, the prospects for greater mutual comprehension appear bleak. Even more unlikely is the possibility that religious and scientific perspectives could ever work together in the study of human life. Yet, that is exactly the goal of this book, and a primary inspiration is the pioneering work of Sigmund Freud, Carl Jung, William James, and other researchers in the psychology of religion. In the early years of the twentieth century they used the most advanced scientific psychology of their day to investigate religion, culture, art, and creativity. The time has come for us in the early years of the twenty-first century to use the most advanced scientific psychology of *our* day to push their investigations in new directions, opening up new vistas of scientific knowledge and spiritual insight.

Wonder, as I will employ the term, is *the feeling excited by an encounter with something novel and unexpected, something that strikes a person as intensely real, true, and/or beautiful.*[1] As will be seen in coming chapters, experiences of wonder have played a significant role in many of the world's religious, spiritual, and artistic traditions from ancient times right into the present day. Experiences of wonder have also been crucial but unappreciated inspirations for new philosophical discoveries, scientific progress, and technological innovations. Wonder may be experienced in a variety of settings, but it occurs with special regularity in four spheres: visionary dreaming, sexual desire, aesthetic experience, and contemplative practice. These four spheres of wonder will be discussed, each in their turn, in the four main chapters of this book.

To feel wonder is to experience a sudden *decentering* of the self. Facing something surprisingly new and unexpectedly powerful, one's ordinary sense of personal identity is dramatically altered, leading to new knowledge and understanding that ultimately *recenter* the self. The profound impact of this decentering and recentering process is evident in both the intense memorability of the experiences and the strong bodily sensations that often accompany them. People speak of being stunned, dazed, breathtaken, overwhelmed, consumed, astonished — all gesturing toward a mode of experience that exceeds ordinary language and thought and yet inspires a yearning to explore, understand, and learn. This is where the noun "wonder" transforms into the verb "to wonder," where the powerful emotional experience stimulates lively curiosity, knowledge-seeking behavior, and critical questioning: "And it makes me wonder...."

If we take any interest in experiences of wonder as a prominent feature of human life — particularly religious life — an opening immediately presents itself to CN because such experiences may be identified as psychophysiological phenomena that involve distinctive (if unusually intensified) modes of brain–mind activation. This is the opening I wish to explore here. The initial question may be stated as follows: What can we say, based on current CN research, about the activity of the brain–mind system during experiences of wonder?

By carefully examining the major findings of current neuroscientific research we will develop a knowledge of the brain–mind processes most likely involved in different types of wonder. We will then use that hard-won CN knowledge to address a second question: What can these findings contribute to the interpretive efforts of scholars who are trying to understand the diverse phenomenology of human religiosity, what William James termed the "varieties of religious experience?" As James did in his Gifford Lectures of 1901–02, I will try to answer that question by making frequent use of case studies of both historical and contemporary people, individuals whose experiences of wonder provide us with evidence of creative new patterns of extraordinary brain–mind functioning. Although cognitive neuroscientists are highly suspicious of the reliability of subjective reports, introspection remains an indispensable source of insight into the fullness of human experience — not the *only* source, but perhaps the best source for some purposes, and certainly a source that has to be taken seriously in brain–mind research. Antonio Damasio puts the point well: "Whether one likes it or not, *all* the contents in our minds are subjective, and the power of science comes from its ability to verify objectively the consistency of many individual subjectivities."[2] This is the spirit that will animate the various case studies to come. I am seeking to authenticate the "consistency of many individual subjectivities" in experiences of wonder.

In addition to case studies of particular individuals, we will also discuss experiences of wonder in relation to diverse forms of cultural expression, from ancient myths and sacred texts to philosophical dialogues, literature, poetry, music, and cinema. Wonder as experienced in creative actions, wonder as evocatively portrayed within a work of art, wonder as felt by audiences when encountering and experiencing cultural creations — these are recurrent themes that will be woven throughout the book as we move from "real" wonder to "fictional" wonder and back again.

At the same time as we use CN to investigate religion and spirituality, we will apply the critical resources of religious studies to brain–mind science in order to elucidate dimensions of meaning and significance that neuroscientists themselves do not, and perhaps cannot, recognize. A good place to start is with the so-called "nature vs. nurture" debate. CN continues the long-standing Western tradition of agitated philosophical puzzlement over the precise relationship between the natural foundations of human existence (e.g., our genes, bodies, instincts) and the nurturing influences of culture (e.g., child-rearing, language, ritual, music). One gets the sense in reading the mainstream works of CN that most researchers assume, despite faint protestations to the contrary, that the nature side is much the stronger, and eventually scientists will be able to explain all the effects of cultural nurturance in strictly naturalistic terms. But CN research is generating a great deal of evidence that demonstrates the direct and measurable impact of human cultural behavior on the physical development of neural circuitry and structuring. *Cultural phenomena shape the brain.* It is a simple point, really, but one that CN researchers themselves have not fully appreciated. Among its many implications, this means that fields such as RS that specialize in the study of human culture are in an excellent position to identify patterns, processes, and interactions that CN researchers are not trained to recognize.

This will be the rhythm of the following chapters — a lively dance between energetics and hermeneutics, a spiraling movement between the explanations of cognitive neuroscience and the interpretations of religious studies. Where, in the end, will this dance lead? To a fuller understanding of certain types of rare but extremely vivid experiences that people throughout history and all over the world have considered to be among the most important and decisive events of their lives, and to a new vantage on human nature that reveals the self-transcending capacities of the human brain–mind system, capacities that have evolved with explosive speed in the brief history of our species and *are continuing to evolve right now.*

The conclusion of the book will discuss one of the most troubling ethical and political implications of the human capacity for wonder — the relationship between wonder and war. From the earliest human prehistory right through to the present, from the thousand-ship siege of Troy to the "shock and awe" assault on Baghdad, martial violence has always had the power to evoke a kind of reverential joy and visceral admiration. CN and RS scholars will find common ground here if nowhere else: The wondrous, awful allure of warfare is deeply rooted in the human psyche.

II. Presidential Proclamation 6158

Following these observations on war and wonder, and as a way of more precisely contextualizing recent developments in brain–mind science, I want to highlight the key symbolic event in the recent history of cognitive neuroscience: the proclamation by President George H.W. Bush announcing that the 1990s were officially to be known as the "Decade of the Brain." Here is the full text of President Bush's proclamation:

> Presidential Proclamation 6158
> July 17, 1990
> By the President of the United States of America
>
> A Proclamation
>
> The human brain, a 3-pound mass of interwoven nerve cells that controls our activity, is one of the most magnificent — and mysterious — wonders of creation. The seat of human intelligence, interpreter of senses, and controller of movement, this incredible organ continues to intrigue scientists and layman alike.
>
> Over the years, our understanding of the brain — how it works, what goes wrong when it is injured or diseased — has increased dramatically. However, we still have much more to learn. The need for continued study of the brain is compelling: Millions of Americans are affected each year by disorders of the brain ranging from neurogenetic diseases to degenerative disorders such as Alzheimer's, as well as stroke, schizophrenia, autism, and impairments of speech, language, and hearing.
>
> Today, these individuals and their families are justifiably hopeful, for a new era of discovery is dawning in brain research. Powerful microscopes, major strides in the study of genetics, and advances in brain imaging devices are giving physicians and scientists ever greater insight into the brain. Neuroscientists are mapping the brain's biochemical circuitry, which may help produce more effective drugs for alleviating the suffering of those who have Alzheimer's or Parkinson's disease. By studying how the brain's cells and chemicals develop, interact, and communicate with the rest of the body, investigators are also developing improved treatments for people incapacitated by spinal cord injuries, depressive disorders, and epileptic seizures. Breakthroughs in molecular genetics show great promise of yielding methods to treat and prevent Huntington's disease, the muscular dystrophies, and other life-threatening disorders.
>
> Research may also prove valuable in our war on drugs, as studies provide greater insight into how people become addicted to drugs and how drugs affect the brain. These studies may also help produce effective treatments for chemical dependency and help us to understand and prevent the

harm done to the preborn children of pregnant women who abuse drugs and alcohol. Because there is a connection between the body's nervous and immune systems, studies of the brain may also help enhance our understanding of Acquired Immune Deficiency Syndrome.

Many studies regarding the human brain have been planned and conducted by scientists at the National Institutes of Health, the National Institute of Mental Health, and other Federal research agencies. Augmenting Federal efforts are programs supported by private foundation and industry. The cooperation between these agencies and the multidisciplinary efforts of thousands of scientists and health care professionals provide powerful evidence of our nation's determination to conquer brain disease.

To enhance public awareness of the benefits to be derived from brain research, the Congress, by House Joint Resolution 174, has designated the decade beginning January 1, 1990, as the "Decade of the Brain" and has authorized and requested the President to issue a proclamation in observance of this occasion.

Now, therefore, I, George Bush, President of the United States of America, do hereby proclaim the decade beginning January 1, 1990, as the Decade of the Brain. I call upon all public officials and the people of the United States to observe that decade with appropriate programs, ceremonies, and activities.

In Witness Whereof, I have hereunto set my hand this seventeenth day of July, in the year of our Lord nineteen hundred and ninety, and of the Independence of the United States of America the two hundred and fifteenth.

GEORGE BUSH

[Filed with the Office of the *Federal Register*, 12:11 p.m., July 18, 1990]

No one could deny that the rapid expansion of CN research during the 1990s would have occurred even without the blessing of a presidential proclamation. The increasing sophistication of neuroimaging technologies during the 1970s and 1980s had already convinced the medical research community to devote major financial resources to further CN studies, so a tremendous surge in new knowledge was bound to come despite what the politicians might say. Even still, the beneficial impact of Proclamation 6158 on the subsequent growth of brain–mind research should not be underestimated. President Bush's formal expression of support from the highest levels of the national government validated the status of CN as a preeminent authority on questions of normal and abnormal modes of human functioning. Most forms of CN research, particularly those involving neuroimaging, are quite expensive, and as a consequence CN is heavily dependent on the financial backing of large private institutions and governmental agencies. In a world of fierce competition between scientists grasping for precious grant monies, the imprimatur of a presidential proclamation must have given an extra competitive edge to CN researchers.

The proclamation starts with a sentence of surprising eloquence, something one might not expect from a president who frankly admitted that he had little interest in the "vision thing." The phrase "one of the most magnificent — and mysterious — wonders of creation" aptly expresses the feelings of many CN researchers who have devoted their lives to the study of an organ they believe holds the key to profound truths and fundamental realities of human existence. The mention of "creation" allows a hint of theism to enter the proclamation, enough anyhow to deflect objections from politically powerful conservative Christians who might take offense at a seeming idolatry of the brain, but not so much as to discomfort the Darwinian sensibilities of the scientists who actually do the research.[3]

Overall, the first paragraph of the proclamation strikes a tone of remarkable humility, openness, and aesthetic appreciation, promoting the idea that a reverential sense of wonder should serve as the primary guiding principle in future studies of the brain. Here is something that nearly all of us — religious and scientific people alike — can agree is worthy of our admiration and deserving of our energetic study.

In the next paragraph, however, the tone abruptly shifts toward more pragmatic concerns with the instrumentality of brain science — what it can *do* for us. Current scientific knowledge is divided into two categories, "how [the brain] works [and] what goes wrong when it is injured or diseased," and the next three paragraphs are devoted exclusively to the latter category, providing an increasingly specific agenda for researchers to pursue in developing treatments for neurological maladies afflicting a significant percentage of the (voting) population.

Any doubt about the influence of political interests in the proclamation is put to rest in the fourth paragraph, where brain research is explicitly recruited into the president's "war on drugs," the controversial, ideologically charged effort to eliminate the use of certain psychoactive substances. Immediately following, in a grudging gesture to the president's political opponents, mention is made of the benefits of future brain research for understanding acquired immune deficiency syndrome (AIDS). Compared to the earlier comments about specific diseases, the sentence about AIDS is notably detached and impersonal, with no expression of any hope for a cure, just the possible "enhance[ment]" of knowledge.

While everyone may agree on the paramount importance of trying to help people with schizophrenia, Alzheimer's disease, autism, drug addictions, and (even) AIDS, the exclusive focus of Proclamation 6158 on "disorders of the brain" represents an unnecessarily narrow vision of what brain–mind science can teach us. *Beyond* curing disorders and malfunctions, brain–mind science has the potential to enhance our understanding of healthy humans in their full vitality and creative flourishing. Lamentably, Proclamation 6158 says nothing about any of that; the "Decade of the Brain" is wholly dedicated to the elimination of pathology and abnormality, as a muscular expression "of our nation's determination to conquer brain disease."

Now that we are well into the first decade of the new millennium, the many benefits from the disease-oriented research agenda of the 1990s are easy to recognize, and many of us owe our very lives to recent advances in the medical treatment of strokes, seizures, depression, etc. But few researchers in either CN or RS have taken on the task of trying to understand what recent discoveries in brain–mind science can tell us about the special dynamics of human health. We know more than we ever did about how to eliminate suffering, but we still do not know nearly enough about the development of a capacity for creative vitality, let alone about spiritual experience and religious revelation. Proclamation 6158 illustrates the problem perfectly. In its rousing call to neuroscientific battle against illness, it never bothers to mention what exactly life without disease might look like. This problem is all the greater because it is so rarely recognized as such. True health is not simply the lack of illness; it has its own phenomenology that can be studied, understood, and consciously guided. I caution readers not to be fooled by the boastful theories of "how the mind works" that permeate CN — these are usually little more than schematic renderings of generic cognitive functioning, with no concern for the experiential richness and dynamism of a flourishing human life. If we want to learn more about the distinctive qualities of human health, we need to look beyond pathology and beyond the mechanical workings of the mind. We need to look carefully, critically, and empathetically at particular experiences in which people's powers of creative living manifest themselves in especially vibrant forms. The following study of wonder is a contribution to that effort.

1

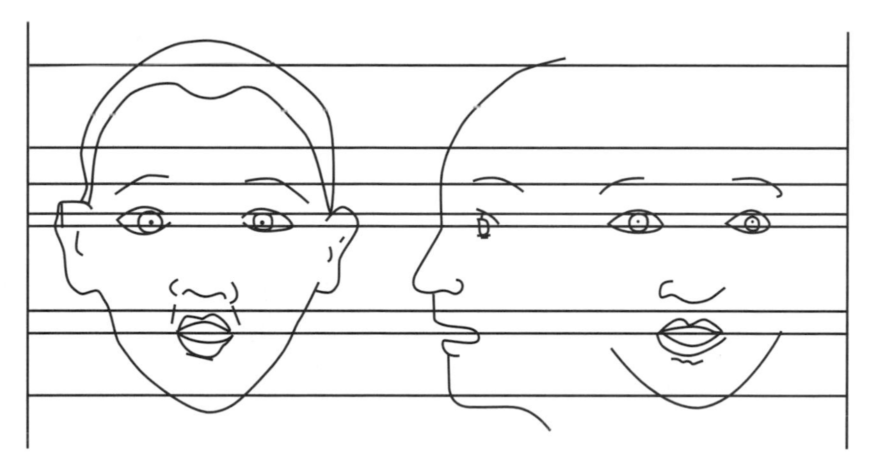

L'Admiration — Wonder

Dreams and Visions

1
Dreams and Visions

I. The Young Man's Dreams

A young man sits alone in a rented room. The fire blazing in the hearth warms his chamber against the cold, snowy winds outside. He is a gentleman, born of an honorable family, so he lacks no material comforts. To all appearances he is a cultured, well-mannered gentleman of leisure. The young man, however, knows better. He has left that respectable, normal family background behind and chosen to follow a very different path. Now twenty-three years old, he has journeyed far from his home, during a time of bitter warfare, to this innocuous little town where he knows practically no one. His father is angry with him; today was to be the day the young man officially entered the family profession, but instead he is here, without a profession, all by himself in a small, warm room. Thinking.

He is thinking about what to do with his life. He yearns for a cause; he wants to give himself wholly to something *real*, something he can trust without any doubt or hesitation, something that is worth the complete devotion of his considerable intellectual energies. Yes, the young man can feel those energies rising up within him, and he can feel grand designs and sweeping plans taking shape in his imagination — but to his increasing frustration he has no distinctly formed idea of what exactly he should *do* with himself. Sitting before the fire, the young man thinks, and thinks, and thinks. In time, a violent agitation rises up and seizes his mind. It feels as if his brain has taken fire, burning like the reddish flames dancing in the hearth, and then he suddenly realizes what it is he is seeking — the *truth*. Nothing more, nothing less than the truth. Pure and everlasting, stripped clean of all the opinions, biases, and superstitions that befuddle ordinary people's minds, the ultimate foundations of Creation and thus the divine commands of God Himself. This is what the young man desires.

Now that he has answered with such perfect clarity the question of *what* he desires, he can concentrate on the practical process of how to achieve it. The quest for truth will henceforth be the supreme, overarching cause of the young man's life — his own personal "profession." Exhausted by his long meditations and yet completely filled with enthusiasm by his new discovery, the young man goes to sleep…

> His imagination felt itself struck by the representation of some ghosts who presented themselves to him and who so frightened him that, thinking that he was walking down the streets, he had to lean to his left side in order to be able to reach the place where he wanted to go, because he felt a great weakness on his right side so that he could not hold himself upright. Because he was ashamed to walk in this way, he tried to straighten up, but he was buffeted by gusts that carried him off in a sort of a whirlwind that spun him around three or four times on his left foot. Even this was not what alarmed him. His difficulty in dragging himself along made him think that he would fall at each step until, noticing a school open along his way, he entered in search of refuge and a remedy for his trouble. He tried to reach the school church, where his first thought was to say his prayers; however, having noticed that he had passed an acquaintance without greeting him, he wanted to retrace his steps to pay his respects but was thrust back by the wind that was blowing against the church. At the same time, he saw another person in the middle of the school courtyard who addressed him by name in kind and polite terms and told him that, if he wanted to go to find Mr. N., he had something to give him. The young man imagined that it was a melon from a foreign land. What surprised him more was to see that those who clustered around that person in order to talk with him were upright and steady on their feet, although he was still bent over and unsteady on the same ground. Having almost knocked him down many times, the wind had greatly abated.
>
> He woke up imagining this and then felt a real pain, which made him fear that it had been the work of some Evil Spirit who had wanted to seduce him. Immediately, he turned over onto his right side, for he had slept and dreamed on his left side. He prayed that God would protect him from the evil effects of his dream and preserve him from all of the miseries that could threaten him as punishment for his sins, which he acknowledged to be great enough to call down upon his head thunderbolts of heaven, although he had led a more or less blameless life in the eyes of men. In this situation, he fell asleep after an interval of almost two hours spent on various thoughts on good and evil in this life.
>
> Immediately, a new dream came to him in which he thought that he heard a sudden, loud noise, which he took for thunder. Terrified, he

awoke at once. Having opened his eyes, he noticed many sparks of fire scattered around the room. He had experienced this phenomenon on many other occasions, and it did not seem too strange to him, when he awoke in the middle of the night, that his eyes sparkled enough that he could make out the objects closest to him, but this time he wanted to find a reason for it, and he was able to reassure himself about his mind/spirit. After having opened and closed his eyes in turn and observed what was represented to him, he saw that his terrors faded away, and he fell asleep again quite calmly.

A moment afterward he had a third dream, unlike the first two, about which there was nothing frightful. In this last dream, he found a book on his table without having any idea who had put it there. He opened it and saw that it was a dictionary, which delighted him, because he hoped that it might be very useful to him. At the same moment, he noticed that another book came to hand which was no less new to him. He did not know from whence it had come. He discovered that it was a collection of poems by different authors, entitled *Corpus Poetarum*. He was curious to read some of it, and, opening the book, he chanced upon this verse:

What way in life shall I follow?

Just then he noticed a man whom he did not know. This unknown man gave him a piece of poetry that began with these words:

Yes and No.

The man recommended it to him as an excellent piece. The young man told him that he knew this verse: It was one of the *Idylls of Ausonius* included in the big anthology of poetry on the table. He wanted to show it to this man and began to leaf through the book, the order and scheme of which he boasted of knowing perfectly. While he searched for the passage, the man asked him where he had gotten this book, and the young man answered that he could not say how he happened to have it, but that a moment before he had leafed through still another book that had just disappeared, although he did not know either who had brought it to him or who had taken it away again. He had not finished when he saw the other book reappear at the other end of the table, but he saw that this dictionary was no longer as complete as the one he had seen the first time.

Nevertheless, he came to the poems of Ausonius in the anthology through which he paged, and, although he could not find the poem beginning with the words "Yes and No," he told this man that he knew another one by the same poet that was still finer. It began with the words "What way in life shall I follow?" The person begged him to show it to

> him, and the young man set himself the task of trying to find it. Then he happened upon several little portraits engraved by copperplate, which led him to remark that this was a very handsome book but that it was not the same edition as the one that he knew.
>
> It was at this point that the books and the man disappeared. They vanished from the young man's imagination, although they did not awaken him.
>
> It is a most remarkable thing that, wondering whether what he had seen was a dream or a vision, he not only decided that it was a dream while he was still asleep but also interpreted it before he was fully awake.[1]

Not, perhaps, the clearest message in the history of divine revelations; still, these three dreams had the tangible effect on the young man of stimulating a powerful sense of wonder. All the qualities discussed in the Introduction appear here in vivid form: the surprise, the strong physiological impact, the memorable encounter with deep truths and realities, the decentering of one's ordinary sense of selfhood, the quickening curiosity, and the impulse to new exploration. In the young man's case, the experience of wonder via dreaming stands in surprising contrast to his waking thoughts of the previous days. Coming the night immediately following his exultant discovery of the new supreme purpose of his life, his dreams are remarkable for their absence of just those qualities he is seeking in his waking life — clarity, simplicity, and unity of purpose. The dreams shuttle him around to various locations where things appear and disappear at random, where people behave in unexpected ways, and where ordinary volitional control of his body has been inexplicably disrupted. The bizarrely disjointed nature of the experience naturally raises the skeptical question: As wonderful as these dreams may appear, could they in fact be essentially meaningless? If so, is there any point or purpose to trying to understand them?

Later in the chapter we will hear what the young man himself made of his decidedly messy and complex dreams and how he interpreted them both during and after their occurrence. Right now, I would like to focus on what the young man said about the *origins* of the dreams. After he wrote out the text of the dreams and their interpretations in a special journal, he went on to explain that the Spirit who had aroused in him the enthusiasm with which he had felt his "brain on fire" for the past several days had predicted these dreams before he had gone to bed. He furthermore insisted that his "human mind had nothing to do with them."

The story of this young man represents an especially dramatic illustration of something that is in fact a widespread phenomenon in human history: experiences of wonder generated in and through extraordinary dreams. Research in the comparative study of religion has made abundantly clear the historical and cross-cultural frequency of intensely memorable dreams that strike people with awe and amazement.[2] What makes this young man's case so interesting is that he guides our attention straight to the vivid paradox that lies at the core of these highly unusual experiences. On the one hand, the young man's dreams are thoroughly *embodied*; he says his "brain is on fire," he feels his body being spun around, he experiences a variety of physical sensations and emotional reactions, he speaks with other people, and he touches various material objects. His physical self is completely immersed in the experience. On the other hand, the young man insists that his "human mind had nothing to do" with the dreams — they happen *to* him, independently of his will. Struggling quite literally to keep his balance, the young man does his best during the dreams to make sense of the strange forces and inexplicable happenings he encounters. When he awakens, he feels an immediate certainty that the dreams are genuine revelations, and he attributes their ultimate cause to Divine powers transcending his embodied self.

Again, a skeptical question immediately presents itself: Could this paradox simply be a meaningless self-contradiction, the inconsequential product of the young man's confused and agitated mental condition? It would be easy to answer "yes" to that question, just as it is always easy to dismiss the significance of anything that does not comfortably fit into our common assumptions about what constitutes the normal range of human experience. But this is exactly what moments of wonder do to us — they forcibly propel us outside that normal range of experience, shattering our preconceptions, disclosing new possibilities, and revealing previously unknown dimensions of reality. To understand the meaningfulness of the young man's dreams and, indeed, to understand any experience of wonder, this first step must be taken: admitting that ordinary modes of analysis and explanation will not be sufficient, precisely because wonder is that which transcends the ordinary. To gain deeper knowledge in this realm of extraordinary experience, we must be open to the surprising and the unexpected, we must resist the skeptic's temptation to reduce and dismiss, and above all we must be patient with the creative labor of integrating widely divergent points of view.

II. "Brain on Fire": A First Look at Cognitive Neuroscience

Let us take as an initial point of departure the young man's comment that he felt his "brain was on fire." Whatever else we may want to say about his experience, its powerful impact on him derived in no small measure from the intense physiological activation of his embodied self, particularly the neural operations of his brain. The nature and functioning of the brain is, of course, the primary concern of cognitive neuroscience (CN), and this is a good time to lay out some basic findings of current research in the field. The brain lies at the terminal end of the central nervous system (CNS) (Figure 1.1), which functions as an information conduit receiving data from the sense organs and transmitting commands to all parts of the body.

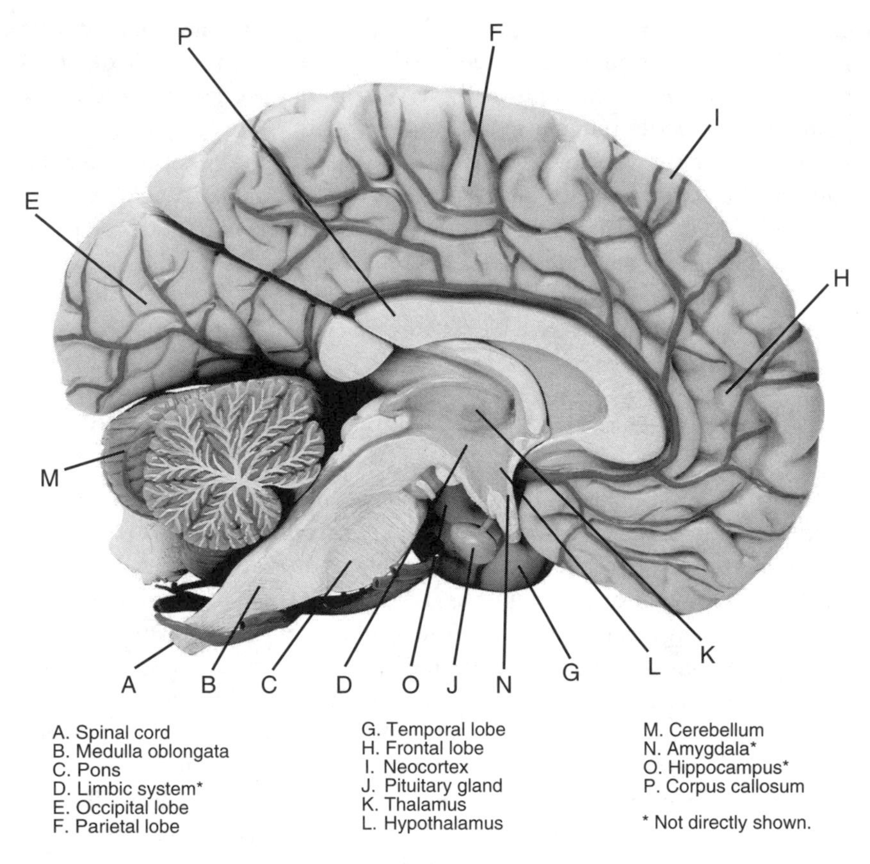

Figure 1.1 Cross-section of the human brain.

The basic anatomical plan of the CNS first emerged in evolution among ocean dwellers such as the jellyfish and sea anemone, creatures that developed networks of nerve cells that increased their ability for coordinated movement and adaptive response to different environmental conditions. In species appearing later in evolution, such as the earthworm, the nerve cells came to be organized in tubular networks culminating in a relatively large bulbous structure in the head that connects and coordinates the various nerve cells running through the organism's body. This neural structure is the anatomical foundation for the human brain.

In humans the central nervous system is commonly divided into seven main parts: the spinal cord, medulla oblongata, pons, cerebellum, midbrain, diencephalon, and the cerebral hemispheres. Compared to other mammalian species, the human brain is distinguished by a vastly expanded cerebral *cortex* (the Latin word for "bark"), the heavily wrinkled outer layer. Although humans do not have the largest brains in absolute terms, we do possess the greatest brain size relative to body size, and much of that can be attributed to the unusually large development of our cerebral cortex. Also known as the *neocortex*, this is the newest part of the brain in evolutionary terms, and its surprisingly fast emergence has puzzled CN researchers. Richard Thompson comments, "The remarkable and still mysterious explosion in brain size of the developing humans took place within the past 3 million years or so, beginning with *Homo erectus*.... As yet we have no very clear understanding of why this happened. The massive change in the human brain over the short span of 3 million years is unprecedented in the evolution of other species."[3]

The cerebral cortex is conventionally divided into four lobes: occipital, parietal, frontal, and temporal. Enough evidence has accumulated from the three main sources of CN research data (lesion studies, animal experiments, and neuroimaging) to provide several insights into the anatomical localization of certain behavioral and psychological functions. Readers who know something of the history of psychology have likely noticed striking similarities between CN and the now disreputable practice of phrenology, a quasi-scientific discipline founded by Franz Josef Gall in Europe in the late 1700s which flourished for several decades and attracted the enthusiastic interest of a broad public audience. Phrenologists boldly claimed they could identify precise correlations between external features of the skull and internal processes in the brain, thus giving them penetrating insights into an individual's personality and moral character. The contemporary echoes of phrenology are real, as CN research does indeed follow the same intellectual program of examining minute physiological details of the cerebrum as a means of gaining new knowledge of human psychological functioning. Not everyone, however, hears these echoes in the same way. Antonio Damasio, whose work we will consider in more detail later in the chapter, rejects any such comparisons between phrenology and CN. Damasio argues that contemporary CN researchers are going far beyond facile anatomical localizations to identify complex neural systems of many functionally integrated brain regions:

> We can now say with confidence that there are no single "centers" for vision, or language, or for that matter, reason or social behavior. There are "systems" made up of several interconnected brain units.... This is most important: What determines the contribution of a given brain unit to the operation of the system to which it belongs is not just the structure of the unit but also its *place* in the system.... I am not falling into the phrenological trap. To put it simply: The mind results from the operation of each of the separate components, and from the concerted operation of the multiple systems constituted by those separate components.[4]

Damasio's phrase "phrenological trap" is a good one to keep in mind as we proceed. A recurrent theme in the pages that follow regards the difficulty of determining with any degree of precision how psychological experience and neural anatomy are connected. By repudiating the phrenological trap Damasio wants to emphasize how contemporary CN research has developed a more sophisticated understanding of that crucial connection between mind and body. Phrenology was too crude, too simplistic, and, worst of all, too speculative; CN, by contrast, is firmly grounded in empirical data produced by new imaging technologies that have revolutionized our knowledge of the brain. CN researchers have developed highly refined models showing how mental functioning depends on systemic interactions of multiple cerebral regions.

Later on we will return to the question of whether or not Damasio and his CN colleagues succeed in their efforts to avoid falling into the phrenological trap. What should not be lost in this mind–body debate, however, is how little of the brain can even speculatively be assigned a specific mental function. Vast regions of neural anatomy remain *terra incognita*, and not simply because CN mapmakers have not yet applied their neuroimaging technologies to those areas; rather, it appears that enormous portions of the cerebral cortex are not innately programmed to perform any one function but are potentially available to play active roles in a variety of neural systems and psychological processes. Thompson describes the state of neuroanatomy like this:

> Authorities disagree on the number of areas in the human cerebral cortex; estimates range from a few to over 200. Everyone agrees, however, on the basic sensory areas and the motor area. The remainder of the cerebral cortex is arbitrarily called *association cortex*. We are only just beginning to understand the functions of some of the association areas, which occupy a great deal of the cerebral cortex in humans and other primates. Interestingly, the basic organization of the primary sensory and motor areas of the cerebral cortex is virtually the same in all mammals, from the rat to the human. As one ascends the mammalian scale of evolution, however, both the brain's absolute size and the relative amount of association cortex increase strikingly.[5]

This large portion of genetically uncommitted cortex plays a vital role in all those mental functions that intervene between sensory inputs and motor outputs.[6] Any time you recollect a past experience, any time you consider different options for a future action, any time you fantasize about something that does not exist, the association areas of your brain are likely to be activated. The integrative power and expansive potential of the association cortex are key features of distinctively human consciousness, and CN researchers have begun to devote more of their resources to improving scientific knowledge of the neural circuitry in these cortical regions.

It is hoped that our study of wonder will contribute to that research, because experiences of wonder by definition push the brain–mind system beyond its normal range of functioning, forcing it to make sense of extremely unusual input. Because experiences of wonder are encounters with the novel and unexpected, they defy conventional associative categories and transgress the normal boundaries of understanding. More than that, they stimulate an expanded development of those crucial mental processes that intervene between sensory input and motor output. Experiences of wonder quite literally stretch our minds.

Deep within the cerebral cortex is a region that Pierre Paul Broca, one of the pioneers of modern neuroscience, termed the "limbic lobe" because of its continuity with the phylogenetically more primitive regions of the brainstem (the term "limbic" comes from the Latin word *limbus*, for "border"). Contemporary neuroscientists no longer speak of a separate limbic lobe but rather of a limbic system located deep within the temporal lobe.[7] The evolutionary appearance of the limbic system in the brains of other creatures seems closely connected with the importance of a sense of smell: "In relatively primitive beasts, such as the crocodile, much of the limbic forebrain has to do with olfaction, the complex analysis of the intensity, quality, and direction of odors."[8] In humans, the limbic system is a multimodal sensory association area that serves the twin functions of emotional evaluation and memory creation. The limbic system receives input from all sensory systems, evaluates that input in terms of its emotional salience, and, if the input is sufficiently important, stores it in memory. Information from the limbic system is then projected to various regions in the frontal lobes, where it is subjected to what most neuroscientists refer to as "the highest brain functions — conscious thought, perception, and goal-directed action."[9]

The limbic system includes several structures that have received extensive study. Most important for our purposes are the hippocampus and the amygdala. The *hippocampus* (Greek for "seahorse") is chiefly responsible for laying down new memories, particularly the spatial features of experiences with a strong emotional charge. Damage to the hippocampus disrupts a person's ability to form new memories. The plight of a hippocampus-deprived life is depicted with great dramatic power in Christopher Nolan's film *Memento* (2001). Adjacent to the hippocampus is the *amygdala* (Latin for "almond"), so named because of its almond shape and size. The amygdala "appears to be involved in mediating both the unconscious emotional state and conscious feeling."[10] It influences rapid physiological reactions to novel, frightening, and/or stressful stimuli (e.g., the startle response, the orienting response, the fight/flight response), and at the same time connects to the prefrontal cortex and thus to the conscious perception of emotion.

Moving outside the limbic system, two other brain organs should be mentioned in this preliminary survey of gross brain anatomy: the thalamus and hypothalamus. The *thalamus* sits above the midbrain and serves as a final relay station for the visual, auditory, and somatic (but not olfactory) sensory systems, collecting and processing information from all of them and then projecting it forward to various regions in the cerebral cortex. The thalamus in turn receives projections back from the cerebral cortex that modulate the treatment of incoming sensory information. The *hypothalamus* is located, as its name indicates, just below the thalamus, at its junction with the midbrain. One of its key functions is to connect the amygdala, hippocampus, and other regions in the limbic system with the pituitary gland, which controls various bodily functions through the secretion of hormones into the bloodstream. Research has suggested that the hypothalamus is directly involved in metabolic functions, drive regulation, and strong emotional experience. According to Thompson, "Electrical stimulation in one part of the hypothalamus (and in certain regions of the limbic system) can elicit full-blown rage and attack behavior in humans and other animals. Stimulation of a closely adjacent region of the hypothalamus produces a feeling of intense pleasure."[11]

The most obvious external feature of the cerebral cortex is its division into two sides or hemispheres. A turning point in the recent history of CN was the discovery that the two cerebral hemispheres are not identical but are in fact quite different from each other, controlling markedly asymmetrical functions. The pioneering research in this area was performed on people with intractable epilepsy who had undergone a complete commissurotomy, in which their corpus callosum (the fiber tract that connects the two hemispheres) was totally severed. This surgical procedure was highly effective in reducing epileptic seizure activity, and, despite its radical nature, it left people's basic personality, intelligence, and behavioral functions intact. What most surprised researchers was the discovery that these "split-brain patients" now had cerebral hemispheres that were operating as independent agents. In the most colorful reports about these patients, they suffered strange manifestations of inter-hemispheric competition: "One of the earliest patients, for example, described the time he found his left hand struggling against his right hand when he tried to put his pants on in the morning: One hand was pulling them up while the other hand was pulling them down. In another incident, the same patient was angry and forcibly reached for his wife with his left hand while his right hand grabbed the left in an attempt to stop it."[12]

Summarizing the effects of commissurotomy on the brain, Roger Sperry says that each hemisphere has its own "private sensations, perceptions, thoughts, and ideas, all of which are cut off from the corresponding experiences in the opposite hemisphere. Each left and right hemisphere has its own private chain of memories and learning experiences that are inaccessible to recall by the other hemisphere. In many respects each disconnected hemisphere appears to have a separate 'mind of its own.'"[13]

Many important discoveries have come from this area of research, and so have many preposterous speculations. The idea that people have "left-brain" or "right-brain" personalities has percolated throughout popular culture, despite the fact that such a notion is plainly unjustified by the findings of current research. Even more outlandish are suggestions that certain religions, philosophies, or whole civilizations have a predominantly "left-brain" or "right-brain" orientation.[14] Speculations of this sort ignore the voluminous CN research showing that almost every type of human cognitive and behavioral function depends on the activation of neural circuitry in *both* hemispheres of the brain. Several CN researchers have warned against "dichotomania" in the popular understanding of hemispheric functioning, and we should heed their cautions.[15]

Having said that, it must also be acknowledged that asymmetrical functioning in the human brain–mind system is a real phenomenon; indeed, it is a striking feature of our species, given that evolution exhibits a strong preference for symmetry. While any complex behavior or cognitive process depends on the activation of both hemispheres, the past half-century of research has identified the following predominant distinctions in their functioning:

- The right hemisphere governs both sensory input and motor output on the left side of the body. The right hemisphere has primary responsibility for manipulospatial activities (i.e., activities involving movement in imaginal space and mental mapping), and it has a central role in the detection of anomalies and novelties. The right hemisphere predominates in musical skills and singing.
- The left hemisphere governs both sensory input and motor output on the right side of the body. The left hemisphere has primary responsibility for speech, language, and the imposition of semantic structure on spoken communication. The left hemisphere is also centrally involved in tasks involving sequential analysis and more generally in the maintenance of a consistent and coherent sense of selfhood.

Research in this area has also pointed toward a distinction in the degree of lateralization in men and women. For men, certain abilities (e.g., language, speech, spatial orientation) are more specialized in one or the other hemisphere, whereas for women these abilities seem to draw more equally on neural systems in both hemispheres.

All the research we have been discussing so far looks at brain anatomy in relatively large-scale terms. We must also take into consideration the workings of the brain on a much smaller scale; specifically, we must include in our reflections an awareness of the intricate patterns of interaction between and among individual neurons (Figure 1.2). Neurons, the "functional elements in a brain,"[16] are biological cells that have a special capacity to transmit information. A neuron typically consists of a *cell body*, an *axon*, and numerous *dendrites* (from the Greek term *dendron*, for "tree"). The axon sends signals to other neurons, which receive those signals via their dendrites.[17] The point of contact between an axon and a dendrite is called a *synapse*, and the axon connects with a dendrite by means of either an electric pulse or a chemical substance. Electrical synapses are more characteristic of the central nervous systems of species from earlier in evolutionary history, while chemical ones predominate in the mammalian brain.

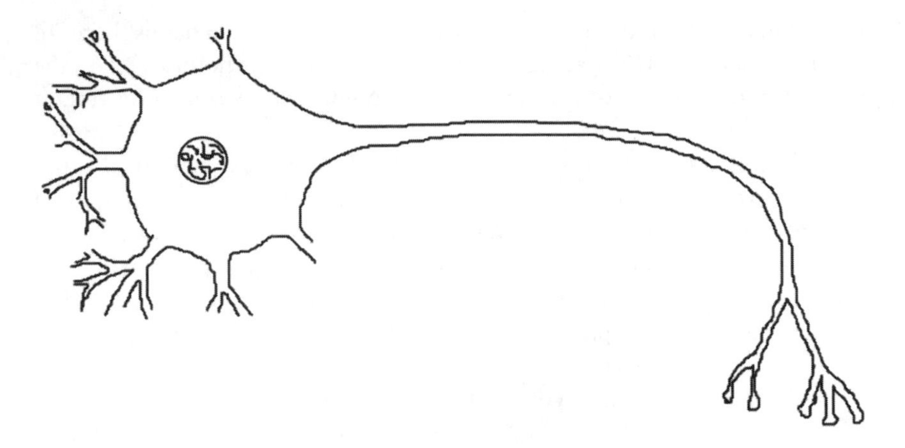

Figure 1.2 The human brain contains approximately one trillion neurons.

The key fact to emerge from research on the microscopic level of neuroanatomy is this: The human brain is structured by a vast, incredibly complex, and powerfully dynamic system of neural circuitry. Our brains are populated by many different types of neurons that vary in the size, shape, and number of their dendrites. Some neurons put out only a few small dendrites, while others have more than 10,000 bushy extensions sprouting forth from the cell body. Neurons also differ in the length of their axons; some connect to dendrites just a millimeter away, while others reach several centimeters across the brain to form synaptic bonds with particular neurons. These few simple characteristics of the average neuron lead to an astonishing mathematics. Our brains have something in the neighborhood of a trillion (10^{12}) neurons, and the average neuron has several thousand dendrites. This means that the neural structuring of the human brain lays the foundation for an almost inconceivable combinatorial power, a power that for many CN researchers is itself a source of wonder. As Thompson says, "The number of *possible* different combinations of synaptic connections among the neurons in a single human brain is larger than the total number of atomic particles that make up the known universe, hence the diversity of the interconnections in a human brain seems almost without limit."[18]

Vilaynur Ramachandran puts it this way: "A piece of your brain the size of a grain of sand would contain one hundred thousand neurons, two million axons, and one billion synapses, all 'talking to' each other. Given these figures, it's been calculated that the number of possible brain states — the number of permutations and combinations of activity that are theoretically possible — exceeds the number of elementary particles in the universe."[19]

Jean-Pierre Changeux's version goes like this: "Exploring this forest of synapses is an endless source of delight for the neurobiologist but also a cause for despair since the number of possible combinations among all these synapses, assuming them to be of equal weight, is of the same order of magnitude as the number of positively charged particles in the universe. The limits of this combinatoric are expanded still further when the functional flexibility of the connections are taken into account."[20]

Even granting the likelihood that in actuality most neurons form connections with only a limited number of their immediate neighbors, the significance of this CN discovery remains momentous. The human brain–mind system is deeply rooted in webs of neural activity whose fathomless complexity creates a radically open-ended potential for new awareness, experience, and insight. A recognition of this potential is, I suspect, part of what inspired that first sentence of Presidential Proclamation 6158: "The human brain, a 3-pound mass of interwoven nerve cells that controls our activity, is one of the most magnificent — and mysterious — wonders of creation."

A leading voice among present-day CN researchers is Antonio Damasio, a neurologist at the University of Iowa who focuses on those regions of the frontal lobe responsible for connecting emotional sensations with rational decision making. Damasio is well aware of the imperfect state of current brain–mind science, and he warns CN researchers against falling into that phrenological trap of making facile, premature generalizations about human life based on limited neuroanatomical information. Nevertheless, Damasio argues that we already have enough information to state with confidence certain important facts about the evolutionary structure of human consciousness. Damasio's first book, *Descartes' Error: Emotion, Reason, and the Human Brain* (1992), was written at the beginning of the "Decade of the Brain," and it provides something of an ideological manifesto for the contemporary CN research agenda. As Damasio presents the field, CN identifies itself philosophically as a scientific refutation of the mind–body dualism of the seventeenth-century French philosopher Rene Descartes. In contrast to Descartes' view that the rational soul is distinct from the physical body, Damasio argues that all our feelings, sensations, and experiences are products of the neural workings of the brain. Damasio's theory rejects Cartesian dualism and affirms in its place a forthright materialism that defines all mental phenomena as the secondary after-effects of natural bodily processes. In the introduction to *Descartes' Error*, he anticipates the objections of readers who may not endorse Cartesian dualism but who still believe there is more to human life than just neurons kicking around in the brain. Damasio insists that a materialist theory of human life should be a cause for celebration rather than despair:

> To discover that a particular feeling depends on activity in a number of specific brain systems interacting with a number of body organs does not diminish the status of that feeling as a human phenomenon. Neither anguish nor the elation that love and art can bring about are devalued by understanding some of the myriad biological processes that make

> them what they are. Precisely the opposite should be true: Our sense of wonder should increase before the intricate mechanisms that make such magic possible. Feelings form the base for what humans have described for millennia as the human soul or spirit.[21]

The key point in Damasio's argument against Descartes, and for a CN-inflected sense of wonder, regards the relationship between emotion and reason. While Descartes and countless other Western philosophers have asserted the primacy of reason over emotion and have claimed that the highest form of human consciousness is a pure rationality without any taint of emotionality, Damasio says reason and emotion *cannot be separated*. In fact, reason cannot function in a normal, healthy fashion without the active and continuous input of emotional information.

The evidence Damasio provides to support this claim comes from an unlikely source: the preserved skull of a nineteenth-century railroad construction foreman named Phineas Gage. One day in the late summer of 1848 Gage was on the job, setting a charge of dynamite to blast away a section of rock that was blocking the way of the track, when the dynamite suddenly exploded in his face. An iron rod three and a half feet long and weighing more than thirteen pounds shot up through his cheek and out the top of his head, landing a hundred feet away (Figure 1.3). Miraculously, Gage was not killed. He was knocked to the ground but never lost consciousness, and when he was brought by horse-drawn cart to the local doctor he managed to walk into the office with little help from his astonished coworkers. While the doctor examined the gaping

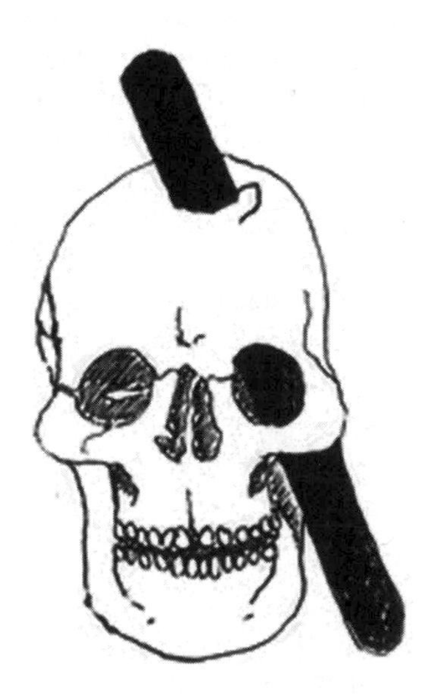

Figure 1.3 Trajectory of iron rod through Gage's skull.

wound in his skull, Gage amiably chatted with the other people crowding into the room. To everyone's surprise, Gage seemed almost completely unaffected by the sudden, violent ejection of a sizable chunk of his brain. (The *Vermont Mercury* ran an article about Gage a few days later with the headline "Wonderful Accident.") It took two months of constant medical attention to protect the wound from infection, but once it healed Phineas Gage was declared completely cured.

This is where Damasio's interest comes in. Although Gage appeared to have maintained a normal degree of rational functioning after the accident, a closer analysis reveals several strange new patterns of behavior. Gage's original doctor noticed the changes, and even though he could not explain why Gage was acting in these ways he still felt it important to mention them. Gage was now "fitful, irreverent, indulging at times in the grossest profanity which was not previously his custom, manifesting but little deference for his fellows." The personality shift was so severe that his old friends told the doctor, "Gage is no longer Gage." He went through several jobs, never lasting long in any of them. For a time he worked in a circus, showing off his wound and the iron bar that caused it to gawking crowds. He then lived for several years in South America before failing health forced him to return to the United States in 1860 to live with his mother and sister. He died a year later from a series of seizures and convulsions. Damasio sees a meaningful pattern in Gage's tragic post-injury life, a tale that reveals vital processes hidden deep within the brain–mind system: "After the accident, [Gage] no longer showed respect for social convention; ethics, in the broad sense of the term, were violated; the decisions he made did not take into account his best interests.... There was no evidence of concern about his future, no sign of forethought."[22] Gage may have seemed rational and conscious, but somehow he had lost an ability that is crucial to ordinary, day-to-day human existence — namely, the ability to *apply* his rationality to the practical exigencies of his personal and social life.[23]

Thanks to the sleuthing efforts of Damasio's neuroscientist wife, Hannah Damasio, the skull of Phineas Gage has been analyzed to determine, based on the precise location of the entry and exit holes caused by the iron rod, what parts of his brain were most likely destroyed and what parts were unaffected. Combined with clinical data from the study of patients with brain lesions in the same regions, Damasio says we can conclude this much about what happened to Gage:

- The iron rod did not affect the cortical and subcortical areas necessary for motor activity or ordinary language.
- The damage was worse in the left than the right hemisphere.
- The damage was worse in the interior areas of the frontal lobe, particularly in the ventromedial prefrontal region.
- The external regions of the prefrontal cortex were not directly damaged.

Damasio then connects the neuroanatomical data from Gage's preserved skull to the behavioral changes in his post-accident life: "It was selective damage to the prefrontal cortices of Phineas Gage's brain that compromised his ability to plan for the future, to conduct himself according to the social rules he had previously learned, and to decide on the course of action that ultimately would be most advantageous to his survival."[24]

This connection between the damage to Gage's prefrontal cortex and his impaired personal and social behavior highlights the key factor in Damasio's model of human consciousness: emotion. Damasio says that Gage and other people with brain injuries in the same precise locations suffer from a radical impoverishment of their emotional lives. Other than occasional short bursts of feeling, these people display a dramatically diminished range of emotion. They show little interest in or concern for others, and they seem oblivious to threats or risks. Having studied many patients with exactly this kind of brain damage in his own laboratory, Damasio says they often maintain a high degree of rational functioning, with normal IQ levels and capacities for abstract moral reasoning. This makes it all the more striking that, after their accidents, they lose the ability to use that reasoning to help them make good decisions in the actual circumstances of their personal and social lives. Their core problem stems from the disruption of a healthy flow of emotional input from the limbic system and other subcortical structures to the reasoning centers of the prefrontal cortex. Phineas Gage lost the part of his brain (specifically, the ventromedial prefrontal area) that facilitates this emotional flow, and this evidently deprived his reasoning abilities of a vital source of information and guidance.

Damasio's rejection of mind–body dualism is based on the notion that "pure reason" cannot function in a normal, healthy fashion without the influence of embodied emotional experience. Once we realize that Descartes was wrong to separate the sensations of the body from the cognitions of the mind, Damasio says, we are free to consider a new way of thinking about fundamental questions of human nature. "Gage lost something uniquely human, the ability to plan his future as a social being. How aware was he of this loss? Might he be described as self-conscious in the same sense that you and I are? Is it fair to say that his soul was diminished, or that he had lost his soul? ... We need to understand the nature of these human beings whose actions can be destructive to themselves and to others if we are to solve humanely the problems they pose."[25]

In Damasio's follow-up to *Descartes' Error, The Feeling of What Happens: Body and Emotion in the Making of Consciousness* (1999), he expands on that crucial reason–emotion connection and proposes a CN-based model of human consciousness that makes clear why emotional sensations from the body are so important to higher-level rational functioning. At the lowest level of the human brain–mind system are those simple biological processes we share with all other living creatures. Next up the scale are the emotions, which Damasio defines as patterned physiological responses to stimuli from the external or internal environment. The *primary emotions* are happiness, sadness, fear, anger, surprise, and disgust, which CN researchers regard as universal and impervious to cultural influence. The *secondary emotions* include embarrassment, guilt, jealousy, pride, and other culturally elaborated extensions of the six primary emotions. *Background emotions* consist of general moods or diffuse sensations of well-being or malaise, calm or tension. At this level, humans possess the basic features of "core consciousness," which Damasio says is a primal form of self-knowledge that precedes the development of language and autobiographical memory but that depends centrally on emotional input from the body: "Core consciousness is *the very evidence, the unvarnished sense of our individual organism in the act of knowing*."[26] Damasio also refers to this level of consciousness as the "proto-self." Continuing up the developmental scale, the emotions then feed into feelings, which depend on a higher-order capacity for creating "mental images arising from the neural patterns which represent the changes in body and brain that make up an emotion."[27] In Damasio's terminology, a *feeling* is a second-order elaboration of the emotional input that enhances its beneficial impact on our functioning. Feelings emerge in tandem with a more sophisticated form of consciousness and a more elaborate sense of self: "Consciousness allows feelings to be known and thus promotes the impact of emotion internally, allows emotion to permeate the thought process through the agency of feeling.... Emotion is devoted to an organism's survival, and so is consciousness."[28] Thus, feelings serve as an imagistic bridge between the unconscious emotional sensations from the body and the conscious mental faculties involved in high-order reasoning. When feelings and consciousness combine with an expanded memory, the stage is set for what Damasio calls the "autobiographical self," a relatively consistent pattern of awareness about the moment-to-moment state of one's own organismic existence. From here, Damasio says, we can at last see the full extension and flowering of human consciousness in the form of language, art, conscience, and scientific discovery.

Of course, not all CN researchers agree with Damasio on every point of his theory, but the model just outlined in its essentials does represent the mainstream view of the CN field. The mind and body are one; rational cognition depends on emotional input; consciousness has evolved in the service of adaptation and survival; the self is a neural construct. These are the basic ideas, and they are shared and fully endorsed by most CN authorities.[29]

In the context of our discussion, Damasio's theory is notable for several ideas it does *not* include in its portrayal of normal, healthy human consciousness. First, he puts so much emphasis on homeostasis and stability of structure in biological life that he neglects the equally important influences of change, adaptation, and transformation on the evolution of life in general and human consciousness in particular. Damasio may express genuine amazement at our revolutionary new vision of the brain–mind system, but unfortunately his theory of that system does not adequately account for the decentering, homeostasis-disrupting effects of his and other people's experiences of wonder. Second, although Damasio admits that CN has gone far beyond Freud in revealing the vast proportions and astonishing complexity of unconscious brain–mind functioning, he thinks there is little value to introspection, and perhaps even some harm in paying undue attention to the workings of one's own unconscious:

> Only a fraction of what goes on mentally is really clean enough and well lit enough to be noticed, and yet it is there, not far at all, and perhaps available if only you try.... I would also add that it is advantageous not to notice yourself noticing. Come to think of it, unless the particular purpose of the mental moment was to reflect on a particular state of your organism, there would be little point in allocating attention to the part of mental contents which constitute the you of the moment, no need to waste processing capacity on you alone. Just let you be.[30]

Damasio's disinterest in introspection is widely shared among CN researchers who make it a point to separate their theoretical models from Freudian psychoanalysis by repudiating subjective data gathered from self-reflection. To the extent that we find experiences of wonder connected with unconscious mental processes that can be directly accessed only by means of introspection, Damasio's theory will no longer be of help.

The third absence regards the realm of sleep and dreaming. Everything Damasio says about consciousness has to do with *waking* consciousness. In the final pages of *The Feeling of What Happens* he speaks eloquently of consciousness as an experience of light: "When self first comes to mind and forevermore after that, two-thirds of each living day without pause, we step into the light of mind and we become known to ourselves."[31] What is missing, naturally, is the darkness, the other one-third of human existence spent in something other than ordinary waking consciousness. The only reason Damasio ever mentions sleep, dreams, and the unconscious is to highlight what consciousness is *not*—namely, clear, coherent, and controlled. He takes no interest in the possible functions of sleep and dreaming, and he gives the strong impression that they do not matter to a scientific understanding of human life.[32]

As insightful as Damasio's neurocognitive model may be, it is by his own admission limited to an understanding of waking consciousness. For the investigation of sleep, dreaming, and any other mode of brain–mind activity that deviates from the standard of waking ego awareness, we must look to CN resources beyond those offered by Damasio. Fortunately, a small but creative community of CN researchers has developed that is devoted to the study of these phenomena, and their findings can help us begin to formulate an answer to the question of what is happening in the brain–mind system during an experience of wonder like the young man's dreams.

The basic CN response to that question is that his dreams were produced by the neurophysiological activation of his brain during rapid eye movement (REM) sleep. The connection between dreaming and REM sleep has been a widely accepted fact for half a century now. In the early 1950s, University of Chicago physiologist Nathaniel Kleitman and his student Eugene Aserinsky began studying the seemingly trivial phenomenon of eye movements during sleep. To their great surprise, they found that during sleep both children and adults experience cyclical periods of highly coordinated eye movements, intensified electrical activity in the cerebral cortex (as measured by the electroencephalogram, or EEG), irregular breathing, loss of muscle tone, increased heart rate, and increased blood flow to the genitals (leading to penile erections in men and clitoral swelling in women). William Dement, who soon joined the Aserinsky and Kleitman research team, coined the term "rapid eye movement" for these stages of sleep, contrasting them with "non-rapid eye movement" (NREM) stages of sleep. Subjects in the sleep laboratory who were awakened during a stage of REM sleep were much more likely to report a dream than people awakened during a state of NREM sleep, and the REM dream reports frequently involved "strikingly vivid visual imagery," suggesting that "it is indeed highly probable that rapid eye movements are directly associated with visual imagery in dreaming."[33]

Following up on Aserinsky and Kleitman's discovery, many other researchers studied the variable physiological patterns of mammalian sleep, and they soon found that a typical night's sleep for an adult human follows a regular alteration of REM sleep and four distinct states of NREM sleep. On average, an adult human experiences each night four to five periods of REM sleep, of between ten and sixty minutes, for a total of approximately one-quarter of their total sleep time. Looking at sleep in other animals, researchers found that all mammals (with the apparent exception of the spiny anteater and the bottlenose dolphin) experience regular cycles of REM and NREM sleep. Birds seem to have a kind of REM sleep, but reptiles do not. Furthermore, in most mammals the percentage of REM sleep is higher among newborns than adults; human babies pass up to 80% of their sleep in REM, a ratio that declines with age to approximately 25% in mature adults.

These findings suggest that REM sleep (and possibly dreaming) serve some adaptive function, developed over the course of evolutionary history, in the activation and maturation of the mammalian brain. Some of the adaptive functions that have been suggested include storing memories and newly learned skills, processing information with a high emotional charge, responding to waking-life crises, making wide-range connections in the mind, and practicing adaptive types of behavior.[34]

Perhaps the most surprising finding in the early years of research on REM and NREM sleep was the intensity of activation in the brain during REM. Contrary to expectations that sleep is a time of quiescence and neural deactivation, researchers found that, in fact, the brain is designed to engage in a cyclical pattern of complex and dynamic activation, whose electrical intensity is often greater than that of brain functioning during wakefulness. According to J. Allan Hobson, "If we were not able to observe that a subject is behaviorally awake in the first case and sleeping in the second, the EEG alone would not be capable of indicating whether the subject is awake or [in REM sleep]."[35] Much of this heightened neural activity can be attributed to the phasic discharge of ponto-geniculo-occipatal (PGO) waves originating in the brainstem and spreading throughout the cortical and subcortical regions of the brain: "PGO waves represent unbridled brain-cell electricity. 'Brain-stem lightning bolts' is hyperbolic but to the point."[36]

Following these discoveries, mainstream scientific theorizing about the connection between REM sleep and dreaming focused on repudiating Freud and depreciating the meaningfulness of dreams. Hobson's activation–synthesis model, with its emphasis on the unidirectional, bottom-up influence of REM-generating brainstem processes on dream formation, has reigned over scientific dream research since its first appearance in 1977.[37] Hobson's theory has been seriously challenged, however, by the recent findings of Mark Solms, a psychoanalytically trained clinical neurologist who has studied the dream lives of 361 patients suffering a variety of brain lesions. Solms found that almost all of the patients suffered one of four distinct syndromes, or patterns, of disrupted dreaming: (1) *global anoneira*, a total loss of dreaming; (2) *visual anoneira*, cessation or restriction of visual dream imagery; (3) *anoneirgnosis*, increased frequency and vivacity of dreaming, with confusion between dreaming and reality; and (4) *recurring nightmares*, an increase in the frequency and intensity of emotionally disturbing dreams. Solms analyzed these four syndromes in comparison to each other and in comparison to those patients who, despite suffering serious forms of brain damage, experienced no disruptions in their dreaming. On this basis, Solms has made several claims about what specific regions of the brain are responsible for the formation of dreams:

- *Dreaming involves activation of both hemispheres.* Solms says that global anoneira "can occur with strictly unilateral lesions in either hemisphere,"[38] suggesting that both left and right hemispheres make necessary contributions to normal dreaming.
- *Dreaming is not modular.* Global cessation of dreaming can occur after damage to several different regions of the brain, which Solms says supports a distributed, nonmodular view of brain–mind functioning: "[C]omplex mental faculties such as reading and writing (and, we might add, dreaming) are not localized within circumscribed cortical centers.... [They] are subserved by complex functional systems or networks, which consist of constellations of cortical and subcortical structures working together in a concerted fashion."[39] In other words, no phrenology of dreaming can exist; dreaming

involves a wide-ranging system of neural interaction that defies simple analysis, localization, or explanation.

- *Dreaming exceeds ordinary language.* Solms found that disorders of spoken language such as aphasia were no more common among his dreaming patients than his nondreaming patients. He comments that "the high incidence of preserved dreaming among our aphasic patients … demonstrates that loss of the ability to generate language does not necessarily imply loss of the ability to generate dreams."[40] Put differently, dreaming does not depend on those regions of the brain responsible for ordinary social communication. This is one likely reason for the difficulty people often have in describing their dreams after they wake up — the images and feelings are neurologically decoupled from regular, everyday language.
- *Dreaming involves an autonomous visionary system.* Most interestingly, for our purposes, Solms finds a "double dissociation" between visual imagery in dreams and visual perception in waking: Patients with visual problems had normal dreaming, and patients with nonvisual dreaming had normal visual abilities. Specifically, he argues that those brain areas in the parietal lobe that are crucial for the processing of external visual signals are *not* necessary for the generation and maintenance of normal dream imagery. Putting his findings in a broader context, Solms provides neuropsychological evidence that the human brain–mind system has evolved with the capacity to generate autonomous visionary experiences whose visceral power and sensory intensity do not depend on external stimuli or volitional self-control. This discovery has surprisingly religious-sounding implications — it would seem we are all natural visionaries.

Of course, such implications do not concern Solms, who focuses more narrowly on the CN task of developing a model of the normal dream process. He argues that several specific brain regions make functional contributions to ordinary dreaming:

- Basal forebrain pathways, which contribute a "factor of appetitive interest" in terms of curiosity, exploration, and expectation
- The medial occipito-temporal structures, which contribute visual representability
- The inferior parietal region, which contributes spatial cognition
- The frontal-limbic region, which adds a "factor of mental selectivity" in separating dreaming from waking (damage to this region leads to reality-monitoring problems in waking)
- Temporal-limbic structures, which contribute a "factor of affective arousal" and may, in their seizure-like behavior during sleep, be the ultimate source of dream generation

Solms claims his neuropsychological findings decisively refute Hobson's activation–synthesis theory:

> [T]he neural mechanisms that produce REM are neither necessary nor sufficient for the conscious experience of dreaming … normal dreaming is impossible without the active contribution of some of the highest regulatory and inhibitory mechanisms of the mind. These conclusions cast doubt on the prevalent notion — based on simple generalizations from the mechanism of REM sleep — that "the primary motivating force for dreaming is not psychological but physiological" (Hobson and McCarley, 1977). If *psychological forces* are equated with *higher cortical functions*, it is difficult to reconcile the notion that dreams are random physiological events generated by primitive brainstem mechanisms, with our observation that global anoneira is associated not with brainstem lesions resulting in basic arousal disorders, but rather with parietal and frontal lesions resulting in spatial–symbolic and motivational–inhibitory disorders. These observations suggest that dreams are both generated and represented by some of the highest mental mechanisms.[41]

Much more could be said about the further details of what CN researchers are discovering about sleep, dreams, and the various states of human conscious and unconscious life.[42] We have enough material, however, to return to the young man's dreams and identify with a high degree of confidence several likely features of neural activation in his brain that occurred during his remarkable oneiric experience. To begin with, the first and third dreams almost certainly took place during REM sleep. Their qualities of emotionality, sensory vividness, imagistic complexity, and narrative unfolding are much more characteristic of REM than NREM dreams; thus, the young man's first and third dreams can be understood as grounded in the neurophysiological processes that take over both hemispheres of the brain during REM (e.g., activation of secondary visual processing systems, memory and spatial recognition systems in the hippocampus, emotional responsiveness in the amygdala). The second dream is more difficult to identify; it could have occurred during REM, NREM, or some other hypnogogic condition totally different from ordinary sleep stages. As Hobson would note, all three dreams are filled with bizarre happenings, thematic discontinuities, and inexplicable metamorphoses; all of this is evidence that the young man's dreams involved a dramatic shift away from those aminergically driven abilities of rational consciousness that normally predominate in waking life. But, as Solms would note, the dreams surely involve the activation of many high-order neural systems as well, with the clearest evidence coming in the second and third dreams: The young man becomes self-aware within the dream state and (re)gains some ability to reflect on the meaning of what he is experiencing. Such a capacity for metacognition usually depends on the operation of executive functions centered in the prefrontal cortex, although it is possible that during dreaming different neural systems not dependent on prefrontal regions emerge to support conscious awareness and volition.

So in terms of contemporary CN research, the young man's dreams are neither totally random nonsense nor perfectly rational cognitions; they are something strangely and provocatively in between, a liminal (and limbic?) phenomenon *par excellence.*

III. "Not My Human Mind": A First Look at Religious Studies

Recall that the young man's explanation of his three wondrous dreams did not conclude with that feeling of his brain being on fire; he also insisted that his "human mind" had nothing to do with their formation. Specifically, he attributed the first two dreams to the influence of malevolent spirits, while the third he regarded as a heavenly revelation. Here, the young man is speaking in the language of Catholic Christianity, and throughout his journal he uses terms and phrases deriving from that religious tradition as a way of explaining both the origin of his dreams and their momentous significance for his life.

What are we to make of this connection between the young man's dreams and his religious life? The only way to answer that question is to look beyond brain–mind science and draw upon the resources of religious studies scholarship. Just as I did earlier in this chapter with the field of CN, I want now to provide an initial overview of the field of RS, with particular attention to what RS researchers have to say about dreams and visions. Once we do that, we will be in a good position to say something new about the primary concern of this book — namely, the evolution of a capacity for wonder.

Religio is a Latin term that originally meant "obligation" or "bond." Related to the verb *religare* ("tie back" or "tie tight"), the word came to be used in the fifth century C.E. in connection with Christian monastic life and the practice of binding oneself to the rule of a given church order. Although still used today in that more strictly Catholic context, from the sixteenth century forward the word "religion" has developed a broader field of reference and now is generally used to describe an interrelated set of phenomena that can be found in human communities all over the world and throughout history. Considered in substantive terms, religion involves the awareness of powers that transcend human control or understanding and yet have a formative influence on and discernible presence within human life. In many traditions these trans-human powers are represented in the form of gods, spirits, mythic beings, and personified forces of nature, and their presence can be felt in experiences of vision, dream, trance, prayer, meditation, and many other states of mind. Most religions venerate certain objects or places because of their capacity to bring people closer to the trans-human powers, and special practices (worship, ritual, ceremony, dance, music) are commonly performed to enhance their benevolent, life-affirming influence on people's lives (Figure 1.4). Although our existence may be filled with suffering, loss, and misfortune, religions around the world express a hopeful belief that the healthiest and most meaningful human life is achieved by

Figure 1.4 Different forms of religious worship.

harmonizing one's thoughts, feelings, and behavior with those transcendent powers.

A different way to characterize religion is to look at what it *does* (i.e., how it functions in the world). One of religion's most prominent historical roles has been to create and sustain a sense of community. Religious traditions all over the globe have developed elaborate cultural systems that have helped to bind (*religare*) large groups of people together over the span of multiple generations and across vast geographic expanses. Aligned with that community-building function, almost all religions propose moral teachings and ethical principles to guide people's behavior in relation to both human and the trans-human powers. Although it can be argued that a capacity for moral behavior does not depend on being religious (more on that later), the historical and cross-cultural evidence is quite strong that religion traditions provide a conceptual language and practical framework for the moral behavior of a large percentage of the human population.

Another widespread function of religion is the *therapeutic*: When people are suffering from some misfortune (e.g., an illness, accident, death of a loved one), most religions provide resources for relieving their distress and restoring some degree of vitality and meaning to the people's lives. In many traditions, this therapeutic function shades into more speculative reflections on death, evil, human nature, the origins of the world, and other philosophical issues. Studying and exploring such ultimate questions are rarely the concerns of every member of a religious community; instead, most traditions have a small number of specialists (e.g., shamans, doctors, mediums, witches, priests, scholars) who are experienced in therapeutic practice and who develop detailed systems of knowledge and wisdom based on that practice.

As even this brief discussion of substantive and functional qualities makes clear, the study of religion requires the use of resources from several different fields of scholarship: history, sociology, anthropology, philosophy, and cultural studies, to name a few. RS as a distinct academic discipline first arose during the nineteenth century in the German university system, with the explicit intention of separating the study of different religions from the confessional advocacy of one's own religion (as is found, for example, in seminaries and theological schools). Today, most colleges and universities in Western Europe and North America have an RS department, although it is usually quite small in comparison to other departments. Most scholars in RS focus on the study of one particular religious tradition, while a smaller number of RS researchers pursue comparative studies across different traditions on such topics as ritual, mysticism, art, ethics, politics, and gender. A good statement of what motivates RS researchers appears in the mission statement of the American Academy of Religion (AAR), the major professional organization in North America:

> AAR members find the academic study of religion intrinsically interesting because people often express their deepest values in forms of religious symbolic behavior, whether in ritual settings, creedal statements, or in their ordinary ways of living. Throughout history religion has been a vital source for some of our greatest artistic and literary achievements. The religious imagination can give us access to insights which could not be garnered in any other way, insights that can play an important role in helping to foster social harmony, especially in times of rapid social change.[43]

Religious studies may be a small field compared to other academic disciplines (the financial resources devoted to its cultivation are tiny compared to the monetary support given to CN), but its object of study is real, sizable, and significant. Looking at religion in the contemporary world, a vast majority of the human population is religious in the sense of people identifying themselves as adherents of a recognizable religious community.[44] The major religions of the world include:

- *Christianity* — Originating as a messianic movement within Judaism and centering on the healing ministry of Jesus Christ, the Christian tradition now counts its membership (including Catholic, Eastern Orthodox, and Protestant branches) as approximately 2 billion people.

- *Islam* — Founded by Muhammad, a visionary and military leader who proclaimed himself to be the "Seal of the Prophets" in the Abrahamic tradition, Islam (which means "surrender") has approximately 1.3 billion members today.
- *Hinduism* — Hinduism originated in the diverse religious beliefs and practices of the people of the Indus Valley (Persian *hindu*, Sanskrit *sindhu* for "river") and is now the faith of approximately 900 million people, including the majority of the population of modern-day India.
- *Buddhism* — Beginning with the enlightenment of an Indian prince named Guatama, by which he became a Buddha ("one who has awakened to the truth"), Buddhism today claims approximately 360 million adherents.

In addition to these four major traditions, the present-day world is filled with dozens of other religions, many of which have histories reaching back thousands of years, such as Chinese traditional religions, 225 million members; African traditional and diasporic religions, 95 million; Sikhism, 23 million; Judaism, 14 million; Baha'i, 6 million; Jainism, 4 million; and Shinto, 4 million.[45] Of course, the people who claim adherence to these faith communities have varying degrees of involvement in worship practices, and not all members share the same exact beliefs or feelings about the tradition.[46] But, by any reasonable standard of demographic measurement, religion has been, and continues to be, a pervasive phenomenon in human life. It is worth emphasizing this ongoing vitality of religion in the present-day world because so many social commentators in the early part of the twentieth century predicted that religion was fated to extinction as a result of the secularizing forces of modernization. The widespread assumption that religion would decline in significance as the world became more rational and scientific has turned out to be false. This is not to say that religions have been unaffected (and in some cases radically transformed) by modernization, only that religious communities are manifestly capable of enduring and thriving in a world of fast-moving scientific discovery and technological change.

I think it is fair to say that the vast majority of CN researchers have little or no interest in religion as a relevant source of material for their investigations. One of my chief goals in this book is to demonstrate why RS research is a vital and necessary complement to CN in any effort to develop a full understanding of human experience and behavior. Here and in the following chapters I will present the work of RS scholars who *accept* the skeptical critique that secular scientists make against religion and go on to develop new, more sophisticated ways of understanding the power and persistence of religion in human life.

I first want to bring the work of Lee Irwin into the discussion. Irwin's research focuses primarily on Native American cultural traditions, but he also studies the history of Western esotericism and trends in contemporary spirituality. As director of the innovative Religious Studies Program at the College of Charleston in

South Carolina, Irwin has a broad and decidedly non-Christian overview of the RS field, and his ideas about the nature and significance of religion bear directly on the issues we are discussing in this book.

In *Visionary Worlds: The Making and Unmaking of Reality*, Irwin wastes little time in passing harsh skeptical judgment on the world's major religions. Beginning in Chapter 1, he castigates the world's religious traditions for their pervasively negative and harmful effects on humans throughout history. Here, for example, is what he says about Hinduism and Buddhism:

> Problematically, in these eastern traditions, human life is given little substantive significance, little social or communal intelligibility beyond what is posited as its illusory, seductive, and mandated character. A multiplicity of teachings in both Hinduism and Buddhism tend to deny the intrinsic worth of ordinary human experience. The incarnate soul or psyche, contracted in bodily life, seeks to liberate itself from the wheel of suffering and rebirth, to discard the outer shell of the physical, to attain in pure awareness the foundational essence of its primal origins. But then, what purpose to life?[47]

Regarding Islam:

> [T]his great teaching has been lost in the formulation of alternate laws which, propagated by the sword, cannot distinguish the true heart from the false and so demands that all bow equally beneath the blade. This visionary world is mediated by legal authorities, *mullahs* and *imams*, who, having established a consensus, apply themselves to executing the law with a rigor and passion that allows for little variance or deviation. Perhaps the most rigorous and dogmatic of all world religions, the teachings of the *Qur'an* are represented as the Seal of Revelation.[48]

And, lest he be accused of going easy on the predominant Western tradition:

> Christianity does not fare better. What presumptions and audacity have marked the history and development of this great tradition! Jesus, as world redeemer, as Christ the anointed, rises out of the grave at Golgotha and his followers proclaim the sanctity of their belief in the resurrected life, an idea long resident in the ancient world, but with the unique stipulation that only those who believe in this miraculous event can be so resurrected — all else are condemned.... Thus in creating a new synthesis and view, a wall of condemnation was constructed as final and absolute.[49]

Freud and Marx could hardly have phrased it better. As these passages indicate, Irwin has an acute awareness of all the suffering and woe that religion has caused in human history, but, for Irwin, aiming a harsh spotlight at religion's worst failings is the *beginning* of RS scholarship, not its ending. His pointed critique clears the way for a new understanding of religion, an understanding that centers on the profound powers of creative imagination that animate human life and connect our species to other biological processes and cosmic forces. "Every religion," Irwin says, "presents us with a pattern of truth. A particular way of conceiving both the structures of human existence and the cosmological counterpart to those structures."[50] These patterns of truth are generated by a visionary capacity that Irwin believes is an innate gift in all members of our species. Everyone, not just priests, kings, or the social elite, has the imaginative capacity to envision possible futures, alternative worlds, and new potentials: "This is the visionary process: to create the world in relation to the arising of what life might be or become. Life without vision is sterile.... To grow we must create."[51]

Irwin's cardinal belief in the revitalizing power of the human imagination prompts his strong criticism of a tradition such as Islam: Any time a religious community uses force to impose an exclusive pattern of truth on people, violence is being done to those visionary powers that make us human and give meaning, purpose, and joy to our lives. The irony is that many religious traditions (such as Islam) first arose in the "fires of passion and vision" but then became "molded into sacred vessels no longer capable of sustaining the intensity nor the primacy of original and foundational experiences."[52] Irwin's charge against Christianity likewise focuses on the exclusivity and grandiosity of its pattern of truth, and he goes on to reject the claims of all monotheistic traditions — Islam, Christianity, and Judaism — insofar as they deny the validity of alternative visions and actively suppress the possibility of future transformations: "The concept of 'universal teachings' is self-limiting because it does not take into account the unknown, the yet-to-be realized, nor the possibility of some other, surpassing synthesis and visionary emphasis."[53] The restless creativity and dynamic pluralism of the human imagination may be a threat to political authorities and a puzzle for discipline-bound scholars, but for Irwin it is an irreducible fact of being human and a key to understanding both the negative and positive effects of religion on our lives.

Irwin's critical concern with Buddhism and (to a lesser extent) Hinduism derives from a different aspect of the visionary process. Although Irwin respects the many wise insights to be found in these religious traditions, he accuses them of neglecting the fundamental reality and goodness of embodied, passionate human life. Their advocacy of the ascetic's path, their hostility toward the body, their rejection of all sensory experience as illusory, misleading, and dangerous — for Irwin this view offers a woefully constricted vision of what actual human life is and can become. Yes, the world may be filled with harmful illusions and, yes, our daily existence may be permeated with suffering and unfulfilled desire,

> ... but passion and desire are also responsible for the creation of much that is beautiful and well-crafted. Science has risen on the fires of passion in the form of knowledge; art has endured through the aspirations of

> both joy and pain; humanistic disciplines of all types have been generated out of curiosity, exploration, and a constant mental activity, immersed in the world of the everyday.... The denial of worldly passion as fundamentally creative is also a "spiritual illusion," one that wishes to substitute the passion of renunciation, meditation, and self-discipline for the passion of world-affirmation, creativity, and social becoming.[54]

Many other religions beside Hinduism and Buddhism have at least partly endorsed an ascetic hostility toward embodied life in all its sensory and emotional dynamism. The goal may be release and liberation, but too often the result is a shriveling of the spirit and a starving of the imagination. For Irwin, the visionary ability depends on everything the ascetic would reject — namely, the messy, complex, emotionally turbulent world of our bodily existence. Trying to escape that world is futile and self-defeating because the cause of suffering is *not* the human body — the worst suffering comes rather from exclusivity, arrogance, and denial. These are qualities that characterize religious *and* nonreligious people alike.

Religion, according to Irwin, is fundamentally constituted by the distinctly human capacity for visionary imagination. Although religious traditions have frequently tried to control, manipulate, and suppress the visionary capacity, it remains the core source of creative energy in all faith communities. Religion does not have a monopoly on it, however. Irwin points to many arenas outside religion where we can see the visionary process at work, manifestations of the "ability to create vivid mental and emotional imagery, to imagine the world as something other than a mere appearance, to give it color and feeling tones."[55] Foremost among these nonreligious manifestations is evolutionary science itself, which has arisen in the relatively short time span of 150 years to assert a sweeping new vision of the origins of all life on the planet. By any means of reckoning, the pattern of truth constructed by evolutionary science has had an enormous effect on the modern world, and its powerful insights have revolutionized everything from medicine and morality to education and politics. But, as Irwin points out, evolutionary science remains but one among many possible visions of the world, and it has no more claim to universal perfection than any other humanly created vision: "It would be extremely naïve to imagine that evolutionary history is not full of remarkable errors, that it will not be written and rewritten and perhaps radically revised or even abandoned in the generations to come."[56] Given his insistence on the bodily roots of the visionary capacity, however, Irwin still embraces the research of evolutionary scientists. He takes their findings seriously and he actively seeks to integrate their creative insights with his own "anthropology of the spirit," which he alternately describes as an "ethnography of becoming, a record of all the transformations and changes so evident in the world around us."[57]

For the purposes of our discussion, Irwin's account of religion, evolution, and the visionary capacity provides an initial basis in RS scholarship for the study of experiences of wonder. To put it the simplest terms, *wonder is the fruit of the visionary capacity.* What I described earlier as the key elements of wonder — a surprising encounter with something that strikes a person as uniquely real, true, and/or beautiful — are, using Irwin's terms, generated by the healthy functioning of the human capacity for visionary imagination. Deeply rooted in the biological processes of the body, defying all externally imposed constrictions, continually decentering and recentering the self in its relation to the ever-changing world, the power to create new visionary worlds is what enables humans to grow and flourish. Extending Irwin's characterization, I would say that the clearest indication that this visionary power is alive and well in people's lives is the frequency with which they experience moments of wonder.

It should come as no surprise that Irwin takes a strong interest in dreams, for dreaming is nothing if not a process of making and unmaking reality: revisiting what has been in the past, experimenting with what is in the present, and envisioning what could be in the future. Irwin's book *The Dream Seekers: Native American Visionary Traditions of the Great Plains* (1994) offers the preeminent ethnographic study of the many different roles dreams have played in the religious lives of various Native American cultures. Most Native American communities have traditionally practiced some form of ritual dreaming by which a person deliberately seeks a visionary revelation in a special dream.[58] The "vision quest" is the best known of these practices, which some readers may know through the writings of pioneering anthropologists such as Irving Hallowell, Paul Radin, and Ruth Benedict.[59] Although Native Americans believe that highly meaningful dreams can potentially come to anyone at any time, they also believe that such dreams can be actively solicited by means of special prayers, ceremonies, and ritual acts. In this sense, going out on a vision quest is simply a way of increasing one's chances of receiving a dream of power — it is a way of intentionally opening oneself to an experience of wonder.

According to Irwin, efforts to evoke a visionary dream are usually propelled by three different motivations:

> The quest as a socially significant rite of passage undertaken around the time of puberty; the individually or communally motivated quest as a response to a particular social condition, crisis, or cyclical event affecting the community; and the quest undertaken as a means of attaining or enhancing personal empowerment. The intentional structure of such motivation, seen from the religious viewpoint, is the same in all three cases: to attain a specific and immediate relationship with the dream-spirits and to acquire the means to transform and enhance the human situation.[60]

The details of these rites vary widely. Some are practiced in hills and mountains, some near rivers, others at the graves of great warriors or medicine men, and still others in specially constructed huts, caves, or treeborne platforms.

The common element in all these locations is a separation from the world of ordinary living — the individual seeking a dream of power must travel to a radically different kind of space, a space where the human and more-than-human realms may come into closer contact. Questing individuals usually fast, going without food and water for long stretches of time, and they pay extremely close attention to the natural environment, alert for any movement, any changes, any hints of meaning among the animals, plants, and weather surrounding them. They sing songs, chant prayers, make offerings, and do everything they can to intensify their devotion and open themselves to the influence of the trans-human powers.

No Native American culture has ever claimed to possess techniques that automatically produce a dream response; even the more gruesome forms of ritual practice, such as slicing away strips of skin and cutting off fingertips, are no guarantee of a successful visionary experience. The goal of vision quest rituals is much more modest — namely, to generate a state of what the Sioux called *wacinksapa*, or "attentive understanding," in which people's awareness is dramatically heightened and their receptivity to new insights and revelatory visions is expanded radically.

Most Native American cultures believe that if a person is fortunate enough to receive a true dream vision, the full meaning of that vision will not be immediately apparent but will only emerge over a lengthy period of reflection. In pointed contrast to those who promise the "instant" analysis of dreams, Native Americans generally regard the interpretation of a powerful dream as the work of a lifetime: "The dream cannot be interpreted or understood in any 'finished' way; it is part of an ongoing process of interaction, dialogue, reflection, and insight unfolding over the years."[61] The fact that a dream vision may have a transformative effect on a person does not necessarily make it a pleasant or enjoyable experience, and most Native American cultures recognize that a genuine encounter with spirit powers often leaves a person feeling overwhelmed with fear, confusion, and vulnerability.

IV. The Young Man's Dreams, Anew

Let us circle back now to the three dreams of the young man described at the beginning of the chapter to see if anything new enters into our understanding of the wondrous qualities of those dreams. As some readers may have known or guessed, the young man is none other than Rene Descartes, the seventeenth-century French philosopher who is now accused of being the originator of that grievous dualistic error that Antonio Damasio and other CN researchers are aiming to correct. Descartes spoke of these dreams as a turning point in his life and thought, and I find it surprising that so few scholars have made any effort to incorporate this profoundly meaningful experience into a broader understanding of Cartesian philosophy. Biographers of Descartes speak of his dreams with obvious reluctance, unsure of how to connect his youthful visions with his mature system of thought, a system that depends so centrally on the seemingly antidreaming capacity of pure reason to apprehend truth and control behavior. I have yet to see any mention of Descartes' dreams in the CN literature. Researchers in this field care only to attack the Cartesian system of thought, and thus take no interest in the man's early life, dreaming or otherwise.

Freud made some brief comments about Rene's dreams, referring to them as "dreams from above" ("this term must be understood in a psychological, not mystical sense"), reflecting the interaction of the young man's waking thoughts with the unconscious desires released in sleep.[62] This is the only instance in all of Freud's writings where he invokes the "dreams from above" category to interpret a dream, and beyond that he says he has very little to add to our understanding of Descartes' dreams, although he cannot resist suggesting that the "melon from a foreign land" in the first dream "might stand for a sexual picture which occupied the lonely young man's imagination."[63] Marie Louis Von-Franz, one of Jung's most talented and prolific followers, wrote an extended essay on Rene's dreams in which she interprets them as "archetypal dreams … [that] contain a suprapersonal message. The dream's basic symbols — the storm, the round fruit, the sparks of fire, and the 'magic trickery' — are all *archetypal images* with a collective meaning showing that the events which took place in Descartes' unconscious and pushed their way into the light of his mind were deeply enmeshed in the general religious and scientific problems of his time."[64] Historian John Cole has closely examined the familial and cultural context of Rene's early life and, by employing psychoanalytic resources Freud himself did not see fit to use, has concluded that the three dreams reflected the young man's strong feelings of guilt over having rejected the law career for which he had been trained and which his lawyer father had wanted him to pursue.[65]

I would like to elaborate on these interpretive perspectives by integrating their important psychobiographical insights with the RS and CN material we have been discussing in this chapter. A fresh look at Descartes' three "Olympian" dreams will help us gain a more detailed understanding of one of the major spheres of wonder, and it will also give us new insight into the anti-Cartesian philosophical foundations of contemporary CN.

You do not have to swallow to the entirety of psychoanalytic dream theory to agree that when trying to understand a person's dreams it helps to know something of his or her personal life history. Rene Descartes was born in 1596 in La Haye, France, into a wealthy and socially prosperous family with many connections to the country's legal and judicial system. His mother died when he was one, during childbirth with her next child; no one ever explained this to Rene, however, and for many years he thought his mother had died in childbirth with *him*. He and his older brother and sister were raised by a nursemaid while their father, Joachim, remarried and started a new family in a faraway town. Joachim was an ambitious lawyer and government official, and he made it clear to all his children that their paramount concern was the social advancement of the Descartes name, with the ultimate goal being an official designation of their family as true nobility. For Rene and his siblings, no other life aspirations were allowed.

From the ages of eleven to nineteen, Rene attended school at the Jesuit College of La Fleche. His education was predicated on the Scholastic philosophy of Thomas Aquinas, and the teachers took as their goal the process of "Christianizing" the students by instructing them in methods of rigorous inner self-control. Rene was an excellent student, particularly in mathematics, but his fragile health was a constant source of concern. The school granted him the special privilege of "lying in" each morning after the other boys were forced to wake up for prayers and classes, and the unusually large amounts of time Rene spent in bed earned him the nickname "*Le Chambriste*." A voracious reader, he developed a special love of poetry, although he felt the inspiration required to create poetry was not a product of intentional study but was rather a "gift of nature," and thus beyond the range of his modest talents.

More than anything, Rene's school years fostered a total contempt for the teachings of philosophy, especially the Scholastic philosophy that dominated his education: "I will say nothing of philosophy except that it has been studied for many centuries by the most outstanding minds without having produced anything which is not in dispute and consequently doubtful and uncertain.... When I noticed how many different opinions learned men may hold on the same subject, despite the fact that no more than one of them can ever be right, I resolved to consider almost as false any opinion which was merely plausible."[66]

At the age of twenty, Rene took a law degree but, in apparent defiance of his father, did not immediately practice it as a vocation. Instead, he spent the next two years leading a dandyish life of fencing, horseback riding, and gambling in Paris (his mathematical skills showing their usefulness). He also spent a great deal of time thinking by himself and sketching out unabashedly anti-Scholastic notes on physics, music, mechanics, and other topics in natural philosophy. In 1618, a bloody new round broke out in the religious warfare that had plagued Europe for decades and would continue to wrack the continent for many decades to come. Having no other practical vocation in mind, Rene decided to try his hand at soldiering, as a reasonably honorable alternative to the legal career still being pushed on him by his father. He went to Holland to enlist in the army, but to his disappointment the troops were poorly organized, badly behaved, and altogether unappealing to Rene's refined moral and intellectual sensitivities; however, while in Holland he had the good fortune of meeting a slightly older gentleman named Isaac Beeckman, who shared Rene's scientific interests and who greatly encouraged the younger man's increasingly ambitious philosophical visions.

Their intimate friendship ended only a year later, however, when Beeckman became engaged to a young woman in another country. Bitter and upset over their parting, Rene left Holland and traveled to Germany, where he hoped to attach himself as an officer to another one of the armies mobilizing for battle. Once again his effort at military service was frustrated. By the time he arrived, the chill winds of winter had begun to blow and the troops were settling into their camps, waiting for the more favorable fighting conditions of spring. Resigned to waiting with them, but not wanting to subject himself to the bawdy, licentious behavior of the common soldiers in the barracks, Rene rented himself private living quarters and gave himself up to the warmth of the fire burning in his hearth and the undisturbed solitude of his own thinking.

This is the period of time during which his three dreams came, and thanks to the scholarly detective work of Cole we can make a reasonable guess at the exact date when they occurred: the night of November 10, 1619. This was Saint Martin's Eve, a pre-Advent carnival commonly celebrated with boisterous public drinking, feasting, and revelry — just the kind of behavior that Descartes studiously avoided. That date was also one year to the day from when he originally met his friend Isaac Beeckman, the first person who had ever responded positively to Rene's grandiose philosophical speculations. Perhaps most significantly, two days later would be Saint Martin's Day After, the official opening of the French judicial year. Magnificent ceremonies were performed on this day all over the country in honor of the legal system, and as part of the festivities new lawyers were formally initiated into the profession. The fact that Rene would once again *not* be among those newly installed lawyers was as much on his mind as on his father's; Joachim made no attempt to hide his disapproval of his middle son's frivolous behavior, and he remained angry about Rene to the end of his life: "Of all my children, only one is a disappointment."

Sitting alone in his warm room, with the early winter winds blowing outside and a complex array of emotions, memories, and ideas swirling within, Rene devoted himself to his own thinking — and suddenly experienced a momentous conceptual breakthrough. He saw for the first time a full picture of his new method of rational inquiry, and he realized with a flash that *this* was to be his vocation: a philosopher, a lover of truth, a teacher and practitioner of a method leading to certain knowledge, moral virtue, piety of soul, and supreme happiness. In his first major publication, *Discourse on Method* (1637), he presented the rules of method he discovered during the course of that remarkable day: First, accept nothing as true unless it presents itself clearly and distinctly to the mind, with self-evident certainty. Second, when facing a problem or difficulty, divide it into smaller parts so a solution may be more easily achieved. Third, start all thinking with that which is simplest and easiest to understand, gradually building up to more complex ideas. And, fourth, review all ideas to make sure nothing has been overlooked or omitted.

What Descartes did not mention in the *Discourse* (or anywhere else in his published corpus) is what happened that night, *following* the day of his great philosophical discovery. It is only within a private journal titled the *Olympica* that he described his experiences. He wrote the *Olympica* in the days immediately following the dreams and then kept the journal secret for the remainder of his life. (The motto inscribed on his gravestone reads, "He lives well who hides well."[67]) In contrast to his sober account in the *Discourse*, written many years after the fact and portraying his experience as one of serene, orderly self-reflection, the contemporaneously written *Olympica* suggests a process of overwhelming passion and sudden revelatory insight: "[H]aving gone to bed completely filled with his enthusiasm, and wholly preoccupied with the thought of having found that very day the foundation of the wonderful science, he had three consecutive dreams in the same night, which he imagined could have come only from on high."[68]

To remind ourselves of the content of those dreams, the first involved Rene being spun around by a whirlwind and blown toward a church and then into a school courtyard, where he was given a melon. The second included frightening sounds of thunder and flashing sparkles of light, and the third was a long narrative involving a dictionary and a book of poetry suddenly appearing and disappearing, with a conversation with a strange but apparently benevolent man.

Toward the end of the third dream Rene realized he was dreaming, and he started to interpret what had happened to him before he fully woke up. He decided that the dictionary represented all the sciences, while the *Corpus Poetarum* stood for the union of philosophy and wisdom. The prominence of poetry in his dream was interpreted as meaning that philosophical reason cannot compare with the quick brilliance of poetic inspiration, "which can bring out the seeds of wisdom that are found in all men's mind — like the sparks of fire in stones." The particular lines of poetry in his dream ("Yes and No" and "What way in life shall I follow") were interpreted as wise moral advice. Regarding the earlier dreams, the powerful winds symbolized an "evil spirit" trying to impede the exercise of his free will. With regard to the "melon from a foreign land" that was given to him by Mr. N., Rene somewhat cryptically wrote that it "signified ... the charms of solitude, but presented by purely human solicitations." The frightening thunder of the second dream was aimed at his conscience and the moral imperfections of his life: "The thunder that he heard was the Spirit of Truth descending to take possession of him."

Overall, Rene took great comfort in the three dreams, and he saw their marvelous qualities as signs of divine encouragement for his new vocation as a philosopher — "he was bold enough to persuade himself that it was the Spirit of Truth that had wanted to open unto him the treasures of all the sciences by this dream." Filled with a nearly overwhelming enthusiasm from both his waking world discoveries and his dreaming world revelations, Rene prayed to God for help in trying to decide what to do with himself in response to all these marvelous visionary experiences. More than that, he "appealed to the Holy Virgin, laying before her this affair, which he considered the most important in his life." The stakes were so high that he felt extraordinary signs of supplication were necessary: "And in his effort to interest the Blessed Mother of God in a more pressing way, he took the occasion of a trip to Italy that he was planning to take in a few days, to vow a pilgrimage to the Notre Dame of Loretto."

As we saw earlier in the chapter, current CN research can give us some insight into the likely neurophysiological processes involved in a series of dreams like those experienced by Rene. Specifically, the formal qualities of the dreams indicate heightened activation of secondary visual processing systems, stimulation of the memory and spatial orientation systems in the hippocampus, chaotic bursts of emotional responsiveness in the amygdala, and, in the case of the second and third dreams, reactivation of selected executive functions in the prefrontal cortex. Now, we can go on to include RS in the discussion, because the overtly religious context in which Rene initially understood his dreams invites the use of RS research to provide a comparative perspective on the experience. Although compatible with the psychobiographical approach taken by Freud, Von Franz, and Cole, the RS perspective focuses more broadly on the historical and cross-cultural patterns that characterize human dreaming. Rene regarded the dreams as highly significant revelations, with a vividness and memorability that distinguished them from ordinary dreams (they came from "on high"). The three dreams involve strong emotions and distinctly formed sensations, particularly visual imagery and feelings of kinesthetic movement. In terms of their function, Rene understood the dreams to be a warning about his moral failings, a prophecy about his future life, and a divine encouragement for his "wonderful science" and his new vocation as a seeker of truth. Whatever else may be said of Descartes' three dreams, they manifestly embody special qualities and themes that characterize rare but highly memorable dreams reported in religious traditions all over the world.

In fact, the phenomenology of his dreams points to a very specific RS conclusion: Rene experienced a spontaneous religious initiation, comparable in many ways to what happens in dream incubation rituals such as the Native American vision quest as described by Irwin and other ethnographers. Consider the following details:

- Rene is in the midst of the developmental transition from youth to adulthood.
- He journeys to an unusual place far from home, family, and friends.
- He deliberately shut himself off from all external stimuli.
- He devotes himself to intense, sustained contemplation.
- His feelings of power and discovery reach their climax on a day of religious celebration, a day laden with strong personal and communal meanings.
- He experiences a series of dreams that are extraordinary in their forceful sensations and vivid images.
- He expresses wonder at the dreams, an awed reverence and excitement mingled with fear and humility.
- He reacts to the dreams with prayer, with gratitude to the ultimate source of the dreams, and with a vow to undertake the ritual practice of a pilgrimage.
- The dreams become emblems of his new adult identity and vocation as a philosopher.

Rene's religious culture did not prepare him for such an event. Unlike Native American youths, he was not raised with the expectation that one day he would journey forth in a quest for a revelatory dream vision. Nevertheless, all the conditions were there for a classic initiatory dream, an experience that would establish a special lifelong connection between him and mighty powers that transcend the ordinary, everyday sphere of human thought and control.

Indeed, the extreme nature of Rene's experience suggests a comparison of what he went through with the even more demanding initiatory ordeals of healers, prophets, and other religious specialists in various indigenous cultures around the world.[69] Rene was not simply passing through a developmental stage — he was caught up in deep, emotionally turbulent struggle with his father over his future vocation. He did not simply travel away from home — he was a veritable family outcast, the target of open disdain and condemnation. Never knowing his mother, largely abandoned by his father, set apart from his peers by his physical debilities and lethargic behavior, bitterly disappointed by his school teachers and, most recently, by his friend Isaac Beeckman, Rene's personal life was pervaded by loss and broken relationships. All of this bears a striking similarity to what many studies of shamanism have indicated are the most common personal conditions that can predispose a person to having a spontaneous initiatory experience: extreme emotional distress, interpersonal conflict, and a propensity to visionary thought. Rene's initiatory experience not only healed his suffering and confusion but also inspired him to heal others as well. He became a type of philosophical therapist who devoted his life to teaching other people about the best path to knowledge of the truth, thus helping them live happier and more virtuous lives.

What I am leading to is a new way of understanding Descartes' life, dreams, and work: I regard him as a *shaman of rationalism*. On that singular day of November 10, 1619, Rene had an astonishing vision of the full power of mathematical reasoning as applied to all of life — not just to physics, biology, chemistry, and the like, but also to ethics, theology, and the practical concerns of daily life. Pure rationality was the key to a brand-new understanding of truth, God, and the cosmos itself. Pure rationality was also the foundation for a new conception of what it means to be human. Throughout his writings Descartes emphasizes the fact that the capacity to think rationally is inherent in all humans; it is what defines us as a species. Whether we are wealthy or poor, Catholic or Protestant, civilized or savage, male or female, all of us have a spark of divine power enabling us to think freely, reflect critically on our behavior, and use scientific reasoning to gain true insights into the nature of reality. Each individual has the strength to rise above the limitations imposed by the physical frailties of our bodies, the entanglements of family and social relationships, and even the oppressive stupidity of political authorities. Out of a life of loss and disappointment, in a world of horrific war and bloodshed, Descartes gave us the "wondrous science" and a vision of the human soul that is free, rational, powerful, and capable of knowing the truth.[70]

According to CN, this is precisely his error. Descartes' vision artificially separates the soul from the body. It cuts the mind off from the brain, which has the negative effect of confusing our understanding of the biological foundations of evolved human nature. In the final pages of *Descartes' Error*, Damasio states the CN position in the bluntest of terms:

> It would not have been possible to present my side of this conversation without invoking Descartes as an emblem for a collection of ideas on body, brain, and mind that in one way or another remain influential in Western science and humanities.... This is Descartes' error: the abyssal separation between body and mind, between the sizable, dimensioned, mechanically operated, infinitely divisible body stuff, on the one hand, and the unsizable, undimensioned, un-pushpullable, nondivisible mind stuff; the suggestion that reasoning, and moral judgment, and the suffering that comes from physical pain or emotional upheaval might exist separately from the body. Specifically: the separation of the most refined operations of the mind from the structure and operation of a biological organism.[71]

Damasio's words reflect a widespread perception of Cartesian philosophy, as the most egregious historical expression of mind–body dualism. If you had nothing other than his *Discourse on Method* and his later *Meditations Concerning First Philosophy* (1641) by which to judge him, you might be warranted in that view, but once we learn about Rene's three Olympian dreams, with their intense emotions, strong sensations, and vibrant physicality, we must question the adequacy of that perspective and consider the alternative possibility that from early in his life Descartes had a much richer and more nuanced understanding of soul and body than is usually conceded to him. Drawing on Paul Ricoeur's ideas about the language of psychoanalysis, I would say anachronistically that Descartes is striving to develop a new kind of "mixed discourse," a synthetic conceptual language that aims to integrate at a higher order of complexity the specialized terminologies of philosophy, theology, and natural science, with a practical interest in using the new knowledge gained by this discourse to care for suffering individuals and promote a more peaceful social world.[72]

The key text in Descartes' effort to work out the details of this mixed discourse is his last published book, *The Passions of the Soul* (1649). Published a few weeks before his death, it responds to questions posed to him by his close friend Princess Elisabeth regarding the proper role of the passions (CN researchers now prefer the term "emotions") in a happy, virtuous, religiously faithful life. Characteristically enough, Descartes starts by saying the "ancients" (i.e., previous generations of philosophers, especially the Scholastics) were completely wrong about the passions when they defined them as purely negative factors in human life that must be eliminated in order to achieve true moral virtue. Descartes argues that our passions are a normal and natural part of being human, even if they can be confusing, obscure, and at times unruly. Passions serve a vital mediating function between the body and soul, conveying particular perceptions and sensations to the soul in order to "incite and dispose the soul to will the things for which they [the passions] prepare their body."[73]

Descartes' ideas in this text bear a striking similarity to the claims of Damasio and other CN researchers regarding the interaction of bodily generated emotions and higher-order "executive functions" such as reasoning and willing. When Descartes speaks of the passions as being modulated by the variable movement of "spirits," which he defines as extremely fine and quick-moving particles coursing through our bloodstream, he is seeking exactly the kind of empirically based physiological explanation that CN researchers have also sought in their work on the role of hormones, nerve signals, and other forms of chemical and electrical communication involved in our emotional experiences.

Even his much-derided notion of the pineal gland as the specific location of the soul in the brain is not as farfetched as many of his critics have made it sound. Descartes was an avid anatomist, spending numerous hours dissecting animal and human cadavers to examine their internal physiological structures. Based on these observations, he claimed the soul's operation within the body was most particularly associated with the pineal gland because its central location in the brain would give it a uniquely powerful ability to connect input from a variety of other brain regions. CN research has obviously developed a much more complex notion of neural functioning than was possible for Descartes, and the pineal gland is now thought to govern the circadian rhythms of sleeping and waking along with the female reproductive cycle — valuable functions, to be sure, but not quite "seat of the soul" material. Still, this should not obscure the fact that Descartes' hypothesis about the pineal gland was based upon a type of reasoning that is still common in CN today — namely, the search for higher-order neural structures that serve as central processors for multiple sources of input and output. The ultimate neural processor, the Holy Grail of CN, is the one that produces a clear, unified, waking state of consciousness. Damasio and other CN researchers are trying, just as Descartes did, to develop ever more detailed understandings of the neurophysiological processes that underlie our abilities to reason, to exercise will, and to reflect self-consciously upon our own lives. The terms may be different, but the fundamental goal is the same.

Thus, Damasio's sweeping denunciation of Descartes, ritually celebrated in the opening pages of numerous CN texts, is revealed to be an act of supreme ingratitude. Rather than committing an error that must be corrected by CN, Descartes' psychological investigations have effectively defined the intellectual agenda that guides contemporary CN research. He is not the primal antagonist of CN; he is in many ways the field's philosophical progenitor.

What, then, of the soul? What of Descartes' insistence that humans are *more* than their bodies, that we are constituted by a mysterious combination of material substance and immaterial soul? Even if Descartes took far more interest in the detailed workings of the body than modern readers give him credit for, does he not still violate the basic tenets of science by appealing to the religious notion of the soul to explain human nature? Answers to those questions will unfold in the coming pages, as we develop a mixed discourse that can help us move beyond the tempting but vacuous simplicities of both the scornful skeptic and the unwavering theist. That kind of mixed discourse is precisely what Descartes was seeking in *The Passions of the Soul*, and my approach in this book takes inspiration from his understanding of the vital role of wonder in the relationship between the soul and the body. Descartes identifies wonder as the first of the principal passions: "Wonder is a sudden surprise of the soul which makes it tend to consider attentively those objects which seem to it rare and extraordinary."[74] Objects of wonder abruptly seize our attention through strong sensory impressions and a quickening of the spirits, which Descartes says produces an expansion in the functional range of brain processing: "It is certain that novel objects of the senses affect the brain in certain parts not usually affected and that these parts, being more tender or less firm than those a frequent agitation has hardened, this increases the effect of the movements they excite there."[75] In keeping with his view of the general function of the passions, Descartes says wonder "is useful in making us learn and retain in our memory things we have previously been ignorant of."[76] The passion of wonder stimulates curiosity and questioning, and Descartes regards it as a fundamental stimulus to scientific investigation.

What distinguishes wonder from all other passions is the way it precedes reflective thought. Wonder strikes us before we can judge something to be good or bad, helpful or dangerous, pleasurable or painful. In its radical novelty and decentering impact, wonder momentarily suspends the ordinary cognitive filtering processes of evaluation and categorization. As Rene well knew from his own personal experience, it heralds a new apprehension of truth, a new vision of the divine, a newly recentered self.

Before the *cogito* is wonder.

2

Sexual Desire

2
Sexual Desire

I. Angela Amid the Roses

Our first view of Lester Burnham, the hapless protagonist of the film *American Beauty*,[1] is of him naked in the shower, masturbating. "This," he informs us in a confessional, self-mocking voiceover, "will be the high point of my day. It's all downhill from here."[2] At first sight, it would seem Lester (played by Kevin Spacey) has a perfectly respectable and satisfying American life. Forty-two years old, employed as a writer for an advertising industry magazine, living in a comfortable house in a clean and quiet suburb, married to a beautiful woman, father to a healthy teenage daughter — he appears to have achieved admirably the basic goals for which most people in our society strive, right down to the home-cooked family dinners served at the dining room table each night. But all is not well with Lester. He admits that he feels unsure of himself, detached from his surroundings, sedated: "I've lost something, but I don't know what." The first several scenes of the film, with their artful mix of comic absurdity and spiritual despair, make it clear that the pleasing appearance of normality in Lester's life is only a disguise for the gnawing sadness and aching desperation that are consuming both him and his family. His wife, Carolyn (Annette Bening), is a real estate agent whose maniacal determination to "project an image of success at all times" requires the strictest possible control of emotion, behavior, and appearance. His daughter, Jane (Thora Birch), despises both her parents, and, while she feigns a cool disinterest in how she looks, she in fact worries about the shape of her breasts and is secretly saving money for an implant operation. Carolyn and Jane make no secret of the contempt they feel for Lester and the clumsy, vacant way he sleepwalks through life. Lester has a dim awareness of the distance that has grown between them — "We used to be happy," he muses — but he does not know when this happened, or why, or what if anything he can do about it.

Then something strange happens to Lester. Something unexpected, bizarre, and profoundly decentering. Something wonderful. Jane has joined the cheerleading team, and Carolyn drags Lester to see their daughter perform during halftime of a school basketball game (Lester morosely complains that he is missing a James Bond movie marathon on television). Carolyn and the bumbling Lester take their seats in the gymnasium stands, and the halftime show begins. As the school band launches into a brassy rendition of "On Broadway," the cheerleaders bounce onto the court and strut through their routine, with Jane giving a hesitant but passable performance. Suddenly, Lester's gaze fixes on one particular cheerleader, Jane's beautiful friend Angela, and in an instant Lester is transformed. The light softens, the noises fade away, all the other people just disappear, and nothing remains in the entire world but Angela, incredibly attractive, vivacious, blond-haired Angela (Mena Suvari). Lester watches with eyes wide and mouth hanging open (in a pose reminiscent of Descartes' *L'Admiration*) as the aptly named Angela, a heavenly vision of budding sexual desire, floats toward him. She slowly unzips her cheerleader uniform and opens up her blouse for him, and a thousand red rose petals flutter through the air.

After the game the star-struck Lester introduces himself to Angela and practically drools as he praises her "very … precise" cheerleading. Jane is first shocked and then disgusted by her father's ardent leering, but Lester could not care less — he sees nothing but Angela. Later that night he lies in bed with a dreamy smile on his face, staring up at the ceiling as red rose petals softly rain down upon him. "I've been in a coma for about 20 years," he says to himself, "and I'm just now waking up." An image of the glorious young woman appears before him. "Spec-tac-ular."

The story of Lester's befuddled midlife epiphany of reawakened libido points to a second major sphere of the human experience of wonder. Sexual desire expresses a primal creative energy, a deep bodily yearning more intense than perhaps any other force in our lives. According to the *Kamasutra*, the third-century C.E. Hindu manual of sensual pleasure, "The emotions and fantasies conjured up in a moment in the midst of sexual chaos cannot be imagined even in dreams.… [W]hen the wheel of sexual ecstasy is in full motion, there is no textbook at all, and no order."[3] Amazingly pleasurable, emotionally overwhelming, supremely decentering of one's ordinary sense of self, the wonders of sexuality represent a tremendously powerful motivating force in human life and a deeply rooted feature of our evolutionary nature. Indeed, to the extent that it leads to procreation, sexuality *is* our evolutionary nature — it expresses the prime biological directive of all life (i.e., to produce new copies of our genes). In humans, the reproductive instinct has developed in ways not found in any other species: We have devised various cultural mechanisms for systematically controlling, regulating, channeling, and enhancing our sexual desires. We have created elaborate kinship systems, detailed codes of moral behavior, vivid myths and religious teachings, and a vast array of laws and customs that define the boundaries of who can have sex with whom and when they can do it, where, and why. This produces what is surely one of the basic existential facts about the human species: We live with a persistent tension between the deep biological urges driving our sexual desires and the vast cultural web of constraints and constrictions we have invented to control the expression and satisfaction of that desire — hence, the spectacle of Lester's lustful fascination with Angela, which is all the more shocking because he is violating so many of the moral rules governing his cultural world (and, by implication, American society as a whole). He is betraying his marriage vows to his wife, he is publicly humiliating his daughter, and he is opening up a host of incestuous fantasies between them; also, in trying to seduce the underage Angela, he is effectively planning to commit statutory rape.

Lester's wondrous yet dangerous experience of renewed sexual desire brings forth many of the issues I want to explore in this chapter. The sheer bodily power of sexual desire is one major theme, and the overwhelming impact of sex on ordinary cognitive functioning is another. I am interested in the interplay in human sexuality of deep biological processes and enhanced states of self-awareness, aesthetic sensitivity, and ontological insight, and I want to consider that interplay from both the cognitive neuroscience (CN) perspective of evolved brain–mind functioning and the religious studies (RS) vantage of culturally elaborated meaning making. To bridge the discussion in this chapter with the focus on dreams and visions in the previous chapter, I will highlight several ways in which human sexual desires are interwoven with our visionary capacity. *American Beauty*, for example, is permeated with dreams, visions, and revelatory shifts of perspective, especially for Lester. His family thinks he has gone totally crazy and lost touch with the real world, but after his experience at the basketball game Lester has absolute confidence in the realness of his visions of Angela, visions that are enabling him to (re)connect with something true, clear, and certain, something that is in danger of dying out in what everyone else considers the "real world." As Lester's ultimate fate suggests, however, the potential for violent conflict between wonder and society is nowhere more explosive than in the sphere of sexual desire.

II. Mating Games and Climactic Mysteries

Because of its key role in the evolution of mammalian life, sexual desire has attracted a great deal of research interest from cognitive neuroscience. More specifically, the branch of CN known as evolutionary psychology (EP) has undertaken a detailed study of the influence of reproductive instincts in the development of the human mind. Drawing inspiration from the sociobiology project of E.O. Wilson, EP researchers apply the logic of evolutionary adaptation to the observable behavior of humans, with particular interest in sexuality, mating, and gender differences.[4] When Wilson's theory first appeared in the 1970s, it generated intense controversy and heated opposition because of its boldly reductionistic dismissal of culture as a significant factor in human life. EP researchers today argue that Wilson's critics fundamentally misunderstood his theory and that subsequent research has amply borne out his original insights.

Among the many notable scholars in this field, I regard Steven Pinker as the best and most articulate exponent of EP thinking about sexual desire. A close look at his ideas, especially in *How the Mind Works* (1997), will provide several benefits. First, Pinker offers a clear and compelling explanation for the basic methods of EP, foremost of which is "reverse engineering": "On this view," Pinker says, "psychology is engineering in reverse. In forward engineering, one designs a machine to do something; in reverse engineering, one figures out what a machine was designed to do.... The rationale for reverse engineering living things comes, of course, from Charles Darwin. He showed how 'organs of extreme perfection and complication, which justly excite our admiration,' arise not from God's foresight but from the evolution of replicators over immense spans of time."[5] Using this method, EP researchers such as Pinker analyze specific human behaviors and cognitive abilities in terms of their adaptive value during the evolutionary history of our species. Language, vision, morality, aesthetic preferences, mating behaviors — all of these and more can be explained by EP in terms of the selective advantages they gave to humans competing for survival in the ancient ancestral environment of the African savanna.

Second, Pinker provides an excellent summation of the major findings of EP in its quest to identify the primary modules of human cognitive functioning. Building on the work of Antonio Damasio and other CN researchers who have made great progress in localizing the neuroanatomical systems that govern various mental functions, Pinker forcefully advocates a modular framework for conceptualizing the basic workings of the brain–mind system ("a universal structure to the mind is not only logically possible but also likely to be true"). Here is what he calls the key sentence of *How the Mind Works*: "The mind is a system of organs of computation, designed by natural selection to solve the kinds of problems our ancestors faced in their foraging way of life, in particular, understanding and outmaneuvering objects, animals, plants, and other people."[6] Pinker relies centrally on the notion of the mind as a kind of neural computer that has evolved a number of specific, task-oriented abilities. The primary function of this computer is to process information in ways that, through the long course of evolutionary history, have helped humans survive and procreate. All humans are born with a set of basic mental modules ("organs of computation") that enable us to perceive, think, remember, plan, and act in the world. Although culture has some influence in steering people's development in one direction or another, for Pinker the fundamental psychological structures of the human mind are genetically determined and essentially impervious to cultural influence.

The third benefit of a focus on Pinker is that he writes with great flair and gusto, and he takes obvious delight in attacking, mocking, and vanquishing his intellectual opponents. This makes his books vastly more entertaining to read than most EP texts, which I think is Pinker's intention. It also reveals quite a bit about his intellectual limitations and shadow preoccupations, which I think is not his intention at all. During the course of *How the Mind Works*, Pinker vents considerable spleen at postmodernists, deconstructionists, feminists, psychoanalysts, and everyone else who advocates the "secular catechism of our age" and grants too much credit to culture as a factor in human life, experience, and development. Pinker's colorful rhetoric and combative tone clearly appeal to a wide audience — his writings have a kind of Rush Limbaugh quality, and he delights in making fun of all the soft-headed, psychologically correct, '60s holdouts who live in a fantasy world and refuse to face the cold, hard empirical data of brain–mind science. Few of Pinker's tirades in *How the Mind Works*, however, make documented reference to any particular texts or scholars, and as the book progresses his visceral animosity toward the human sciences becomes increasingly evident. This animosity is particularly evident in his discussion of sexual desire.

As Pinker's intellectual comrade-in-arms Wilson describes it in *Sociobiology*, the fundamental evolutionary value of sexuality is the way it mixes genetic materials during reproduction in order to increase the adaptive flexibility of the species:

> "[T]he advantage of sexual reproduction lies in the much greater speed with which new genotypes are assembled.... Each step peculiar to the process of gametogenesis and syngamy serves to increase genetic diversity. To diversify is to adapt; sexually reproducing populations are more likely than asexual ones to create new genetic combinations better adjusted to changed conditions in the environment. Asexual forms are permanently committed to their particular combinations and are more likely to become extinct when the environment fluctuates. Their departure leaves the field clear for their sexual counterparts, so that sexual reproduction becomes increasingly the mode."[7]

Different species have devised different strategies for taking advantage of the opportunities afforded by sexual reproduction. Mayflies, for example, spend three years as underwater nymphs living in ponds then develop into flying adults that immediately mate and, a few hours later, die. Their sexual lives are compressed into one final developmental stage, as spectacular as it is brief. Likewise, the Pacific salmon dwells in the open ocean for most of its life but then returns to the river where it was born, swimming heroically upstream through churning rapids and over steep falls and finally reaching its natal headwaters, there to spawn and expire. In most insects, the sexual behavior of males is driven by highly programmed responses to the perception of pheromones and other signals indicating the presence of a receptive female. The insect's abdomen rather than head is the control center of male copulatory behavior, and as Wilson (whose primary scientific training was in entomology) notes, "The total removal of the brain of a male insect — chopping off the head will sometimes do — triggers copulatory movements by the abdomen. Thus, a male mantis continues to mate even after his cannibalistic mate has eaten away his head."[8] In mammals the control of sexual behavior shifts completely to the brain, where preprogrammed cycles of hormone secretion work to initiate reproductive activities. Humans have the distinction of being comparatively free of hormonal determinism in our reproductive activities. Female fertility does not depend on limited periods of estrus, and male sexual arousal does not require the perception of hormonal cues.

The most striking feature of sexual evolution is the almost universal prevalence of male competition and female choice. These twin behaviors derive from the physiological differences in what males and females typically contribute to the reproductive process. Because males in most species need only invest a small amount of genetic material to reproduce successfully, their maximal evolutionary advantage is served by mating with as many fertile females as possible — over the long run, the most effective strategy is for a male to spread his genes. By contrast, females make a far greater investment of time, energy, nutrients, and risk in reproduction. Mammalian females, besides providing the larger sex cell of the egg, continue to carry the fertilized egg for a lengthy period following conception, nourishing it with their blood and nursing and protecting it after it is born. In precocial mammalian species such as humans, the postpartum caregiving stage typically extends for another lengthy period of time. This large investment means that the optimal reproductive strategy for females has little to do with the number of males she mates with and much more with the need to discriminate between competing males in terms of the quality of their genetic contribution and their willingness to feed and protect offspring. Pinker explains it this way: "Male competition and female choice are ubiquitous in the animal kingdom. Darwin called attention to these two spectacles, which [in *The Origin of Species*] he dubbed sexual selection, but was puzzled as to why it should be males that compete and females choose rather than the other way around. The theory of parental investment solves the puzzle. The greater-investing sex chooses, the lesser-investing sex competes. Relative investment, then, is the cause of sex differences."[9] Pinker points out that, in animal species where the males make the greater investment in reproduction, the exact same pattern is found but with a switch in the gender roles: "In some fishes, the male broods the young in a pouch. In some birds, the male sits on the egg and feeds the young. In those species, the females are aggressive and try to court the males, who select partners carefully."

Evolutionary psychology researchers such as Pinker take special interest in the sexual behavior of such higher primates as chimpanzees, orangutans, gorillas, and bonobos. Humans share nearly all the same genes with these species (up to 99%, according to some estimates), and EP researchers have studied primate mating strategies as a source of insight into human sexual behavior. Several important points have come out of this research. First of all, quite a bit of diversity exists among primates in terms of male–female relations. Gorillas, for example, typically live in groups of one dominant male and several females, with males constantly fighting for control over the females. Orangutan females live on their own, but males still compete to mate with as many as they can. Chimpanzees live in large mixed groups that no one male dominates, thus each male has an opportunity to mate with at least a few females. Bonobo females are remarkably promiscuous, allowing virtually all males in the group multiple reproductive opportunities. As a consequence, bonobo males engage in violent conflict less often than do the males of other primate species.

Pinker argues that these different sexual behaviors represent different evolutionary strategies that can be traced in the contours of primate physiology. The winner-take-all approach of gorilla males has made physical size and strength their premium attribute, and the males are generally twice as large as females. By contrast, chimp males are not much bigger than the females (no point in wasting energy in extra physical prowess when plenty of females are available to have sex with); however, chimps have enormous testicles, far larger than those of the mammoth gorillas. Because each chimp male is mating with females who have been mating with other males, the competition in their species has shifted from external to internal combat, where the male with the most vigorous and plentiful sperm will have the best reproductive chances. Gorillas, by contrast, put little physiological emphasis on sperm production. Their main concern is gaining sexual access to females in the first place; if they succeed in that, whatever amount of sperm they produce will have no competitors within the female's vagina for access to her egg.

Using this information from primatology as a comparative context, Pinker asks the question we are all wondering about:

> What kind of animal is *Homo sapiens*? We are mammals, so a woman's minimum parental investment is much larger than a man's. She contributes nine months of pregnancy and (in a natural environment) two to four years of nursing. He contributes a few minutes of sex and a teaspoon of semen. Men are about 1.15 times as large as women, which tells us that they have competed in our evolutionary history, with some mating with several women and some men mating with none.... Men have smaller testicles for their body size than chimpanzees but bigger ones than gorillas and gibbons, suggesting that ancestral women were not wantonly promiscuous but were not always monogamous either.... Until recently, men hunted and women gathered. Women were married soon after puberty. There was no contraception, no institutionalized adoption by nonrelatives, and no artificial insemination. Sex meant reproduction and vice versa.... These conditions persisted through ninety-nine percent of our evolutionary history and have shaped our sexuality. Our sexual thoughts and feelings are adapted to a world in which sex led to babies, whether or not we want to make babies now. And they are adapted to a world in which children were a mother's problem more than a father's.[10]

This, in essence, is what comes from applying the EP method of reverse engineering to human sexuality. The males of our species are, by evolutionary design, motivated to seek multiple reproductive partners, although the ultimate procreative success of human males is also enhanced by making post-conception investments in the nurturance of offspring. Human females are innately motivated to choose among potential reproductive partners those with the best genes and greatest resources to invest in children. This means human females typically seek fewer sexual partners than do males, though not necessarily to the point of absolute monogamy.

Pinker also highlights several consequences that flow from this EP analysis:

- Males are much more easily aroused sexually than females (although, once aroused, women seem equally responsive as men), which accounts for male interest in pornographic images of "anonymous nude females eager for casual, impersonal sex."
- The sex lives of gay men provide an especially clear view on male sexual desire: "Homosexuals do not have to compromise [with choosy females], and their sex lives showcase human sexuality in purer form."
- Males are more prone to jealousy than females are because males fear that females with whom they are having sex may secretly be having sex with other males as well. "A cuckolded male is worse than a celibate one in the evolutionary struggle"; at least the celibate male is not actively aiding in the nurturance of another male's genetic offspring.
- Males of low social status and poor genetic quality must compete more intensely, with greater violence, for sexual access to females; "the fiercest competition can be at the bottom, among males whose prospects teeter between zero and nonzero."
- The universal propensity of males to view females in terms of a "Madonna–whore" dichotomy represents an "optimal genetic strategy" for the males: They jealously guard their females (the Madonnas) against sexual advances by other males, while at the same time actively seeking to reproduce with any and all willing (or, in the case of rape, unwilling) females who can be found (the whores).
- Males are most attracted to females who show signs of good health and genetic fitness (e.g., youth, symmetrical features, intact teeth, clear eyes, luxuriant hair, and a waist-to-hip ratio of .70).
- Females are also attracted by health and fitness, but compared to males they are more interested in signs of wealth, status, and the capacity to protect and nurture offspring.

For those readers who are already familiar with the basic findings of EP, I apologize for this review of well-known arguments. For those readers who do not have prior familiarity with EP and who may be horrified at one or many of the points just noted, I apologize for not immediately launching into a full-scale critique of Pinker's claims. For the moment, I want to focus not on what Pinker says but on what he neglects to say. For all the learned discussion of mating strategies, parental investments, and reproductive behaviors, *How the Mind Works* says practically nothing about sexual desire itself — nothing about what sex feels like as a physical, emotional, and sometimes even religious experience. Here, as elsewhere, Pinker represents the EP mainstream by effectively dismissing the felt experience of passionate desire as a significant element in our understanding of human sexuality: "Sex means reproduction, and vice versa."

If Pinker and other EP researchers are right about reproduction being the primary function of sexuality, a puzzle immediately presents itself: What is the function of female clitoral orgasm? The pleasurable intensity of male orgasm seems easily explainable as a reward for successful reproductive efforts, a behaviorist's positive reinforcement *par excellence*; however, the clitoris has no direct connection to the female reproductive system (successful procreation can and does occur without it), thus its sensitivity to sexual stimulation has no obvious evolutionary value. Indeed, female orgasm has no reliably observable features at all. It produces no external physical evidence similar to the male ejaculate, and it is difficult to distinguish a genuine orgasm from a fake one — as Sally Albright (Meg Ryan) proved to Harry Burns (Billy Crystal) in the famous diner scene of *When Harry Met Sally* (1989). The use of pelvic thermography can provide some evidence that women's sexual responsiveness is not pure illusion but is similar to men's in its strong increase of blood flow to the genitals, which produces a swelling sensation of heat and energy. Research in such matters is notoriously difficult, however, as the same kind of "lab effect" found in sleep laboratory studies of dreaming also impedes the study of sexual pleasure using conventional CN tools, at least on humans. One clear finding is that orgasm in men and women involves the release of the neurotransmitter oxytocin, which evidently promotes intimate social bonding (oxytocin also plays a key role in women's bodies during childbirth and breastfeeding). Sexual desire in men is associated with higher activation in the amygdala, but actual orgasm is accompanied by decreased amygdala activity.[11] Animal studies have suggested that the hypothalamus and other limbic regions are crucially involved in the experience of sexual pleasure, and researchers have found that electrically stimulating the hypothalamus of rats, monkeys, and several other species has the immediate effect of producing a seminal discharge in the males. The effect of such stimuli on females is currently unknown.

Several theories have been developed to explain the human clitoral orgasm in evolutionary terms. Behaviorists have suggested that the infrequency of women's orgasm creates an "intermittent reinforcement" effect (i.e., a reward is more ardently sought the more unreliably it occurs). Looking more closely at the physiology of reproduction, some researchers have proposed what they call a "polcax" hypothesis: The deep relaxation following orgasm encourages a female to stay in a prone position immediately following sex, thus enabling the male's semen to swim toward the ovum with less gravitational opposition. A similar theory, inelegantly dubbed the "upsuck" hypothesis, identifies potential evolutionary value in the way the contractions of the vagina and uterus during orgasm propel the male's semen faster on its journey through the reproductive tract.[12]

The tremendous pleasure of orgasm, combined with its relative unpredictability in females, has prompted some researchers to suppose that female orgasm has evolved as a means of identifying males who will invest their resources in nurturing offspring — the first test of which is the male's willingness to invest in the female's sexual pleasure. To the extent that the human species uses pair-bonding as a primary evolutionary strategy (even if extra-pair-bonding also occurs with surreptitious regularity), the mutual sexual pleasure of males and females can be understood as an evolutionarily advantageous behavior in promoting the intimacy and durability of such bonding.

None of these theories has much empirical evidence to support it. Each of them sounds plausible, as EP arguments usually do,[13] but for the moment no consensus exists among researchers in support of any one of these explanations for the female orgasm. In fact, some scientific authorities have dismissed these theories entirely and argued that female orgasm has no function or adaptive value whatsoever and is merely an accidental byproduct of other evolutionary developments. Stephen Jay Gould points out that the clitoris develops *in utero* from the same embryonic tissue as the penis, and this leads him to argue that female orgasm only occurs as a vestigal expression of male orgasm, similar to the way a male nipple stands in relation to a female breast. Male orgasm has evolved as a true adaptation and is necessary for reproduction, while female orgasm remains only because natural selection has not (yet) seen fit to remove the clitoris from the female anatomy.[14] Pioneering EP researcher Donald Symons fully endorses Gould's line of thinking:

> If … adaptive design can be recognized in such features as precision, economy, and efficiency, it seems to me that available evidence is, by a wide margin, insufficient to warrant the conclusion that female orgasm is an adaptation…. The female orgasm may be a byproduct of mammalian bisexual potential; orgasm may be possible for females because it is adaptive for males…. The ability of females to experience multiple orgasms may be an incidental effect of their inability to ejaculate.[15]

When Freud was developing his psychoanalytic integration of neuroscience and philosophy, he did not have all the EP information available to Gould, Symons, and other contemporary researchers. But, just like them, Freud regarded the clitoral orgasm as an unnecessary and developmentally immature phenomenon that a normal adult woman should strive to overcome (with the help, if necessary, of psychoanalytic therapy). Here is the prescient passage from *Three Essays on Sexuality* (1905):

> The leading erotogenic zone in female children is located at the clitoris and is thus homologous to the masculine genital zone of the glans penis .... If we are to understand how a little girl turns into a woman, we must follow the further vicissitudes of this excitability of the clitoris. Puberty, which brings about so great an accession of libido in boys, is marked in girls by a fresh wave of repression, in which it is precisely clitoridal sexuality that is affected .... When erotogenic susceptibility to stimulation has been successfully transferred by a woman from the clitoris to the vaginal orifice, it implies that she has adopted a new leading zone for the purposes of her later sexual activity .... When at last the sexual act is permitted and the clitoris itself becomes excited, it still retains a function: the task, namely, of transmitting the excitation to the adjacent female sexual parts, just as — to use a simile — pine shavings can be kindled in order to set a lot of harder wood on fire.[16]

Freud's distinction between clitoral and vaginal orgasm is questionable in light of current research. Although some woman have special sensitivity in certain areas of the vaginal wall, this does not seem to be true for all women. Nevertheless, Freud's basic claim — that female clitoral orgasm has no directly adaptive function or healthy purpose — clearly anticipates the EP claims of Gould, Symons, and Pinker in its axiomatic identification of sexuality with reproduction. Even though EP researchers are generally quite hostile toward psychoanalysis, on this point the conceptual continuity is unmistakable. This should not be surprising, given that Freud greatly admired Darwin and imagined that psychoanalysis would strike as heavy a blow to humanity's self-regard as had evolutionary theory.

Sarah Buffer Hrdy has challenged the Freud–Gould–Symons view for its unashamedly masculine bias, and she points to the great cultural variability of the frequency of female orgasm, ranging from the highly satisfied women of the Mangia people of Polynesia, where young males are taught that "a 'good' man is able to bring his partner to climax two or three times for every one of his," to the rather drearier lives of women in the Irish island community of Innis Beag, where open discussion of sexuality is forbidden and where female orgasm is almost unknown.[17] American women lie somewhere in the middle of this spectrum. According to the 1994 *Sex in America* sociological survey, 29% of American women said they always experience orgasm during sex with their primary partner, while 8% reported rarely or never experiencing orgasm (the figures for men are 75% and 2%, respectively). The authors of the survey say they were surprised to find that male partners were poor judges of women's sexual pleasure. "Although just 29% of women said they always had an orgasm, 44% of men said that their female partners always had an orgasm. In contrast, women guessed correctly about their male partners."[18] Here is further evidence of the frustrating (to men) opacity of female sexual responsiveness.

Hrdy also gives an alternative interpretation of the female capacity for multiple orgasms, which contrasts with the male need for a refractory period following ejaculation. Among more promiscuous primates such as chimpanzees and bonobos, the females regularly mate with multiple males, often in rapid succession during insatiable ecstasies of what, to the primatologist's eye, appears to be orgasmic sexual pleasure. Interestingly, this same behavior among humans was observed by Yashodhara Indrapada, the thirteenth-century C.E. Hindu commentator on the *Kamasutra*, who wrote,

> When a man has ejaculated he has accomplished what he set out to do and stops moving, even if she is still working quite hard at it. And if a woman experienced the sensual pleasure of ejaculation like a man, she would then loosen his penis from her and stop. But this does not happen. When the man stops, she wants another man. For sometimes when a woman has made love with one man she may make love with other men who happen to be there. And so it is said:
>
> "A fire is never sated by logs,
> nor the ocean by the rivers that flow into it;
> death cannot be sated by all the creatures in the world,
> nor a fair-eyed woman by men."[19]

According to Hrdy, the strategic value of multiple orgasms for the female primate lies in the way it confuses paternity — none of the males she has mated with can be sure her subsequent offspring are not his own, and this improves the chances of her ultimate genetic success. At the least, Hrdy says, this orgasmically driven promiscuity provides the female's children with some protection from infanticidal males. At its best, this strategy means that each of the males will be motivated to invest nurturance resources in the female's offspring.

Following Hrdy's feminist critique, Marlene Zuk suggests that "maybe female orgasm is so variable and cryptic because it allows females to deceive males about men's sexual prowess. Only the woman can tell a man if he satisfied her in bed."[20] Zuk goes on to raise a crucial question that illuminates a deeper-lying problem, beyond even the glaring gender biases that distort so much EP research in this area: Why does sexual pleasure exist in the first place, of either the male or female variety? As we noted earlier, the common assumption is that orgasm provides males with a positive incentive to engage in reproductive activities, but Zuk argues that this assumption must be challenged: "Why do men need the reinforcement of orgasm while women can reproduce perfectly well lying back and thinking of England?"[21] Zuk identifies two problems with the "reinforcement" theory of male orgasm. First, it runs contrary to basic evolutionary logic. Because females make the larger investment in reproduction, it should be them rather than males who need the extra motivation of sexual pleasure, but, as already noted, pleasure is not necessary for successful female reproduction. Second, doubt is cast on the theory by the fact that "many, perhaps most, animals in the world reproduce perfectly effectively without any signs of the same type of sexual climax experienced by humans."[22] Zuk herself does not claim to have an ultimate answer to the question of what evolutionary function, if any, is served by human sexual pleasure, and she ends her analysis by saying that we should at least be honest about the full extent of our ignorance: "The point is that it is foolish to puzzle over why women can conceive without orgasm, over what possible function this trait should serve in females, when we do not wonder why males evolved the same trait."[23]

Well said. The mystery of the female orgasm has for so long been contrasted with the seemingly obvious utility of the male orgasm that we have deceived ourselves into thinking we know more about human sexuality than we really do. And, here, at this unsettling moment of wonderful ignorance, we reach the boundary of EP and CN understanding — where orgasm is decoupled from exclusive service to the goal of genetic reproduction, where sexual pleasure takes on a life of its own in human culture.[24]

III. Sex and the Sacred

If the study of the evolution of sexuality leads directly to fundamental questions about evolution itself, it is equally true that the study of sexuality in world religions quickly leads to important questions about the nature of religion: "[H]ow religions conceive of what it is to be truly human, as well as life's meaning, is reflected in each religion's models and mandates for human love and sexuality and for the understanding of gender."[25] Many traditions have used sexual imagery as a symbolic means of expressing religious feelings, beliefs, and experiences. *Sexual desire opens a way of relating to the divine* — that sentiment courses through the Song of Solomon of the Hebrew Bible, the rapturous poetry of medieval Christian mystics, the amorous myths of the Hindu avatar Krishna and his many female disciples, the bawdy rituals of Haitian Vodou, and many other types of religious expression around the world. The idea that the world itself is a product of divine sexuality underlies the creation stories of ancient Egypt, India, Greece, and several indigenous cultures of the Americas, all of which portray gods, spirits, and supernatural beings engaged in various sexual acts that ontologically engender the world and all its living creatures.

Granting the many nuances of cultural variation in religious treatments of sexuality, several recurrent cross-cultural themes stand out that relate to our interests. First is that nearly all religions regard reproduction as the predominant function of human sexuality: "And God said to them, 'Be fruitful and multiply.'" According to historian of religions Amy Lavine, "Procreation is the most sanctioned use of sexuality in every religious tradition. Every religion holds, to varying degrees, that women [and men] should engage in sexual intercourse for the purpose of propagating the human race. Frequently, this is the only form of sexual activity that is accepted by the tradition."[26] This, of course, makes perfect sense from an EP perspective — religious teachings can be seen as cultural reflections and elaborations on the underlying biological processes that govern human existence.

A second recurrent theme in world religions is that female sexuality is almost universally feared by males as impure, insatiable, and dangerous. This fear has motivated the construction of pervasive networks of religious, social, and psychophysiological control that aim at regulating the expression of female sexuality. Consider these four major traditions:

- *Hinduism* — The female body is considered a dangerous source of pollution, and strict laws govern women's sexual behavior — ideally, a bride should be a virgin, and she should never have sex with anyone but her husband, whom she should revere like a god. In some Hindu communities, the practice of *sati*, by which a wife joins her dead husband on the funeral pyre, expresses the ultimate female ideal: "By ending her life she precludes any possible sexual interaction with other men; she also brings merit and auspiciousness to his lineage for generations."[27] As Lavine points out, "The view that women have insatiable sexual appetites is portrayed iconographically in Hindu scripture in the image of the sexually aggressive goddess."[28]
- *Buddhism* — Like Hinduism, the Therevada and Mahayana branches of Buddhism have taught that the polluting nature of female bodies is so great that not only are women incapable of reaching the ultimate state of *nirvana* but they are also dangerous obstacles to men in their quest for that supreme religious ideal.[29]
- *Christianity* — In the Catholic tradition women are prohibited from the priesthood because of the belief that they are by nature incapable of performing the ritual tasks that mediate between the divine and human realms. Male priests take vows of celibacy, and even in the context of legal marriage sexual pleasure is merely tolerated. The fact that sexual pleasure exists at all is a shameful sign of our sinful, fallen nature, and the ideal means of reproduction would dispense with it entirely.
- *Islam* — The practice of veiling is the most overt expression of Muslim control over female sexuality; the practice of cliterodectomy is the most gruesome. Marriageable girls are regarded as property whose economic value stands or falls with their virginity, and as a general matter women are defined as inferior in status to men. The *Qur'an* requires men to abstain from intercourse with their wives (each man is allowed up to a total of four) during menstruation, but encourages it otherwise: "Do not touch them until they are clean again. Then have intercourse with them as Allah has enjoined you.... Women are your fields; go, then, into your fields as you please."[30]

Again, these views correspond very closely with what EP has argued are the evolutionarily derived propensities of human male sexual behavior. Further evidence of this widespread male fear of female sexuality can be found in abundance in the historical and cross-cultural study of dreams. Christian priests and monks have long complained of the seductive temptations of women in their dreams; during the era of the New England witch trials a man's dream of a particular woman could be taken as sufficient proof to convict her of witchcraft. The males of the Kuma people of New Guinea suffer recurrent nightmares about making love to strange girls whom they subsequently realize are *masalai*, or evil bush spirits, masquerading as humans. The Babylonian *Talmud* attributes frightening sexual dreams to the nefarious activities of the demon Lilith, who takes pleasure in torturing men with guilt-provoking erotic fantasies. Dark, dangerous females populate the dreaming imagination of males in both Hindu and Buddhist traditions. According to Serinity Young, "Goddesses such as Durga and Kali personify these dream women, as do the many female ghouls, ogresses, and wrathful yoginis of South Asian literature; they are all depicted as disheveled, with dark skin and adorned with bloodied body parts; and they have great power, are frightening and unpredictable.... [D]reams of such women predict death."[31] Members of the Hamadsha religious brotherhood of Morocco frequently have sexual dream encounters with the she-demon A'isha Qandisha. According to anthropologist Victor Crapanzano, "Belief in A'isha Qandisha is widespread throughout northern Morocco. She is usually portrayed as a female *jinn* or *jinniyya*, capable of appearing as a beauty or a hag, but always with the feet of a camel or some other hoofed animal.... She is always libidinous, quick-tempered, and ready to strangle, scratch, or whip anyone who insults her or does not obey her commands."[32] What Young points out in regard to Buddhist dreaming seems to be a more broadly cross-cultural phenomenon: Women have tremendous power in men's dreams but very little in their waking world.

In addition to the value of procreation and the male fear of women, a third recurrent theme in religious treatments of sexuality concerns its prevention, in the form of chastity, and its total renunciation, in the form of asceticism. Chastity as a religious ideal has always been emphasized more for women than for men, and it is, in effect, a practical combination of the other two recurrent themes mentioned so far. Chastity codes aim to regulate the precise timing of a woman's first sexual experience and control her ability to engage in sexual relations with men other than her lawful husband. As historian of religions Trevor Wade notes, "Religious authorities usually idealize the chaste woman as a paragon of virtue and devotion and promise her spiritual fulfillment, religious merit, or divine salvation.... [R]eligious texts overwhelmingly focus on female chastity, claiming it a paramount religious duty, describing how to ensure its preservation, and recommending harsh punishments for its loss."[33] In any religious tradition where lineage, class, or caste distinctions are an important part of the social structure, female chastity is essential in proving paternity and establishing the purity of one's generational identity. Asceticism, on the other hand, is usually a male practice, although women in some traditions (e.g.,

Buddhism and Christianity) are also allowed to pursue a life of worldly renunciation, including a vow of lifelong chastity. Many religions teach that achievement of the highest levels of divine–human communion requires a repudiation of human–human sexuality: "Hinduism reveres the sannyasin or renouncer ascetic, Buddhism enjoins non-attachment, and Roman Catholicism is committed to a celibate priesthood."[34]

A few religious traditions can be found where sexuality itself (not its metaphorical imagery, but its physical, embodied actuality) is regarded as a legitimate source of religious growth and transformation. Tibetan Buddhist traditions teach that orgasm provides, even for religiously untrained people, a brief experience of clear light consciousness. The Kabbalist mystics of Judaism recognize a sacred power in sexual experience (at least within the confines of marriage), and the medieval text the *Zohar* (*The Book of Splendor*) says, "The Divine Presence rests on the marital bed when both male and female are united in love and holiness."[35] Tantric ritual practices in both Hinduism and Buddhism periodically involve overtly sexual behavior, although this occurs far less often than is commonly supposed, and the focus is almost exclusively on the spiritual/sexual experience of the male: "[I]n many texts, when ritual sex does occur, the man is instructed not to ejaculate; instead, the goal is to reverse the flow of semen and in some cases to absorb the female's sexual fluids, thus enhancing the male's spiritual powers and denying the female any share of the spiritual power thought to be contained in his semen."[36] For Tantric practitioners, spiritual transformation is sought by means of forcible reversal of the ordinary direction of procreation, with the male drawing in the sexual fluids and "conceiving" new life and energy within himself.

At this point I want to bring the work of historian of religions Wendy Doniger into the discussion. Doniger is a comparative mythologist who has devoted much of her abundant linguistic and analytic skill to the study of sexuality in world mythology. She has produced numerous translations of classic Hindu texts such as the *Rig Veda* and the *Kamasutra*, as well as of Aeschylus' tragedy *The Oresteia* and Yves Bonnefoy's massive compendium *Mythologies*. Along with her translations, Doniger has written several works of comparative analysis that start with focused examinations of ancient Indian and Greek mythologies and then range out into analogical engagements with myths from other traditions, theology, politics, psychoanalysis, feminism, and film. She has a special fondness for mythic stories I would call "epistemological thrillers," narratives in which the characters and/or the audience are unexpectedly jolted by a radical shift in perspective — stories that provoke a powerful experience of wonder. The mind-bending dream-and-reality narratives of the *Yogavasistha*, the bed trick discovery of Jacob realizing he has slept not with Leah but with Rachel, Arjuna confronting the raw spectacle of Krishna's true divinity, the awestruck Job hearing God speak out of the whirlwind, Alice tumbling down the rabbit hole into Wonderland, Dorothy finding herself back in Kansas — these are the kinds of tales Doniger loves because the "trick of the illusion-shattering epiphany" generates an extremely high degree of existential tension, conceptual fluidity, and imaginative expansion. Both a connoisseur of wonder and a textual instigator of it, Doniger is particularly skillful at retelling these stories in her writings, producing in her readers the same vertiginous sense of multiperspectival insight that is the main subject of the myths themselves.

Like Pinker, Doniger writes with great flair, profound erudition, and entertaining playfulness. Although her wit is not as biting as his, she shares with Pinker a reverence for language and a deep concern with trends in postmodern scholarship that overemphasize cultural difference and devalue comparative research. Most significantly for our purposes, Doniger's findings about myths of sexuality have surprisingly strong affinities with the claims of Pinker and other EP researchers regarding innate human mating patterns. This offers a particularly good opportunity to build a case for integrated research across the religion–science divide, leading to new insight into the phenomenology of wonder.

Doniger says it is easy to state what a myth is not: It is not a lie, a false statement, or a superstitious explanation for natural phenomena, nor is it a transcendent archetypal structure fixed in the laws of nature or God. "What a myth is is a story that is sacred to and shared by a group of people who find their most important meanings in it; it is a story believed to have been composed in the past about an event in the past, or, more rarely, in the future, an event that continues to have meaning in the present because it is remembered; it is a story that is part of a larger group of stories."[37] Doniger originally planned to write a single massive volume on sexual myths, but ultimately (and appropriately) divided the project into two volumes — *Splitting the Difference: Gender and Myth in Ancient Greece and India* and *The Bed Trick: Tales of Sex and Masquerade*, both published in 1999.[38] The former takes as its object of comparative study the widespread phenomenon of "gendered narratives of doubling and bifurcation, stories that people (mostly but certainly not only men) have told about other people (mostly but certainly not only women) who have been split in half in various ways; split into an original and a double or a male and a female (in tales of androgyny and/or bisexuality), or severed head from body (or mind from body, soul from body, or left from right), or seduced by gods who appear as the doubles of mortals."[39]

The chief heroines of *Splitting the Difference* are the Indian princess Sita of the *Ramayana* and the Greek queen Helen of the *Iliad*. Their mythic life stories are very much alike: Both were married to great kings, both were abducted by a rival to the king, and both were the cause of a great battle in which their husbands fought to retrieve them and restore their honor. What interests Doniger is not, however, the "Cliff Notes" version of the archetypal skeleton shared by the two myths. She wants to track the multiple variants of the myths that have been told and retold in various places and times, including our own current moment in cultural history. In many of these variants, Doniger finds that the heroine of the story (Sita, Helen) is split or doubled in such a way that the woman who was abducted turns out to be a shadow or phantom of the "real" woman, whose dignity, virtue, and sexual purity remain untouched. In the smaller number of stories that involve a sexualized splitting or doubling of a male (human or nonhuman), the goal is usually to seduce an unsuspecting and/or actively resistant woman: "Thus women more often than men produce doubles in order to get away from the men who pursue them, in order not to be in a particular bed, while men (Indra, Zeus) more often than women double themselves in order to get into a bed where they are not wanted.... By and large, men split women in two to dichotomize them and women create doubles to protect themselves from sexual violence."[40] While granting that myths can and do serve to perpetuate unjust treatment of women by men, Doniger provides strong evidence that myths simultaneously express subversive female voices and provide vivid images of female ingenuity, cunning, and resourcefulness.

The Bed Trick complements the doubling theme in *Splitting the Difference* with its focus on the wild variabilities of coupling — who is having sex with whom. Doniger's concern in this book is the vast corpus of myths that portray alternating moments of cruel deception and revelatory insight as the paradoxical essence of human sexuality: "These myths imagine a situation in which a man or woman goes to bed with someone s/he is crazy about and wakes up to discover the astonishing fact that the body in the bed belongs to someone entirely different, someone hated or alien or just different."[41] From the deceptive sexual exchange of Leah for Rachel in Jacob's bed to the birth of Arthur following the rape of Igerne by Uther Pendragon, magically disguised as her husband Gorlois; from Helena substituting for Diana in Bertram's bed in *All's Well That Ends Well* to Mariana substituting for Isabella in Angelo's bed in *Measure for Measure*; from the amnesiac uncertainty of *The Return of Martin Guerre* to the gender-bending revelation at the end of *The Crying Game*, the bed trick as a basic plot "should make it onto anyone's list of the Ten Greatest Hits of World Mythology." Doniger goes on to argue that a careful study of these bed trick myths can enrich our understanding of the actual, embodied reality of human sexuality: "Now, this is not just a myth. It happens to all of us, all the time, for that ol' black magic, sexual passion, is transformative, at least transformative of our perspective; it changes our view of our partner.... [T]he sexual act is simultaneously the most deceptive and the most truth-revealing, the most alienating and the most intimate, the most fantastic and the most real of human acts."[42]

After considering several myths in which humans are tricked into having sex with animals and animals are tricked into having sex with humans, Doniger examines zoological research for insights into the phenomenon of sexual deception in various animal species. She reminds us that the word "cuckold" originated from the practice of cuckoo birds laying their eggs in the nests of other birds as a means of tricking those birds into nurturing the cuckoo offspring. She describes with obvious delight the cunning behavior of "sneaker males" among the bluegill sunfish (which imitate females in order to elude ordinary males and surreptitiously mate with actual females) and the orgiastic "mating balls" of red-sided garter snakes (in which a small percentage of males are "she-males" who produce female pheromones that distract the other males and thus diminish their reproductive chances relative to those of the she-males). Such examples certainly demonstrate that "animals are capable of both perpetrating and detecting bed tricks." More than that, Doniger argues that sexuality is by its very evolutionary nature a process of mutual deception. In humans, the inherent deceptiveness of sexuality manifests itself in the asymmetrical power relations between men and women: "The biological paradox, embodied in many of our myths, argues that it is biologically advantageous for men to be polygamous (the drive to scatter their genes everywhere, promiscuously) and for women to be monogamous (the drive to concentrate on raising one set of children).... [A] biological basis underlying the double standard may also contribute to the fact that, in life as well as in our texts, the consequences for men's adultery are so much milder than the consequences for women's adultery."[43]

As her discussion of zoology proceeds, it becomes clear how much Doniger's general understanding of mythology depends on the same basic evolutionary concepts advocated by EP researchers such as Pinker. In addition to her recognition of various cross-cultural regularities in human life and her contributions to the structural study of the human mind, Doniger explicitly links the historical prevalence of mythology to evolutionary forces that are the biological soil out of which the human species has grown. Her application of the "bottom-up" approach to myths of sexuality offers a surprisingly strong substantiation of the major claims of EP regarding gender asymmetries (likely accounting for the fact that both Doniger and Pinker argue against postmodernism and deconstructionism). However, this rapprochement has limits — any given myth is a bricolage (to use one of her favorite Levi-Straussian terms), a complex mix of the old and the new, the borrowed and the diffused, thus Doniger sees little value in quasi-scientific genealogical studies of sacred narratives: "There are no Galapagos Islands for myths."[44] More forcefully, Doniger rejects the scientific model as the appropriate one for her work: "The idea that the study of mythology is a scientific enterprise has haunted and perverted this discipline from Max Muller to Jung and Levi-Strauss.... But if we acknowledge our debt to art rather than to science, we do not have to submit to criteria like falsifiability."[45] Comparative studies exist in the liminal space between art and science, drawing on the aesthetic sensitivities of the former while identifying the lawful patterns that are the goal of the latter.

An EP approach that shows a greater awareness of and respect for the creative depths of the human imagination, a RS approach that focuses more intelligently on the ceaselessly dynamic interaction of biology and culture — these two methods are not the same. The affinities are not complete, but at least they are close to each other, close enough that we can use them in tandem to generate a unique form of stereoscopic knowledge. The vision(ary) metaphor itself provides a bridge between the two lenses: Doniger makes much of the telescopic and microscopic viewpoints provided by classic myths, while Pinker devotes lengthy discussions in *How the Mind Works* to the evolution of the eye, the cognitive operations that subserve ordinary vision, and the tremendous advantages provided by our ability to perceive objects in three-dimensional space. I suggest that we use EP and RS methods as two closely aligned perspectives that, when trained on a single object, can give us new insights into several dimensions of meaning.

By way of illustration, let us take a look at eyes themselves. EP in particular and CN generally have made perhaps their greatest achievements in mapping out the development and functioning of the human visual system. Partly because vision is the most highly refined perceptual modality in humans and partly because it is easily examined by all the modes of CN research (neuroimaging, brain lesion studies, animal experiments), we now have an abundant knowledge of what happens in the brain when our eyes see something. Much of this research has concentrated on the constructive qualities of vision, showing the various ways in which our perceptual system imposes order on the stimuli coming into it. This, of course, correlates very closely with postmodernist claims regarding the mediated nature of perception and knowledge and also with traditional Buddhist notions of the illusory nature of reality. The ease with which experimenters can trick human subjects with visual illusions may explain the cross-cultural frequency of bed trick myths. We keep telling ourselves these stories because we know how vulnerable we are to being visually fooled.

Ironically, the human eye was regarded by Darwin's earliest theological critics as evidence affirming the masterful role of Providence in creation and as a *prima facie* refutation of the theory of evolution, which the critics said could not account for the appearance of a bodily feature as intricately designed and perfectly suited to our lives as the eye. Today, a theological "argument from design" like this seems especially untenable in light of scientific advances in the past few decades. Pinker is at his best in *How the Mind Works* when he shows exactly how the eye evolved from light-sensitive receptors found in earlier creatures to its current human form and how in the specific mechanisms of their functioning our eyes serve valuable adaptive purposes that make a tangible contribution to our abilities to survive and procreate. The complexity of the human visual system, far from refuting Darwin, is a perfect example of evolution's amazing resourcefulness and creativity.

Francis Crick has pushed the primacy of visual perception to what, for CN, is the ultimate extreme: Vision is the key to consciousness itself. In his combative book *The Astonishing Hypothesis: The Scientific Search for the Soul* (1994), Crick argues that the best way to study the phenomenon of human consciousness (and, incidentally, to debunk religious notions of the soul) is to focus on visual perception: "[H]umans are very visual animals and our visual awareness is especially vivid and rich in information. In addition, its input is often highly structured yet easy to control. For these reasons much experimental work has already been done on it."[46] According to Crick, CN research has shown that the processes by which all the elements of visual processing are brought together provide the fundamental neural basis for consciousness. This processing does not occur in one specific place or location; Crick, like Damasio, Daniel Dennett, and many others in the CN field, insists that no "homunculus" dwells inside the brain, no little person who "sees" a complete picture of what our eyes are perceiving (the homunculus theory founders on the problem of infinite regress, as the homunculus must also have a little person inside its head, and so on). Crick argues instead that the binding of visual input into a coherent subjective sense of sight is achieved by a carefully maintained synchronization of massively parallel neural networks operating throughout the whole brain. More specifically, Crick and his colleague Christopher Koch have suggested that "the beat of a gamma oscillation (in the 35- to 75-Hertz range) might be the neural correlate of visual awareness."[47] Consciousness, in this view, is essentially a trick of timing, an *über*-rhythm created from the variable beats, pulses, and firings of multiple neural systems engaged in simultaneous information processing.

If we take seriously these ideas of Pinker, Crick, and other EP/CN researchers, we gain a new appreciation for a particularly intriguing feature of human vision, which has been known by researchers for half a century and involves the different role that vision plays in male and female sexual responsiveness. Compared to women, men are typically more aroused by explicit visual stimuli of sexual activities: "Men … are more likely than women to be aroused by the sight of a naked body, a nude pictorial representation, or a depiction of a couple making love."[48] Stephan Hamann and colleagues used functional magnetic resonance imaging (fMRI) to show that, when viewing identical sexual imagery, men's brains show greater activation in the limbic region (specifically, the left amygdala and hypothalamus) than occurs in women's brains.

The huge industry in male-oriented pornographic magazines and movies, combined with the ever-increasing amount of pornographic imagery on the World Wide Web, offers obvious cultural and economic evidence of this fundamental difference between men and women. Likewise, the prevalence of the "male gaze" in mainstream Hollywood filmmaking testifies to the predominance of visual sensations in male sexuality.[49] Drug makers have been more reluctant to acknowledge this. Recently, the Pfizer pharmaceutical company announced that, after eight expensive years of study, it had reached the unfortunate conclusion that its popular male impotence drug Viagra® does not work on women. "There's a disconnect in many women between genital changes and mental changes," stated Pfizer's lead sex researcher. "This disconnect does not exist in men. Men consistently get erections in the presence of naked women [or their visual representation] and want to have sex with them. With women, things depend on a myriad of factors."[50]

This is not to say, of course, that women are never sexually responsive to visual stimuli, but it does suggest that for men the eyes are especially sensitive organs of sexual pleasure. This, in turn, suggests that whatever affects men's eyes — whatever threatens them, enhances them, destroys them, transforms them — is likely to affect the men sexually as well, not just in the symbolic terms of a Freudian "upward displacement" but directly in the embodied, psychophysiological functioning of male sexual responsiveness.

Let us consider briefly a couple of myths that involve eyes, males, and sexuality. An ancient, well-known Indian story tells of how the god Indra pretends to be the human sage Guatama in order to seduce Guatama's wife, Ahalya. Different versions of the myth vary in assigning motives and blame to the characters (e.g., in some variants, Ahalya is fooled but in others she knows it is really Indra), but in most versions Guatama reacts to the discovery of the adulterous liaison by casting a rather spectacular curse on Indra: A thousand vaginas shall appear all over his body. Here is one version of the tale, recounted by Doniger in *Splitting the Difference*:

> Guatama cursed Indra, saying, "Since you have committed this false and violent act for the sake of a vagina, let there be a thousand of them on your body, and let your penis [*linga*] fall." Indra was so ashamed that he hid in the water for a long time. There he praised the goddess in her aspect of Indrakshi, and when she offered him a boon he asked her to cure his deformity. But she said, "I cannot destroy the evil created by a sage's curse; only gods like Brahma can do that. But I can do something so that people will not notice it: you will have a thousand eyes in the middle of the female organs, and you will have the penis and testicles of a ram."[51]

Not all versions of the myth include the actual castration of Indra, but, as Doniger notes, that extra narrative detail further emphasizes the idea that Guatama's curse is aimed at emasculating Indra. The thousand vaginas brand Indra's body with the defining physical feature of femaleness, visible for all the world to see. Combined with the loss of his penis, the result is to push Indra as far away from procreative male sexuality as possible. "Revenge of the cuckold" might be a good subtitle for the myth. Thanks to the mercy of a goddess, Indra has some degree of masculinity restored — he is still marked by the curse and he will never again have his own penis, but at least he regains a raw animal potency, and the manifold eyes offer him the possibility of renewed sexual pleasure. "The eyes are not vaginas but un-vaginas or ex-vaginas or even anti-vaginas; in this sense, at least, they are penises."[52]

At the opposite end of the visionary spectrum, the famous Greek sage Teiresias experienced a quite different curse involving eyes and sexuality:

> Teiresias once came upon two huge snakes coupling; when both attacked him, he struck at them with his stick and killed the female; at that moment, he was changed from a man to a woman. But seven years later he came upon two snakes again, struck them again, this time killing the male, and was changed back into a man.

> Now one day Jupiter, in his cups, was joking with Juno; he asserted that women had greater pleasure from love than men did. She disagreed, and they decided to ask Teiresias to decide for them, since he had made love both as a man and as a woman. Teiresias sided with Jupiter, and Juno was so angry that she condemned him to eternal blindness, while Jupiter, to mitigate her curse, gave him the power to see the future.[53]

Teiresias has several different visual experiences in rapid succession here: seeing the sexual union of the snakes, seeing (and making love) as a female, then seeing the snakes *in coitu* once again, returning to the visual perspective of a man, and finally losing his physical eyes but gaining the prophetic power to see into the future. For Teiresias, eyes are alternately informative, dangerous, and irrelevant. His testimony that women enjoy greater sexual pleasure than men do has echoes in texts from other cultures. One version of the Indra–Ahalya story includes an episode in which a female messenger (sent by Indra) tells Ahalya that "to be born a human being is the best result of many good deeds. And to be born as a woman is luckier still, for women have the ultimate desire and pleasure in sex."[54] Yashodhara Indrapada's commentary on the *Kamasutra* includes a respectful acknowledgment (from a man) about the greater sexual passion of women: "Women love producing the climax even if it takes a long time, because the climax is the most important thing. Women hate a quick man because he cannot take a long time to produce the climax. Indeed, women want a climax that takes a long time to produce, because their desire is eight times that of a man."[55]

This brings us back to the EP mystery of female orgasm. Could it be true that, while men are more sensitive to sexually arousing visual stimuli, women experience an overall greater intensity of sexual pleasure? Juno certainly does not like that answer (or at least she does not like having her husband Jupiter aware of it), and her curse, like Guatama's against Indra, has the effect of sexually maiming Teiresias; however, from this wound a new perceptual capacity emerges. Teiresias is granted the gift of internal eyes — he becomes a seer, a visionary. As we know from the neuropsychological work of Solms, humans do not need their physical eyes to see — our brain–mind system has evolved with a visionary capacity that can operate independently of external visual perception. A heightened proficiency with this capacity is what Teiresias gains in compensation for his blinding. The experience of having sex as both a man and a woman (another form of stereoscopic vision) unexpectedly and violently propels Teiresias beyond the sphere of ordinary human knowing; neither a woman nor a (complete) man any longer, he is now possessed of a vastly expanded awareness of time, fate, and the will of the gods. As indicated by the tremendous reverence with which Teiresias is treated in later Greek mythology, his visionary skills enabled him to make metaprocreative contributions to his community — looking beyond the given realities of the present to envision signs of future life potential.

Teiresias plays a key role in another well-known myth involving sexuality and male eyes: the tragic tale of Oedipus Rex. As Sophocles tells it, the father of Oedipus, having learned from an oracle that his son would one day kill him, takes the infant out into the wilds, tightly binds his feet, and leaves him to die. By good fortune, Oedipus is saved by a kindly shepherd and raised in a royal family, but later he discovers he is subject to an incredible curse: He is destined to slay his father and wed his mother. Determined to avoid this abhorrent fate, Oedipus leaves his home and wandered into strange lands, where by both fortune and skill he saves the people of the city of Thebes from the monstrous Sphinx. The grateful Thebans make him their new king, and he soon thereafter weds the recently widowed queen Jocasta. They have children, and peace and prosperity reign for many years, until a plague suddenly strikes the city. Oedipus prays to Apollo for relief, and the god replies that the plague will cease as soon as the man who killed the previous king is caught and punished. Oedipus immediately sends for Teiresias, whose visionary abilities are by now legendary, and asks him who the guilty man is. At first Teiresias refuses, but finally confronts Oedipus with the truth: "You are the man who pollutes our city." The king is outraged at this accusation and heaps abuse on the aged prophet: "[Y]ou are blind in eyes and ears and brains and everything.... You live in darkness; you can do no harm to me or any man who has his eyes." But the awful evidence accumulates, and when Oedipus finally puts it all together — his real father is Laius, former king of Thebes, whom he unwittingly killed in a fight on a wilderness road, and his mother is Jocasta, now his wife and bed companion — he realizes his own eyes have betrayed him. In a desperate spasm of self-loathing and remorse, he gouges them out: "For why should I have sight, when sight of nothing could give me pleasure?... What have I left, my friends, to see?.... [C]ould I look for pleasure in the sight of my own children, born as they were born? Never!"

Blinding is the punishment Oedipus must suffer for what in most human cultures is the ultimate sexual crime, incest. Simple castration would not be enough, for that would simply prevent his further reproductive efforts. No, he must sever all connections with the human community and cut off any further stimulus to sexual desire or pleasure. By destroying his eyes, Oedipus directly repudiates the source of his earlier pride and self-confidence; he relied too much on visual appearances, and now he must pay by sacrificing the very means of those deceptive perceptions. The first sight of his shocking act against sight evokes a dark sense of wonder in the chorus: "O horrible, dreadful sight. More dreadful far than any I have yet seen. What cruel frenzy came over you? What spirit with superhuman leap came to assist your grim destiny? Ah, most unhappy man! But no! I cannot even bear to look at you."

Now let us turn to the other end of the body and consider the feet. According to Doniger, a recurrent theme in myths is the foot as a sign of mortality and the human condition. From the vulnerable heels of the Achaean hero Achilles and the Hindu demon king Ravana to the tail-turned-into-legs of the

Little Mermaid, feet represent our primary point of contact with the earth, "grounding" us in the world of animal desire, instinct, sexuality, and death. The story of Oedipus is of continuing interest here, for his name literally means "swollen foot." His defining physical feature (until he blinds himself) is his lameness, the mark of his abandonment by his father Laius. The mutilated feet of Oedipus are bodily reflections of his cursed life, emblems of the unnatural fate he is bound to suffer and the twisted path of sexual desire he will follow, ultimately to his doom.

Here is another specific place where CN can make a rather surprising contribution to RS and where RS in turn can elucidate new implications of brain–mind research. The work of clinical neuropsychologist Vilaynur Ramachandran offers many points of contact with RS,[56] and here I want to focus on his research on the so-called "phantom limb" syndrome. Why do people who have lost limbs through accident or disease continue to report feeling sensations from those parts of their bodies? How does the brain generate such a compelling illusion of the presence of something that is plainly absent? Ramachandran's answer is that the brain is far more flexible and ready to adapt to new circumstances than has been assumed. When a body part is lost, the region of the brain responsible for mapping that part is taken over by adjacent neural systems. The brain apparently does not tolerate a vacuum; if one region of neural activity is no longer receiving the input it needs to do its work, the brain will use that space for some other purpose. The speed with which these transformations take place is surprisingly fast, and I agree with Ramachandran that the "implications are staggering." Not only does this suggest new possibilities for the treatment of neurological disorders long thought to be incurable, but it also justifies renewed investigation of the cultural forces that actively work to stimulate the experience of specific neuropsychological states (as we will discuss in the next two chapters). The brain–mind system is characterized by remarkable plasticity and flexibility, and we are just beginning to grasp its astonishing dynamism, complexity, and sophistication.

Ramachandran uses Wilder Penfield's work on the cerebral mapping of the body surface as a way of determining the exact neural basis of phantom limb phenomenology. Penfield was the first to identify the portion of the brain (in the central sulcus of the temporal lobe) devoted to the primary processing of tactile sensations from various parts of the body. The hands and face (particularly the lips) command the largest cortical areas, reflecting their acute sensitivity and importance in our behavioral engagement with the world. Penfield's findings (by far the most phrenological in modern CN) give Ramachandran a kind of road map to use in explaining the conditions of various clinical manifestations of phantom limb syndrome. For example, the fact that the face receptors in the brain are adjacent to the hand receptors means that, for a person with an amputated hand, phantom limb sensations can be deliberately induced by stimulating certain regions of the face. Touch a spot near the chin, and the person feels it in her phantom thumb; touch a spot up by the earlobe, and she feels it in her nonexistent pinkie. Of special significance for our interests, Ramachandran notes a strange connection between the feet and the genitals, whose primary sensory receptors just happen to lie next to each other in the brain. Here is an account of a telephone conversation Ramachandran says he had with an "engineer from Arkansas":

> "Is this Dr. Ramachandran?"
>
> "Yes."
>
> "You know, I read about your work in the newspaper, and it's really exciting. I lost my leg below the knee about two months ago but there's still something I don't understand. I'd like your advice."
>
> "What's that?"
>
> "Well, I feel a little embarrassed to tell you this ... Doctor, every time I have sexual intercourse, I experience sensations in my phantom foot. How do you explain that? My doctor says it doesn't make sense."
>
> "Look," I said, "One possibility is that the genitals are right next to the foot in the body's brain maps. Don't worry about it."
>
> He laughed nervously. "All that's fine, doctor. But you still don't understand. You see, I actually experience orgasm in my foot. And therefore it's much bigger than it used to be because it's no longer just confined to my genitals."[57]

Ramachandran admits that he was surprised to discover this rather kinky neural development in people who have lost a limb: "The journeys of science are often tortuous with many unexpected twists and turns." He mentions other cases in which both men and women with amputated feet experienced striking phantom limb sensations during sexual activity, and he comments: "This is what you'd expect if input from the genital area were to invade the [neural] territory vacated by the foot."[58] He goes on to suggest that CN may provide an alternative explanation for the sexual appeal of the foot among people with all appendages intact: "The traditional explanation for foot fetishes come, not surprisingly, from Freud. The penis resembles the foot, he argues, hence the fetish. But, if that's the case, why not some other elongated body part? Why not a hand fetish or a nose fetish? I suggest that the reason is quite simply that in the brain the foot lies right next to the genitalia."[59] So, the connection between feet and genitals not only is symbolic but is also the bodily consequence of neural cross-wiring in the brain. Just as CN enables us to recognize a deeper relationship between visual perception and sexual responsiveness, it also shows us a precise neurophysiological linkage between feet and human sexuality.

This apparent linkage offers new insights into certain myths about feet, particularly myths about wounded or painful feet:

- The feet of Oedipus are bound so tightly by his father that he is maimed for life; his misshapen feet physically manifest the awful, unnatural, inhuman character of his sexuality.
- The glass slippers of Cinderella (in European versions of the story) have the effect of both rigidly encasing the girl's feet and attractively displaying them for the handsome prince at the ball, whose openly stated desire is to find the young lady who is most beautiful, who (in EP terms) shows evidence of the greatest procreative potential. And it works — despite all the odds, Cinderella wins the marriage contest. How did she do it? As Alan Dundes comments, "It is clear that the glass slipper which occurs in several versions of the tale of Cinderella is an appropriate symbol for virginity. Glass is fragile and once broken cannot be repaired."[60] Of all the girls in the kingdom, only Cinderella's foot fits into the slipper; more than any of those other girls, her chastity is guaranteed. That is all a prince needs to know.
- The Little Mermaid may be immortal, but she cannot dance ("a euphemism for the sexual act," says Doniger), so when she falls in love with a handsome human prince she can only join with him by mutilating herself — slicing her tail in two and crudely fashioning a facsimile of human feet. The new limbs bleed profusely and cause her constant suffering, but at least now she can dance with the prince. Now she can marry him, mate with him (the violent splitting of her tail presumably created human genitals as well as feet), and bear him children. She has to give up her voice in the process, but being able to speak or sing (or have an orgasm) is not necessary for human female reproduction. The moral of the fairy tale, at multiple levels of significance, is this: No feet, no sex, no procreation.
- *The Little Mermaid* and many other mythic stories about feet in the Western tradition echo the terrible curse Yahweh casts upon Eve and the Serpent in Genesis 3:14–16, following his seducing her to eat of the forbidden fruit (which opened her eyes and gave her awareness of her body):

  The Lord God said to the serpent,

  "Because you have done this,
  Cursed are you above all cattle,
  And above all wild animals;
  Upon your belly you shall go,
  And dust you shall eat
  All the days of your life.
  I will put enmity between you and the woman,
  And between your seed and her seed;

He shall bruise your head,
And you shall bruise his heel."
To the woman he said,
"I will greatly multiply your pain in childbearing;
In pain you shall bring forth children,
Yet your desire shall be for your husband,
And he shall rule over you."

Here, in just a few harsh words, is laid bare the sexual burden borne by Eve and all her daughters: a terrible physical suffering in childbirth, made all the worse because they bring it on themselves — women will be compelled by an irresistible physical desire to continue seeking sexual relations with their husbands, even to the point of submitting to their total control. Along with that will come a constant battle with the serpent and his progeny, with a special focus on the violent interaction of human feet and serpent heads. In later Christian iconography, the foot imagery is carried to a new level of sexual significance in the numerous portrayals in medieval sculpture of Mary standing triumphantly in bare feet on the serpent. Her virginal purity enables her to overcome the curse of Eve, and the serpent cannot harm her when she steps on him.

Signs of chastity, manifestations of mortality, zones of intense sensual pleasure, targets of violence and coercion — our feet may be lowly, but they provide a remarkably powerful and deeply sexualized means of interacting with the world.

Religion and Psychology Interlude I: How Freud Fares

The specter of Freud has been a haunting presence throughout this chapter. We have noted Freud's comments (so congenial to EP) about the uselessness of female clitoral orgasm, we have taken a new look at the psychoanalytic ur-myth of Oedipus Rex, and we have reconsidered the sexual dimensions of classic Freudian symbols — the eyes and feet. We have also spoken of Freud's role as a historical foil in the development of CN, a field that understands itself as a correction to and scientific advance upon the outdated theories of psychoanalysis. Pinker, Hobson, Crick, Changeux, and many other CN researchers openly denounce psychoanalysis and argue that any further attention to such a scientifically useless theory is detrimental to the future advance of psychological knowledge. Freud is effectively treated as a ghost from the past, a malevolent ancestral spirit who continually threatens to break into the present and who must be firmly and decisively prevented from doing so.

I do not share this hostile view of Freud. On the contrary, I think the best thing to do is invite his ghost into our discussion (as one spectral guest among many) and welcome his continuing relevance to our investigations of religion and scientific psychology. The trick to living comfortably with the ghost of

Freud is to acknowledge the full force of the criticism against him. Referring again to the terms of Paul Ricoeur, we can no longer take psychoanalytic ideas in a precritical, first naïveté fashion. We must submit them to the fiery trial of skeptical analysis and find our way, if possible, to a second naïveté whereby Freud's texts can once again say something meaningful to us.

Ironically, the most severe criticism against Freud in recent years comes not from CN but from an English scholar, Frederick Crews. Once a leading champion of psychoanalytic literary theory, Crews had something of a deconversion experience and is now a leading voice in the attack on Freud (he identifies himself "as a one-time Freudian who [has] decided to help others resist the fallacies to which I had succumbed in the 1960s"[61]). Although it is tempting to turn the skeptical tables and explain Crews' career in psychoanalytic terms as a disillusioned disciple swinging around in Oedipal rage against his former master, the ease of making such a counter-charge should not seduce us into thinking we are absolved from taking Crews' criticism seriously. Crews and his compatriots in CN must be heeded if any intellectually responsible future use is to be made of psychoanalytic theory. To do otherwise is to disrespect Freud himself, by acting as if his ideas are conceptual museum pieces to be carefully preserved in perpetuity and guarded against any change or modification.

Crews lays out his case in two books, *The Memory Wars: Freud's Legacy in Dispute*, which reprints his controversial anti-Freud essays that appeared in *The New York Review of Books* in 1993 and 1994, and the edited work *Unauthorized Freud: Doubters Confront a Legend*, in which he presents twenty chapters by critics from several different disciplines. The charges against Freud made in these works can be summarized as follows. First and foremost, psychoanalysis is not a science. The clinical data Freud used to construct his theories (i.e., the free associations offered by his patients during therapy sessions) are worthless as evidence because they are indelibly tainted by Freud's self-interested position as the analyst. Second, his symbolic interpretations of dreams and slips of the tongue are absurdly idiosyncratic, baroquely elaborate, and utterly impossible to refute or disprove. Sometimes a symbol means this, sometimes it means that, sometimes it means one thing and also its opposite — anything and everything is possible, and only Freud has the unassailable authority to declare with Gnostic certainty which interpretation is the right one. Calling Freud "an intellectual megalomaniac," Crews says, "Classical psychoanalytic theory is best regarded not as a set of sober if perhaps improvable inferences from 'clinical experience' but rather as a perpetual motion machine, a friction-free engine for generating irrefutable discourse."[62] Further doubt is cast upon the credibility of Freud's theories by his dismal record as a therapist (psychoanalysis does not cure people of mental illness any better than several other simpler and less expensive methods) and by his authoritarian behavior as the secretive, quasi-religious leader of the "psychoanalytic movement." Regarding his metapsychological model of the human mind, Freud tells us nothing we did not know before:

> Freud deserves no credit for having introduced us to "the unconscious," a Romantic commonplace with ancestry stretching to Plato. Nietzsche in particular anticipated most of what sounds deep in Freud, and he did so with spirited wit instead of with diagrams and with false and self-aggrandizing tales of healing. Nor should we confuse Freud's psychodynamic unconscious — an unsubstantiated portion of the mind that allegedly schemes and subverts, lusts, atones, remembers, symbolizes, plays on words, encodes its thoughts in symptoms, and quarrels within itself while the subject remains oblivious — with unconscious mental functioning, whose existence is uncontroversial and can be readily demonstrated.[63]

In the end, Crews regards Freud as nothing but a charlatan who forcibly imposed his preformulated ideas onto his patients and called it "therapy" and who cunningly crafted an evasive, critically impregnable dogma and called it "science."

Even granting the obviously deep-seated animosity he feels toward Freud, Crews' mastery of the theory and history of psychoanalysis is impressive. For anyone who takes Freud's writings at face value, Crews' critique is devastating, and no amount of complaining about Crews' personal resistance to the truths of psychoanalysis can make his arguments disappear. Killing the messenger is not allowed in honest scholarly inquiry. This does not mean, however, that those of us in CN, RS, and other fields who still find some enduring value in psychoanalytic thought have no hope of developing a forceful response to Crews. It just means we cannot do so on the basis of an orthodox, unreconstructed reading of Freud's texts. My response to Crews begins with the observation that he makes his arguments against psychoanalysis without substantive reference to any other theory of how the brain–mind system works. Each time I have spoken with Crews I have probed him on this point, and he has consistently denied his need to offer any such alternative psychological theory. I can accept that. Crews has set himself the narrower task of evaluating the logical (in)consistency of psychoanalysis and its (non)empirical foundations, and he has admirably succeeded in that critical task. But, as a consequence of this self-imposed limitation on his approach, Crews has little to offer in the post-critical process of reevaluating Freud in the light of contemporary CN and RS. For the constructive purposes of this book, the purely destructive work of Crews can take us only so far, and then we must set it aside.

We should grant at the outset the dubious efficacy of psychoanalytic therapy. Freud's own texts provide ample evidence of his bullying clinical manner, as is painfully clear to anyone who has read the case of Dora (*Fragment of an Analysis of a Case of Hysteria*, 1905). Studies of Freud's patients following their therapy indicate that, his triumphant claims of successful cure notwithstanding, the people's conditions were not markedly improved by his treatment. Speaking more generally about the various schools of psychotherapy that have been inspired by Freudian psychoanalysis, the evidence is mixed for the consistency of their healing powers (though the clinical literature abounds with success stories), and they fare rather poorly when compared with behavioral and psychopharmacological methods of treating mental illness. The best that can be said is that psychoanalytic therapy provides a deepening of self-knowledge that may, for people without severe psychopathology, have a beneficial effect on their moods, attitudes, and relationships, although this usually falls far short of making people feel happy, contented, or "cured."

We should also grant that Freud's clinical experience, whether therapeutically successful or not, does not have the supreme evidentiary value he claims for it. His own personal involvement in the doctor–patient relationship, which he only belatedly recognized as "counter-transference," produces such a pervasive bias in his writings that none of it can be accepted at face value. Still, I do not follow Crews in categorically dismissing all the evidence from Freud's clinical experience. If we develop a good familiarity with his life context, if we use his admittedly biased clinical insights in conjunction with other sources of evidence, and if we follow Damasio's CN injunction to seek the "consistency among many individual subjectivities," we can still benefit from a critical engagement with psychoanalytic theory.

Last on the list of immediate concessions, we should grant that Freud behaved as a petty tyrant in his leadership of the sociological cult he called the "psychoanalytic movement." Psychoanalytic therapy has all the elements of a religious conversion, and the process of becoming a psychoanalyst resembles nothing as so much being initiated into a sectarian faith community. How many psychoanalytic patients develop a strong wish to become analysts themselves? How many of them actually do so? Regarding all the miserable little cruelties of psychoanalytic politics, the bitter quarrels with Jung, Adler, Rank, etc., there is no denying their venality, and I agree with Crews that an excessive idealization of Freud makes it difficult if not impossible to pursue a fair and open-minded evaluation of his theories. The fact that Freud may have been a despot among his colleagues, however, has no direct bearing on his theories themselves, which should stand or fall on their own merits. Remember, no killing the messenger.

A more interesting question regards the status of psychoanalysis as a science. According to Pinker and most of CN, the answer is an obvious "no," for all the reasons Crews has articulated. In this view, we should simply forget everything Freud said, wipe our theoretical slates clean, and construct a new psychology based on experimental evidence rather than subjective introspection. For Doniger and many RS scholars, the answer is also "no," but for a different reason. In their view, it does not really matter that psychoanalysis fails to qualify as true science because the "good" parts of Freud are those dealing with symbolic interpretation, and using those ideas does not require buying into the "bad" Freud's pseudo-scientific metapsychology.

Neither of these negative answers stands up to closer scrutiny, however. Taking the RS view first, Freud's scientific self-understanding cannot simply be waved away as an irrelevant quirk — it was central to the development of his ideas, and to ignore this is to misunderstand psychoanalysis in a fundamental way. I recall Bert Cohler once asking if Freud were alive today where would he most likely want to go: the Sorbonne in Paris to study deconstructionism and literary theory or to the Salk Institute in La Jolla to study brain research and cognitive neuroscience? An honest reading of Freud's life and works makes it clear he would far prefer the latter, and he would probably be horrified at the discovery that psychoanalysis has been all but banished from mainstream psychological science while being embraced by English departments and Cultural Studies programs. Recall that Freud was originally trained as a neuroscientist and published several well-received articles on various brain disorders; recall also that his 1895 *Project for a Scientific Psychology* expressed a vision that he never gave up on, even though he despaired of achieving it himself: a vision of a psychology that could integrate the neurophysiology of the brain with the subjective experiences of the mind. Freud was a real scientist, at least at the beginning of his career and according to the professional standards of his time.

Defending the authenticity of Freud's scientific identity may seem to give the game away to Crews and the CN critics because, starting with his 1899/1900 work, *The Interpretation of Dreams*, Freud's ideas strayed farther and farther away from conventional science, and it quickly became impossible to defend psychoanalysis according to the basic rules of evidence and argumentation adhered to by other scientists. But this is where Ricoeur's work is so important, in that it emphasizes that the development of Freud's thinking involved a constant tension between energetics and hermeneutics — between brain and mind, instinct and meaning, *das Es und das Ich*. Freud did not fail science; rather, he tried to enlarge its scope to include a deeper, more sophisticated engagement with the realm of subjective psychological (and religious) experience. Crews rejects this appeal to Ricoeur, but he is only correct in cases where Ricoeur is taken to authorize a purely hermeneutic use of psychoanalysis, which of course deviates fundamentally from Freud's own thinking. Crews misses Ricoeur's larger point, about the fruitfulness of seeking a mixed discourse between scientific and humanistic modes of inquiry.

Let us turn to some of the key notions of psychoanalysis to see how they fare in relation to recent findings of CN. We can start with the unconscious, which Freud may not have "invented" but which he certainly did explore in great depth and detail. Crews warns us that a sharp distinction should be made between contemporary research on unconscious mental functioning and the specifically psychoanalytic view of an unconscious region of the mind populated by scheming, deceiving, symbolizing agencies warring against one another. Recent evidence from CN suggests, however, that such a distinction is more difficult to make than Crews assumes. Consider this from Damasio:

> The world of the psychoanalytic unconscious has its roots in the neural systems which support autobiographical memory, and psychoanalysis

is usually seen as a means to see into the tangled web of psychological connections within autobiographical memory. Inevitably, however, that world is also related to the other kinds of connections.... The unconscious, in the narrow meaning in which the word has been etched in our culture, is only a part of the vast amount of processes and contents that remain nonconscious, not known in core or extended consciousness. In fact, the list of the "not known" is astounding. Consider what it includes:

1. all the fully formed images to which we do not attend;
2. all the neural patterns that never become images;
3. all the dispositions that were acquired through experience, lie dormant, and may never become an explicit neural pattern;
4. all the quiet remodeling of such dispositions and all their quiet renetworking — that may never become explicitly known; and
5. all the hidden wisdom and know-how that nature embodied in innate, homeostatic dispositions.

Amazing, indeed, how little we ever know.[64]

For Damasio, recent CN research has wondrously expanded our sense of the range and functional complexity of the unconscious regions of the mind. Contrary to the sharp distinction Crews wants to maintain, it now appears that the autobiographical unconscious of our personal memories and experiences is thoroughly intertwined in a much broader system of brain–mind functioning that operates outside the limited sphere of conscious awareness. More to the point, there is now good reason to agree with Freud in his view on the dynamic complexity of the unconscious. CN research has discovered neural correlates to the psychoanalytic defense mechanisms of denial, repression, confabulation, projection, and reaction formation. People with brain lesions to the right hemisphere often suffer, in addition to paralysis on the left side of their bodies, a syndrome known as *anosognosia* ("unaware of illness"). These severely impaired people will say they feel fine and their bodies are working perfectly well, and no amount of questioning or counter-evidence can shake their assertions. Ramachandran recounts the following exchange with a patient:

I gripped a woman's lifeless left hand and, raising it, held it in front of her eyes. "Whose arm is this?"

She looked me in the eye and huffed, "What's that arm doing in my bed?"

"Well, whose arm is it?"

"That's my brother's arm."

"Why do you think it's your brother's arm?"

"Because it's big and hairy, doctor, and I don't have hairy arms."[65]

People with brain lesions to the left hemisphere suffer no such denial about the fact that half their body is paralyzed. Ramachandran takes these clinical observations as support for the idea that the right cerebral hemisphere specializes in the detection of anomalous information, while the left hemisphere works to create and maintain a stable belief system. In normal people, the two cognitive styles work together more or less smoothly, but in patients with anosognosia the right hemispheric contributions are gone, and we can see the unconstrained functioning of the left hemisphere in the absolute denial of all evidence that might contradict the people's preexisting world view:

> What your left hemisphere does is either ignore the anomaly completely or distort it to squeeze it into your preexisting framework, to preserve stability. And this, I suggest, is the essential rationale behind all the so-called Freudian defenses — the denials, repressions, confabulations and other forms of self-delusion that govern our daily lives. Far from being maladaptive, such everyday defense mechanisms prevent the brain from being hounded into directionless indecision by the "combinatorial explosion" of possible stories that might be written from the material available to the senses.[66]

Ramachandran says he originally had little interest in Freudian theory, but after working with anosognosia patients he could not help but see the connection with psychoanalytic defense mechanisms, and he adds his voice to Damasio's when he says, "Freud's most valuable contribution was his discovery that your conscious mind is simply a façade and that you are completely unaware of 90 percent of what really goes on in your brain."[67] The picture of the unconscious emerging from CN includes, *race* Crews, a tremendous amount of self-delusional scheming, subversive symbolizing, and conflict-ridden cognitive calculation.[68]

These clinical observations correspond very closely to the findings of split-brain research (discussed in Chapter 1). Several remarkable experiments have been performed in which patients are shown images that only the left eye can see, thus only the right hemisphere can process the images. When the patients are asked to answer questions about the images they respond with a strange mix of knowing and not-knowing. The now-classic example (from a study performed by Michael Gazzinaga and Joseph Ledoux) involved showing each cerebral hemisphere a different image projected on a screen, and then asking the subject to choose from a group of cards the ones with images relating to the images on the screen. A subject named Paul was shown an image of a chicken claw to his right eye (left hemisphere) and an image of a snow-covered house to his left eye (right hemisphere). From the group of cards he chose a chicken head to go with the claw and a shovel to go with the snow scene. These were the correct choices according to the experimental design, and they demonstrated that each of Paul's hemispheres was still functioning in terms of basic cognitive abilities. But, the really striking discovery was that Paul insisted he still had a full understanding of his own choices, even though his left (verbal) hemisphere had no access to the visual image his right hemisphere saw on the screen. When the investigator asked Paul why he chose the claw and the shovel Paul quickly replied, "Oh, that's easy. The chicken goes with the chicken head and you need a shovel to clean out the chicken shed."[69] Paul's left hemisphere accurately knew the reason for its choice of the claw, but did not know why the right hemisphere had chosen the shovel — and so, determined to maintain a coherent belief system, his left hemisphere quickly fabricated a plausible, face-saving story to cover up his underlying ignorance.

Here is another account of a split-brain patient, a California housewife known as N.G., whose experience is more to the point of our interests:

> Once again the patient [N.G.] is asked to fixate on the dot on the screen. A picture of a nude woman is flashed to the left of the dot.
>
> N.G.'s face blushes a little, and she begins to giggle.
>
> She is asked what she saw.
>
> She says, "Nothing, just a flash of light," and giggles again, covering her mouth with her hand.
>
> "Why are you laughing then?" the investigator inquires.
>
> "Oh, doctor, you have some machine!" she replies.[70]

N.G.'s right hemisphere processed the image well enough to generate a normal physiological response (blushing and giggling) to the sexual stimulus, while the response of her verbally dominant left hemisphere was first to deny the image and then obliquely refer to it in a flirtatious aside to the investigator. Sprenger and Deutsch comment, "It is very common for the verbal left hemisphere to try to make sense of what has occurred in testing situations where information is presented to the right hemisphere. As a result, the left brain sometimes comes out with erroneous and often elaborate rationalizations based on partial cues."[71]

Further unexpected support for the psychoanalytic theory of unconscious defenses comes from EP in its discussions of the surprisingly adaptive benefits of not knowing our own motives, interests, and desires. Countless experiments in social psychology have demonstrated that people's self-perceptions regularly exaggerate their own benevolence and success while minimizing their personal flaws and weaknesses. According to Pinker, Robert Trivers, and other EP researchers, the evolutionary value of these self-deluded beliefs relates to the innate sociability of the human species (what Pascal Boyer calls our "hypertrophied social intelligence"). Our reproductive success depends on forming reliable social alliances with other humans; thus, we have developed extremely sophisticated skills both in giving a good public show of our trustworthiness and in detecting the possible untrustworthiness of others who are seeking our help. In such a species, the evolutionary advantage would go to those individuals who could best hide any personal weaknesses, misgivings, or secret wishes, and the best way to do that is first of all to hide them from oneself: "In a world of walking lie detectors the best strategy is to believe your own lies. You can't leak your hidden intentions if you don't think that they are your intentions … the conscious mind sometimes hides the truth from itself the better to hide it from others."[72]

Pinker is anxious to deny the connection of this line of thinking to Freud's view of unconscious defenses, but it is too late for that. Robert Wright, in his influential EP manifesto *The Moral Animal* (1994), shows a more generous and open mind in acknowledging the important continuities between psychoanalytic and CN/EP visions of the unconscious:[73] "What is best in Freud is his sensing the paradox of being a highly social animal: being at our core libidinous, rapacious, and generally selfish, yet having to live civilly with other human beings — having to reach our animal goals via a tortuous path of cooperation, compromise, and restraint. From this insight flows Freud's most basic idea about the mind: It is a place of conflict between animal impulses and social reality."[74] Although Wright's ultimate ambition is for EP to surpass psychoanalysis ("Freudianism remains the most influential behavioral paradigm — academically, morally, spiritually — of our time. And to this position the new Darwinian paradigm aspires"[75]), he is willing to recognize the continuing relevance of Freud's ideas about denial, repression, and unconscious conflict. For Wright, EP gives us a far more powerful means of exploring the unconscious and discovering its remarkable autonomy from, and frequent antagonism toward, our conscious sense of self: "Thus, Freud's model of the human mind may have been — believe it or not — insufficiently labyrinthine. The mind has more dark corners than he imagined, and plays more little tricks on us."[76]

Let us turn to another central element in psychoanalytic theory, the interpretation of dreams. How far can we travel on the *via regia* before we get bogged down in contradictory empirical evidence? Not very far, it turns out. Freud was right that dreaming is psychologically meaningful and offers a valuable source of knowledge about the unconscious functions of the mind. He was hardly the first to recognize this, however, and his insistence that the true meaning of a dream lies hidden beneath the empty façade of its surface has been refuted by a multitude of studies showing the rich meaningfulness of manifest dream content. Freud was also correct in suggesting that dreaming uses symbols and metaphors in ways analogous to art, folklore, and myth (hence, his enduring appeal to literary and cultural studies). But, other than that, none of Freud's major claims about the origin and function of dreaming have been confirmed by contemporary research. G. William Domhoff's *The*

Scientific Study of Dreams (2003) summarizes the past several decades of work aimed at testing the different elements of psychoanalytic dream theory, and the overall picture is not favorable: Dreaming is not the guardian of sleep; children's dreams are not always transparently wishful; adult dreams do not always contain references to early childhood memories and fantasies; day residues are not always present in dreams. Most problematically, Freud's key assertion that every dream is the fulfillment of an unconscious wish cannot account for the widespread phenomenon of posttraumatic stress disorder nightmares. Domhoff points out that these repetitive, painfully unwishful nightmares have significant features in common with recurrent themes in the dreams of healthy people, thus Freud cannot dismiss them as a minor, theoretically unimportant exceptions: "Far from being an exception to a general theory, the dreams of posttraumatic stress disorder are a strong test of the adequacy of any new theory of dreams. At the very least, traumatic dreams and recurrent dreams show that wish-fulfillment dreams are only a subset of all possible dreams."[77]

Psychoanalysis is thus turning out to be a poor guide in the quest for an overarching theory of dream function; however, we can admit that criticism and still appreciate Freud's insightful (though scientifically improvable) observations about dream symbolism and its relation to cultural creativity. My approach, illustrated earlier in this chapter, is never to use Freud alone but always in tandem with insights from other fields of study, as a complement to both CN and RS.

Id, ego, superego — these basic psychoanalytic terms may still be useful insofar as they reflect one fairly simple way of mapping the brain–mind system. The id can stand for the instinct-driven, emotion-generating limbic region (the amygdala, hypothalamus, etc.); the ego can be taken as referring to the so-called executive functions of the prefrontal cortex; and the superego can refer to those neural systems involved in self-monitoring, impulse control, and moral judgment — what Damasio calls "adaptive supraregulations." Many other ways of conceptualizing the brain–mind system are possible, of course, and the continued use of Freud's terms should not impede attempts to develop alternative visions.

This is not the place to launch into a full-scale retrospective evaluation of psychoanalytic theory. I have beckoned the ghost of Freud with the specific purpose in mind of adding his voice to our discussion of wonder and sexual desire. In terms of the psychoanalytic model of the mind, wonder can be defined as the feeling evoked by an encounter with stimuli from either external (conscious perception) or internal (unconscious id) sources that surprise the ego and defy its ordinary structuring of personality. If, as Solms says, the ego is best understood as a system of stimulus barriers that modulate arousal, then the dynamic effect of an experience of wonder is to overwhelm the ego with a sudden, extraordinary flood of stimulation that at least temporarily washes those barriers away.

The closest thing to a specific discussion of wonder in psychoanalytic theory comes in the notion of "the uncanny" (*das Unheimliche*), a feeling of dread and horror that Freud explains as the "return of the repressed," the sudden reemergence in conscious awareness of long-forgotten sexual fears and fantasies. Whenever people experience this strange and unsettling feeling, whether watching a play, reading a story, or (for males) seeing female genitals, Freud says the cause of the feeling is the linkage between the conscious perception and unconscious, deeply repressed sexual anxieties, particularly Oedipal fears of castration. Although this will not do as a total explanation of wonder, it is worth keeping in mind as a possible dimension in some wonder experiences. More generally, Freud's notion of the uncanny opens the broader possibility that experiences of sexual wonder may share a similar quality of merging the present moment of ego-jolting astonishment with early childhood feelings of sensuality and intimacy. Consider the following passage, from Freud's *Introductory Lectures on Psychoanalysis* (1916/1917):

> If an infant could speak, he would no doubt pronounce the act of sucking at his mother's breast by far the most important in his life.... Sucking at the mother's breast is the starting point of the whole of sexual life, the unmatched prototype of every later sexual satisfaction, to which phantasy often enough returns in times of need. This sucking involves making the mother's breast the first object of the sexual instinct. I can give you no idea of the important bearing of this first object upon the choice of every later object, of the profound effects it has in its transformations and substitutions in even the remotest regions of our sexual life.[78]

This passage can be taken as a microcosm of psychoanalytic theory: intellectually grandiose and unashamedly patriarchal, yet undeniably insightful and thought-provoking. Freud accurately recognized that sexual desire is a primary motivating force in human life, a constant source of tension and conflict in the individual unconscious, a driving impulse in many of our dreams, and a frequent conspirator in the various denials, defenses, and self-deluded rationalizations that fill our daily lives. He saw the importance of acknowledging the full range of human sexual behavior — our "polymorphous perversity" — and he taught us to recognize the manifold ways in which adult sexual desire is developmentally rooted in the earliest experiences of childhood. At the same time, Freud was an absolute and unrepentant misogynist. His perspective is decidedly that of a heterosexual male, and when he famously asked "What do women want?" he was being honest; he really did not know. His insistence that a mature, healthy woman must surrender the sensual enjoyment of clitoral orgasm goes along with his absolute privileging of reproduction as the sole legitimate aim of sex and his dismissal of all other forms of sexual activity as "perversions." Pleasure, particularly female pleasure, is to be strictly regulated and made subservient to the goal of (male-controlled) procreation. Freud saw it as part of his therapeutic duty to enforce this regime on his patients (most of whom were female) and batter down any psychological resistance they might put up against him. The libidinous passions of women must be tightly reined in — no wonder for them — and they must be made morally and psychologically fit to serve as passive screens for the infantile projections of men. Where whore was, there Madonna shall be.

IV. The Passion of Lester Burnham

It is not Freud the therapist we should follow; it is Freud the interdisciplinary thinker who points our attention toward meaningful symbolic connections between the body, dreams, religion, politics, and art. Some of his most powerful insights into human nature appear not in his clinical case studies but in his cultural writings, when he is analyzing sculptures, novels, fairy tales, and sacred texts. Freud had little contact with movies (he died in 1939), but legions of psychoanalytic thinkers since have explored films in quest of similar revelations about the deepest strata of human desire. From early on, filmmakers themselves learned about psychoanalysis and deliberately responded to it in their works, in direct portrayals of therapy (e.g., *Spellbound*, *Zelig*, *Analyze This*, the television series *The Sopranos*) and also in startling evocations of wonder as it emerges in sexual desire (*La Dolce Vita*, *Blue Velvet*, *Fatal Attraction*). By starting and now ending this chapter with a discussion of the sexual wonder in *American Beauty* I want to highlight the way movies can provide unique windows into the dynamic interplay of brain–mind functioning and cultural creativity.

The opening scenes of *American Beauty* portray a condition of spiritual anemia that is simultaneously absurd, normal, and horrifying. Lester Burnham's life has no wonder, no genuine feeling, no creative energy, no driving passion. His genetic interests are literally washing down the drain as he monotonously masturbates in the shower each morning, but, after his ecstatic, otherworldly vision of Angela at the basketball game, Lester's life is radically transformed. He is now filled with energy, purpose, and a renewed sense of self-determination. His lustful awakening sets in motion a cascading series of consequences that affect the lives of everyone around him, propelling them into their own profoundly decentering experiences of wonder and awe.

At first, Lester's newfound vitality is driven entirely by his genitals. After overhearing Angela say that if he worked out and built up his muscles she would definitely have sex with him ("I'd fuck him 'til his eyes rolled back in his head," she declares with cruel delight to Lester's daughter Jane), Lester throws himself into a new regimen of weightlifting and bodybuilding, surrendering himself to masculine sexual yearning at its most obtuse and single-minded. One day he joins his neighbors, a gay and very fitness-conscious couple named Jim and Jim, on a run and asks them for exercise advice. Jim asks, "Are you looking to lose weight, or do you want to have increased strength and flexibility as well?" Lester's answer gets right to the heart of it — "I want to look good naked." It is all about the bodies: Angela as ethereal vision of radiant beauty is now transformed into Angela as physical prize to be won by the strenuous cultivation of sexualized masculine muscularity.

Angela, it turns out, is no helpless naïf. She knows exactly how much she is worth in the reproductive marketplace, and she displays a skill at calculating sexual cost–benefit analyses that would make an EP theorist proud. She enjoys bragging to Jane about her multiple sexual experiences, and she admits she likes the idea that lots of guys at their high school masturbate while thinking of her. Jane is disgusted by the thought, but Angela has a keener appreciation for the economic implications — "If people I don't even know look at me and want to fuck me, it means I really have a shot at being a model." The heavenly Angela, supremely idealized object of Lester's reanimated desire, has her feet planted firmly in social reality. She fully understands the power of her sexuality and its strategic value in promoting her personal interests, and she knows how easy it is to manipulate men by means of visual fantasy.

At first Jane tries to be a good friend by offering support and encouragement for Angela's modeling aspirations, even though it means Jane must endorse a cultural definition of female beauty that excludes her own physical appearance. If Angela is right, that having males sexually fantasize about you is a sign of female power, then Jane is in a desperately weak position as she enters into womanhood. It is no surprise she is saving her money for breast augmentation surgery; it is a perfectly reasonable response to the reality of her situation.

Just like her father, though, something strange happens to Jane, something that brings a renewed sense of wonder into her life and radically shifts the ordinary bounds of her reality. It comes from the most ordinary of directions — the boy next door. A new family has moved in, the Fittses, with a stern military father (Chris Connell), a nearly catatonic mother (Allison Janney), and a teenage son named Ricky (Wes Bentley). Angela warns Jane to stay away from the strange, dark-eyed young man who shows up for school in a black suit and skullcap and who stares with unabashed admiration at Jane ("I mean, he didn't even, like, look at me once," Angela sniffs). At first Jane is frightened by Ricky's creepy intensity and omnipresent video camera, but she is also drawn to his self-confidence, and she cannot help but notice all the flattering attention he is giving to her and not to her far more conventionally beautiful friend. Indeed, this makes Jane suspicious (there must be something wrong with a guy who stares at her rather than Angela), and she accuses Ricky of being an obsessive psycho. "I'm not obsessing," Ricky replies, "I'm just curious." We get the impression that no one has ever spoken to Jane like this before, and no one has ever looked into her eyes like that. Out of nowhere, a spark of genuine romance has appeared in Jane's life, the wonder of first love.

At the same time, Ricky and Lester strike up an unlikely and largely illicit friendship. Lester is killing time at the bar of a big social event for Carolyn's real estate colleagues when Ricky, working as a waiter, sees his new neighbor and introduces himself. After a few moments of polite conversation, Ricky invites Lester to go outside and get high. Pre-Angela Lester would probably have come up with some lame excuse to decline the offer, but post-Angela Lester only hesitates a moment before saying yes. Once outside, Lester discovers more than the almost-forgotten pleasure of smoking a joint. When the manager of the club comes outside and angrily orders Ricky back to work, Ricky calmly says no and quits the job. Here is Lester's second life-changing moment of wonder, a jaw-dropping revelation not of raw sexual desire but of independence, composure, and self-respect. Gazing at Ricky with open amazement, Lester gasps, "I think you just became my personal hero." Soon thereafter Lester quits his own job in a rousing display of self-assertiveness. The new neighbor thus becomes an agent of wonder for both Jane and Lester, and his decentering, consciousness-altering presence in their lives counteracts the nearly irresistible sexual power of Angela.

Lester's wife, Carolyn, who wears an impeccably tailored suit of emotional armor every minute of the day, would seem the least likely candidate for an experience of life-altering wonder, but she, too, has an encounter with something marvelous and surprising, and as with Lester it initially takes the form of an immoral sexual passion. While Lester is in the back alley of the club smoking pot with Ricky, Carolyn is having a pleasantly inebriated conversation with the "King of Real Estate," a suavely handsome man named Buddy King (Peter Gallagher). Before she knows it, Carolyn is with Buddy in a hotel room, her legs thrown skyward as he grunts, "You like getting nailed by the King?" The bawdy comedy of this scene is fueled by the recognition that this really is what Carolyn desires, a procreative union with economic power and social success. She has been stuck for years now with the useless Lester, a beta male if there ever was one, a petty serf to Buddy's virile Lordship, and suddenly she finds herself joined loin-to-loin with the "King" in an ecstasy of sexual passion. For her, this is truly the stuff of wonder.

The key scene of the film (key in the sense of providing an especially clear expression of the ultimate creative insight of the film) comes soon after this, when Ricky invites Jane to come over to his house.[79] After showing Jane his father's weapon collection and war memorabilia, Ricky asks her, "You want to see the most beautiful thing I've ever filmed?" Jane says yes, so they sit down, he puts in a videotape, and on the screen appears the silent spectacle of a white plastic bag blowing in the wind in front of a red brick wall. Ricky tries to tell Jane what it was like filming this amazing scene, and the closer he gets to the truth of it the more difficult it is for him to express himself in words:

> It was one of those days when it's a minute away from snowing. And there's this electricity in the air, you can almost hear it, right? And this bag was just … dancing with me. Like a little kid begging me to play with it. For fifteen minutes. That's the day I realized that there was this entire life behind things, and this incredibly benevolent force that wanted me to

> know there was no reason to be afraid … ever. Video's a poor excuse, I know. But it helps me remember … I need to remember.… Sometimes there's so much beauty in the world I feel like I can't take it … and my heart is going to cave in.

Something softens in Jane as she listens to him, and the look on her face at this moment has greater claim to the term "angelic" than any expression ever shown by Angela. As Ricky finishes his almost mystical confession of a deeply spiritual and devastatingly romantic vision of life, tears start to fall from his eyes, and there is nothing else to do but for Jane to lean over and kiss him. While both her father and mother are consumed by reckless, deceitful, and essentially impersonal sexual fantasies, Jane finds herself in a relationship of true intimacy and mutuality — one might even say an adult relationship. Later, when Jane stands at her bedroom window and allows Ricky to watch (and video) her while she undresses, the effect is less of crude sexual arousal than of awe at Jane's willingness to share such profound vulnerability with him. The wonder here is that, despite all the odds and despite a dysfunctional family, an oppressive society, a thoughtless best friend, and an unconventional body, Jane is able to find in herself the capacity to transcend all of that and give herself to a real, emotionally honest relationship that is both intensely sexual and something much more than sexual.

At the very beginning of the film, before we see Lester, Carolyn, or anyone else, we see a video image of a young woman lying in postcoital repose on a bed. We later realize this is Jane being filmed by Ricky in his room, but in the opening sequence we do not know who this young woman is or what she is doing there. All we know is that she is talking about how much she hates her father for his sexual advances on her friends and how she would like to do away with him. The offscreen voice of the person with the camera asks "Want me to kill him for you?" and Jane sits up, stares hard at the camera, and says with cold parricidal certainty "Yeah, would you?" The emotional effect of this initial scene strikes me as a perfect example of the Freudian "uncanny," an inexplicable horror and dread, a sense of foreboding at the dangerous eruption of primal sexual fantasies and conflicts.[80] There is another moment in the film of even greater uncanniness, a moment when a character suddenly encounters something that is overtly revolting and yet inexplicably alluring. It comes when Col. Fitts, Ricky's righteously homophobic father, happens to look out the window and sees Ricky over at Lester's house. Already suspicious from seeing Lester out running with Jim and Jim, Col. Fitts stares with a strange mix of horror and fascination as Lester and Ricky appear to engage in a homosexual tryst. The intensity of feeling here has little to do with homosexuality *per se* (there is nothing uncanny about the resolutely normal Jim and Jim) and everything to do with the intensity of Col. Fitts' unconscious repression of any feelings or desires that deviate from the hypermasculinity of his public identity.[81] In this scene, as with the opening video of Jane, the uncanny appears as a frightening species of sexualized wonder that has been bent, deformed, and fragmented by the dark prism of frustrated desire.

Lester is going to die. He told us that at the start of the film, and as his story approaches its inevitably fatal conclusion we become prey to an acute emotional tension — we know his death is just ahead, and yet we see him growing stronger, faster, more confident every day, vital energy coursing through his body, his life hurtling forward toward a sudden, certain doom. He has impressively achieved his goal of reshaping his body, cultivating a bulging masculine virility to match Angela's bewitching feminine allure, and on the night he will die he finally gets the opportunity to claim his prize. Angela sits alone in his darkened house while a torrential rain beats down outside. Jane has abruptly broken off their friendship, and Ricky has told Angela that she is boring and ordinary, "and you know it." Possessed of few introspective resources, Angela is crushed by this harsh confrontation with her own secret emptiness. Now the well-built, genuinely handsome Lester walks up to her, gently takes her in his arms, and tells her, "You are the most beautiful thing I have ever seen." Angela submissively lies down on the living room couch and allows Lester to slowly remove her pants, and then open her shirt. Lester's fantasy is becoming real — the otherworldly vision he first saw at the basketball game is now an actual physical presence in front of him, a supple, receptive body, his for the sexual taking.

Then Angela blurts out a hasty confession — "This is my first time." Lester laughs, unable to believe what he is hearing. Ashamed, Angela says she hopes he will not be disappointed by her inexperience. Lester suddenly realizes what that means, and in an instant the whole situation changes for him.[82] This startling revelation marks his third moment of wonder. Lester is abruptly forced into a radical revisioning of who Angela is: She is no whore — she is a Madonna, a virgin — and this realization provokes a new understanding of who Lester is in relation to her.

What is striking to me is the way this new recognition of Angela should, according to EP theory, raise her value as a target of sexual desire. Lester has the ultimate EP fantasy in front of him: A willing virgin. Yet, he turns away — *he turns away.* Something else enters his life here, and Lester now finds himself guided by a strange force even more powerful than that of sexual desire. Angela is no longer the mystical ideal of his ardent erotic longing; she is just a poor, confused teenage girl who needs a blanket. Lester is no longer the monomaniacal slave of his genitals; he has been spun around, decentered, and radically changed once again. Now he has become ... what? He is not sure, but when Angela asks him how he is doing, Lester can smile and say with absolute honesty, "I'm great." He picks up a framed family portrait, a picture of him, Carolyn, and Jane laughing and having fun at an amusement park. Whatever has happened to him now, whatever this utterly unexpected metasexual insight has done to him, it is drawing him back to his family, back to the actuality of these two women in his life. He gazes at the picture and sighs with rediscovered appreciation, "Man, oh, man...."

At that moment Lester's head explodes. More precisely, a gun shoots at him at point-blank range, spraying bright red blood on the white tiled kitchen wall. Lester's death is the effect, most immediately, of a violent explosion of repressed male sexuality. The trigger is pulled by Col. Fitts, whose awkward pass at Lester left him humiliated and exposed as a person driven by those same homosexual desires he had always claimed to despise. But, Lester's death is more than that. It is also the spiritual apotheosis of his life, a release from the bonds of brute sexual instinct and an achievement of a joyful, transcendental wisdom. Although *American Beauty* makes no direct reference to organized religion, it speaks directly to the existential questions, numinous encounters, and visionary experiences I regard as central to human religiosity. Lester's discovery of a realm beyond sexual desire — a realm of joy, honesty, and compassion — transforms him in a way that is familiar to nearly all religions. He has been enlightened, awakened, saved. Suddenly everything makes sense, fear just fades away, and he overflows with gratitude for "every single moment of my stupid little life." One last time, Ricky, the romantic visionary, enterprising drug dealer, and young master of thaumaturgy, is there to bear witness to Lester's metamorphosis. Though half of his head has been blown off and he is lying dead in a pool of blood, Lester has a faint but unmistakable smile on his face.

3

Creative Madness

3
Creative Madness

I. Teen Spirit

Just before dawn on the morning of April 5, 1994, Kurt Cobain, singer and guitarist for the Seattle band Nirvana, injected a massive dose of heroin into his arm, put the barrel of a .12-gauge shotgun into his mouth, and fired. His lifeless body was found three days later, along with a carefully written letter addressed to Boddah, his imaginary friend from childhood. The letter expresses a variety of painful, negative emotions — sadness, guilt, anger, self-loathing, and a wistful desire to regain the "enthusiasm I once had as a child." He repeatedly comes back to the word "empathy" and his acute sensitivity to the feelings of other people, something that fills him with both love and misanthropic hatred. The note closes with the words, "Thank you all from the pit of my burning nauseous stomach for your letters and concern during the past years. I'm too much of an erratic, moody baby! I don't have the passion anymore and so remember it's better to burn out than to fade away."[1]

The news of Cobain's suicide was received with shock, sorrow, and, in some cases, harsh moral criticism. The reaction was most intense in Seattle, where radio stations devoted all-day coverage to Cobain's death and where 7000 people gathered at a community center for a candlelight vigil. Similar vigils with smaller but no less emotionally distraught fans were held all over the United States and in Europe. *The New York Times* devoted a front-page story to the suicide, making a point of questioning Cobain's unstable character and lack of moral responsibility. In so doing, the newspaper anticipated the judgmental response of numerous mainstream media commentators who denounced Cobain as a failure to his generation. The moral condemnation of his suicide was intertwined with the controversial mourning behavior of his wife, Courtney Love, who read aloud to the audience of the Seattle vigil portions of Cobain's note to Boddah: "I'm not gonna read you all the note, because it's none of your fucking business. But some of it is to you. I don't really think it takes away his dignity to read this, considering that it's addressed to most of you. He's such an asshole. I want you all to say 'asshole' really loud." The crowd complied with a loud chant of "Asshole!" Sobbing, Love went on to read the note, which she repeatedly interrupted with rageful tirades against her husband ("Shut up! Bastard!"), concluding with a furious denunciation: "Just remember, this is all bullshit! ... I have to go now. Just tell him he's a fucker, okay? Just say, '*Fucker*, you're a *fucker*.' And that you love him."

In death, as in life, Kurt Cobain provoked a dark, pain-ridden, viciously self-critical experience of wonder. Without burdening his already over-analyzed career with undue cosmic significance, I want to draw upon his music as a source of reflection and insight for this study of creativity as a third major sphere of wonder. Creativity in this view is the process of bringing something new into being, something original and surprising, something that reveals a vital aspect of truth, reality, beauty — *to be creative is to work wonders*. Cobain's life as a musician embodies the cluster of themes I want to explore in this chapter: creativity, madness, drugs, music, religion, death, and mourning. Using the resources of cognitive neuroscience (CN) and religious studies (RS) to investigate the dynamic interplay of these themes will enable us to understand better the phenomenology of wonder in aesthetic experience, wonder in the artist's creative activity, and wonder in the reactions of audiences and the broader culture.

II. The Neuroscience of Creativity and Madness

The best place to start a discussion of CN research on creativity is with the phenomenon of *neurogenesis*, which refers to the process by which neurons are formed and take their places within the broader neural networks of the brain. To some degree, neurogenesis is driven by the evolutionary imperatives of our genes. According to Richard Thompson, "The major circuits in the brain are basically the same in all mammals: there is a high degree of predetermination, or 'hard-wiring,' in the mammalian brain."[2] New advances in human genetics have shown, however, that the influence of genes on brain development is far less than many CN researchers had initially expected. According to the latest estimates of the Human Genome Project, the DNA of our species is distinguished by a collection of approximately 30,000 genes — not a small number but not a very big number, either, considering that the lowly earthworm has around 15,000 genes. The capacity of humankind to create a highly complex and variegated mental life with only 30,000 genes to work with is one of the great mysteries of contemporary CN. Thompson, writing in 2000 when the consensus estimate was 100,000 genes in the human genome, says there is no way that our brain development could be totally determined by genetic control: "Simple arithmetic argues against this. There are literally trillions of synapses in the human brain, far too many connections to be specified in detail by the genes."[3] Schwartz and Begley call it "the genetic shortfall: too many synapses, too few genes. Our DNA is simply too paltry to spell out the wiring diagram for the human brain."[4]

The growing brain of the human fetus produces far more neurons than it will eventually use. Neurogenesis in the fetus reaches a peak total of approximately 200 billion neurons, but only half of these will actually be used in new synaptic networks, while the other half die away before birth. "Pruning" is the term used to describe the prenatal process of trimming and shaping the early proliferation of bushy dendritic sproutlings. Of special interest for our purposes in this chapter, the fetal brain is subject to repeated bursts of random neural activity by which nascent synaptic circuits are formed, tested, and either preserved or discarded. Some of this chaotic activation is necessary for the formation of basic human capacities such as vision: "The spontaneous but synchronous firing ... excites a local group of target neurons [involved in processing retinal input] and such synchronized activity appears to strengthen those synapses," thereby preparing the fetus for vision well before the eyes have opened.[5]

Although genetic programming does specify the cerebral localization of many important neural systems, the brain of a newborn human retains a huge capacity for structural change and flexible adaptation. This capacity is most vividly displayed in neuropsychological cases of young children who, because of chronic, life-threatening seizures, have undergone the radical treatment of hemispherectomy. As Schwartz and Begley explain it: "The brain of a child is almost miraculously resilient, or plastic: Surgeons can remove the entire left hemisphere, and thus (supposedly) all of the brain's language regions, and the child still learns to talk, read, and write as long as the surgery is performed before age four or five. Although in most people the left cerebral hemisphere supports language, the brain, it seems, can roll with the punches (or surgery) well enough to reassign language function to the right cerebral hemisphere, all the way over on the other side of the head."[6]

Taken together, research on neurogenesis suggests that the creative power of the brain depends fundamentally on how the brain itself is created. A huge number of neurons are produced, subjected to intense stimulation, and then pruned into functional networks of increasing complexity and sophistication. Neurogenesis occurs most vigorously in the fetus and newborn, but that is not the end of it. Another major burst of new neural production occurs in adolescence, particularly in the frontal and parietal lobes. The frontal lobe is responsible for "'executive' functions [such] as self-control, judgment, emotional regulation, organization, and planning"; the latter for integrating "information from far-flung neighborhoods of the brain, such as auditory, tactile, and visual signals."[7] Developmental psychologists from Freud on have noticed similar experiential dynamics in early childhood and adolescence, and now CN has provided a neurological account of the connection between the two different stages of life: "The teen brain, it seems, reprises one of the most momentous acts of infancy, the overproduction and then pruning of neuronal branches."[8] Neurogenesis can and does extend farther into adulthood — how much farther is an open question. For now, the main point is that the prenatal creation of functional neural networks in the brain provides humans with the physical foundation for postnatal creativity in all its varied and colorful manifestations.

Several contemporary neuroscientists have examined the relevance of brain–mind research for the understanding of creativity, art, and aesthetic experience. Jean-Pierre Changeux makes a number of interesting points about this branch of CN research that relate to our discussion. Most importantly, Changeux openly states what is for many CN researchers the unspoken subtext of their interest in creativity: Art is superior to religion, and one can hope that it will replace it as an ultimate source of meaning and guidance in human life. Changeux does not accept Ricoeur's notion of an "inspired dimension" of experience that stimulates madness, artistic genius, and religious enthusiasm: "There is nothing ineffable in the creative work of the artist that would justify making of it a [new] level superior to the others, as Nietzsche wished to do."[9] For Changeux, human creativity is an outgrowth of the "projective style of the functioning of our brain," by which our perceptions of the world are shaped by the filtering processes of our cognitive system. We never know reality "as it is." We only know what our brains have been able to process, based on our past experiences and future expectations. (This is one of the main reasons for the paradoxical appeal of CN research to idealist world views such as that of Zen Buddhism, best illustrated by James Austin's *Zen and the Brain.*) In a very literal sense, we are neurologically creating our reality every moment of our lives.

Changeux goes on to note the prevalence of exploratory behavior in various animal species, suggesting that human creativity reflects a dramatic expansion of the curiosity, daring, and desire for new experience that drive such behavior. Exploration helps us avoid being trapped within the confines of our neurally generated expectations, and it maintains our freedom to adapt and change in the face of new circumstances. Exploration leads to surprise, discovery, innovation. At its best, it leads to wonder. What humans are able to do especially well, thanks to the tremendous flexibility and processing power of our brains, is to make adaptive use of the new knowledge gained by our exploratory behavior. In this view, the creativity of a painter, a musician, or a dancer is a highly sophisticated, freely flowing expression of the basic neural machinery that characterizes every member of our species: "[I]t seems reasonable to suppose that creativity results from epigenetic combination at the level of the evolution of individual thought, involving the highest cognitive and/or affective representations. It may be that spontaneous combinatorial variations are the source of new ideas."[10] On this last point Changeux echoes the CN research on neurogenesis we just mentioned. Whether the source is internal or external, in the brain or out in the environment, it appears that creativity depends in large part on the spontaneous stimulation of new synaptic connections and neural networks. Changeux envisions a time in the near future when

CN researchers will be able to specify with great exactitude the "cerebral architectures of aesthetic pleasure," and contrary to Ricoeur's evocation of religious powers he affirms the dignity of purely human creativity and proclaims the supreme importance of art in the life of civilized society:

> [A]rt possesses ... the faculty of stimulating the mind, the evocative power that makes images, memories, recollections, and gestures suddenly appear in the brain of the viewer or listener and, in so doing, provides food for thought and gives rise to dreams — to the shared dream of an authentically good life.... I would replace your [inspired] level by the more down-to-earth notion of *conatus*, the joyous effort and striving of the creator. This quite terrestrial enterprise makes no appeal to any extrahuman inspiration or mystical ecstasy whatever. The brain of the artist holds center stage here, and the finished work results from a long process of trial and error in which the history of the work itself is merged with the artist's own personal history and, of course, the history of the art he practices.[11]

This is why Changeux feels emboldened to assert the advantage of art over religion in the basic goal of bringing people together (*religare*). Art not only stimulates the brain, expands the adaptive range of cognitive functioning, and brings pleasure and joy into life, but it also promotes an ethical engagement with others, helping us bridge our differences and communicate vital meanings: "The emotional power of forms, the capacity to surprise and to shock, the singular perception of coherence, rhythm, and novelty give art a force of communication that makes it an effective rival of religion.[12]

Another prominent scientific voice affirming the evolutionary benefits of art is E.O. Wilson. Although not as hostile to religion as Changeux (Wilson was raised as a Southern Baptist and continues to speak respectfully of that tradition), Wilson is even more grandly assertive in his CN interpretation of artistic creativity. Evidence is accumulating, he says, that "innovation is a concrete biological process founded upon an intricacy of nerve circuitry and neurotransmitter release. It is not the outpouring of symbols by an all-purpose generator or any conjuration therein by ethereal agents."[13] No special part of the brain makes people talented at different kinds of artistic expression; rather, CN research suggests that highly creative artists make a *broader* use of the same neural systems possessed by all humans. The difference between artists and ordinary people is a matter of quantitative improvement in brain functioning, not some intangible quality or mysterious endowment. For example, Wilson says that "experiments using brain imaging ... have failed to disclose singular neurobiological traits in musically gifted people. Instead, they show engagement of a broader area of the same parts of the brain used by those less able."[14]

As would be expected given Wilson's sociobiology project, he seeks to explain art, creativity, and aesthetic experience in terms of the same ecological pressures and genetic influences that have always been the driving forces of human evolution. For Wilson, the key factor in the development in *Homo sapiens* is an extremely high degree of intelligence, which has had as a negative side effect "the shocking recognition of the self, of the finiteness of personal existence, and of the chaos of the environment.... *Homo sapiens* is the only species to suffer psychological exile."[15] Humans have borne great misery because of this shocking (one might also say wonderful) self-discovery, and artistic creativity is fundamentally motivated by an urgent desire to relieve that misery: "The dominating influence that spawned the arts was the need to impose order on the confusion caused by intelligence."[16] The explosive advances in human civilization over just the past few thousand years have occurred at a much faster rate than our genetic programming has been able to keep up with, compelling our species to invent the arts as a means by which we can create order, structure, and meaning amid the frightening, chaotic vastness of self-aware existence. From the earliest periods of prehistory right into the present, artists have served the valuable function of transforming our inborn existential terrors into manageable, meaningful shapes and forms. These creations are best measured, according to Wilson, by their fidelity to human nature, their accuracy in portraying our basic genetic drives, and their effectiveness in prompting us to adopt adaptive, survival-enhancing behavior: "[T]hat is what we mean when speak of the true and the beautiful in the arts."[17]

Changeux and Wilson draw upon the latest CN research to argue that artistic creativity is an innate characteristic of the human species, improving our chances for survival and reproductive success. This is an eminently sensible perspective and is quite helpful for our project; yet, it neglects something crucial about creativity, something that Freud, Jung, and James all recognized clearly, as did many earlier generations of Western thinkers: *Creativity is a kind of madness.* It involves struggle, effort, and moments of intense concentration; it generates strong emotions, unusual body sensations, and strange slippages of time. For many people, the experience of artistic creativity involves bursts of manic passion intertwined with suffering, distress, and confusion. CN researchers have tended to domesticate creativity, emphasizing its happy benefits and ignoring its darker roots in disordered neural functioning. This is perhaps not surprising, given that the primary mission of CN is to make madness go away. As Presidential Proclamation 6158 makes clear, a major goal of contemporary CN is to find treatments and cures for a variety of brain–mind injuries, diseases, and disorders. From 1990 to the present, huge strides have been made in identifying the underlying neuropathology of many forms of mental illness, and even greater progress is sure to come in the very near future from investigations in molecular genetics, neuropsychology, and brain imaging. The proven ability of CN research to help alleviate human suffering has earned the field widespread moral approbation and expanded financial support, and the time has already come when most of you reading this book will benefit in some way or another from this brain–mind revolution — by

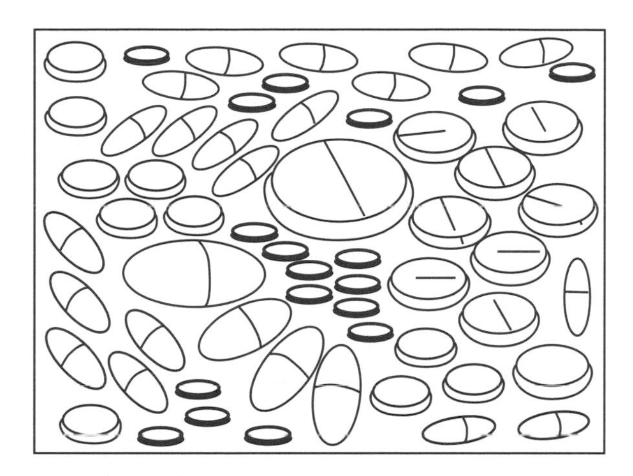

Figure 3.1 According to the U.S. Drug Enforcement Agency, prescriptions for psychiatric medications for children grew by more than 600% in the 1990s.

taking a psychoactive medication (Figure 3.1), undergoing positron emission tomography (PET) or functional magnetic resonance imaging (fMRI) scans, or having a blood sample taken for a genetic screening test.

Still, questions should be raised about where this research is leading us, and what it is leading us *away* from. One of the most obvious trends is the move away from insight-oriented psychotherapy as a method of treating mental illness. Long-term psychotherapy focusing on family history, early life experience, unconscious dynamics, and moral/existential conflicts is playing less and less of a role in the treatment of brain–mind disorders. Psychotherapy, the CN criticism goes, is too expensive, takes too long, and has a spotty record of curing people with severe forms of mental illness. In relatively mild cases of mental illness, psychotherapy is granted a degree of utility, but even then the expense and time factors incline psychiatrists and patients alike to turn with increasing frequency to pharmacological methods of treatment. This, as everyone knows, is the other major trend in the CN approach to mental illness: an ever-growing reliance on psychoactive drugs to help alleviate the worst symptoms of different forms of psychopathology. Many of these drugs work to regulate faulty neurotransmitter systems, and their rates of clinical success are very impressive.

Both of these trends — a reduction in the use of insight-oriented psychotherapy and an increased use of psychoactive drugs — are likely to continue. To the extent they do, I believe several questions should be kept in mind both within the CN research community and among scholars from other fields and the general public. The first of these questions harkens back to a point we discussed at the beginning of this book: Health is not simply the absence of pathology. Health has its own vital dynamism and experiential integrity, its own subtle rhythms and complexities that cannot be defined as that which is left over after the egregiously bad symptoms have been removed. The question to ask, then, is whether psychiatric medications are making people truly healthy or just not painfully sick. There is a real difference between the two, and I wonder if paying closer attention to that difference would change our evaluation of the overall effects of these medications on people's lives.

A second question to consider also relates to something mentioned in the introduction — the linkage in Presidential Proclamation 6158 of neuroscientific research on mental illness with the "war on drugs." What exactly is the connection between the government's efforts to eliminate the use of heroin, LSD, cocaine, ecstasy, marijuana, and other psychoactive substances and its simultaneous effort to expand the use of psychiatric medications such as lithium, Prozac®, and Chlorazine® (an effort strongly supported by the financially and politically powerful pharmaceutical industry)? At one level, a huge difference exists between illegal narcotics and the medicines prescribed by psychiatrists. The latter help to restore order and calm in the brain–mind system, while the former work to disrupt and overstimulate it; the latter allow people to behave in a more self-controlled and socially appropriate fashion, while the former dramatically and unpredictably alter people's ordinary ways of thinking, speaking, and relating to others. At another level, of course, the difference is nil — all drugs, the legal and the illegal, are at base substances that change neurological functioning, emotional experience, and self-awareness. In this regard, instead of a "war on drugs" we can more accurately speak of a "war *of* drugs," with political and medical authority joining forces to promote the use of some psychoactive substances and prohibit the use of others. How the boundaries are drawn between legal and illegal drugs is an issue that demands continuing scrutiny.

The remarkable thing at this stage of CN research is how little is known about the exact reasons why certain medications have the positive effects they do. Chance and serendipity have played a surprisingly large role in the discovery of many common drugs, and useful medications have been found and administered for years before anyone could provide a theoretical understanding of why those drugs have such a beneficial impact.[18] This raises a rather basic question: Do mental health professionals really know what they are doing as they prescribe increasing amounts of psychoactive substances to an ever-larger percentage of the population? Yes, they do, according to the medical profession, the pharmaceutical industry, and the Food and Drug Agency officials charged with monitoring the safety tests and clinical trials that any medication must satisfactorily pass before its legal clinical use. While we can take some comfort in those assurances, we should still be mindful of the intense pressure on researchers to discover new drugs that can quickly be brought to market. The combination of suffering patients desperate for new cures and corporate interests seeking higher profits creates a constant push for faster approval and wider distribution of psychiatric medications. The danger is that in such a highly pressurized context researchers and government regulators will only focus on a narrow set of questions oriented around short-term pathology: Will this drug make people's symptoms better or worse right now? Will it have any immediately negative side effects? Left unasked are questions about how the drugs will affect people's longer-term capacity for health and creative living. The general psychiatric assumption is that removing the symptoms will automatically lead to health, and again I want to challenge that assumption.[19]

Psychiatric researchers are now looking very closely at the genetic factors that predispose people to different kinds of mental illness. The ideal result of these investigations is "OGOD" (one gene, one disease). A few instances of this happy one-to-one connection have indeed been found, but on the whole OGOD is turning out to be a poor theoretical ideal, as most illnesses have far messier origins than the ideal suggests. What researchers are finding with increasing frequency is that mental disorders derive from a complicated relationship between multiple genes interacting with a variety of personal life experiences and environmental circumstances. It seems that every step forward in scientific knowledge regarding the role of genetics in mental illness also brings us to a new realization of the corresponding role of lived experience and cultural context in causing brain–mind dysfunction. Are psychiatric researchers paying enough attention to the latter side of that equation? Are the same financial and technological resources being used to investigate those nongenetic factors in psychopathology? If they were, could it perhaps lead CN back to a renewed appreciation for insight-oriented psychotherapy, with its rich tradition of exploring precisely those unique personal contours and idiosyncratic growth patterns that characterize an individual's life?[20] These are questions that cannot be asked as long as OGOD remains the privileged research ideal of psychiatric science. Not until OGOD is dead will a more realistic and sophisticated understanding of mental illness emerge, one with the potential for even greater advances in relieving people's suffering and promoting their full health and flourishing vitality.

How, then, can we understand the connection between creativity and madness in terms of current CN research? We have already seen in our earlier discussion of neurogenesis that the creative power of the brain–mind system is rooted in the spontaneous activation of new neural circuits that grow into increasingly complex and sophisticated webs of connectivity. We have also seen that CN research on the projective nature of perception means that all of our experience is, in strictly neurological terms, a wholesale creation of the brain–mind. Also, from Changeux and Wilson we learned that the arts may be interpreted in evolutionary terms as highly effective means of promoting social cohesion, psychological composure, and extra-genetic adaptation. Taking these findings together, we can say that creativity and madness are both characterized by a dramatic profusion of new and unusual brain–mind activity stimulated by novel sensory perceptions and/or spontaneous neural impulses. As an inevitable consequence, both creativity and madness have the effect of disrupting, disorienting, and decentering ordinary brain–mind functioning. Creativity and madness are not different in kind nor are they simply different in degree. The distinction between the two is ultimately a pragmatic one: Creativity produces works of integrity and meaning, and madness does not. To paraphrase William James paraphrasing the Gospel of Matthew, *by their fruits shall ye know them*. In cases of mental illness, the unusual neural activation is experienced as painful, damaging, and a potential threat to survival. Individuals suffer impaired mental and physical functioning, engage in socially inappropriate behavior, and lose the ability to care for themselves. The newly stimulated neural connections are so unstable and the degradation of older, more established connections is so severe that what most people think of as a normal, healthy life becomes impossible. In cases of artistic creativity, the unusual neural activation may also be experienced as intensely painful and horribly disruptive of ordinary life. All the symptoms of mental illness may be there, yet somehow the individual manages to create an artistic work of beauty, honesty, and imagination.

Cognitive neuroscience researchers do not like to grant any magic or mystery to the creative process, but their own findings are leading to an insight right at the heart of Romanticism, that aesthetic and philosophical protest against the Enlightenment progenitors of CN. Creativity is indeed a kind of madness, a madness that is not overwhelmed by the powerful new neural connections generated within the brain–mind system but somehow survives the onslaught of those novel patterns and rides with them, plays with them, follows and explores and elaborates on them, and finally crafts them into meaningful symbolic expressions that communicate the experience to others. Being mad does not necessarily make one an artist, but being an artist does make one mad — the madness of greater mental and physical instability, vulnerability to acute suffering, deep ambivalence to ordinary social relations, and openness to nonvolitional, chaotic neural stimulation (i.e., inspiration). What the creative artist does is bring a work of value out of the madness, something that stimulates in other people a comparable sense of insight, discovery, and awareness. Something that provokes wonder.

III. Religion, Music, and the Brain

Cognitive neuroscience has taken us this far, to a new appreciation of the unpredictable dynamism of human creativity. Turning now to the resources of RS and its investigation of the religious and spiritual traditions of the world, we find that human creativity is fundamentally linked to divine creativity. Whatever creative power humans possess depends on the far greater creative powers of trans-human beings and sacred realities. The ultimate act of divine creativity is the formation of the cosmos itself, and nearly every religious tradition tells stories of how the world and the life upon it came into being. As noted in Chapter 2, several of these creation myths involve sexual motifs that symbolically connect human and divine procreativity.

The Taoist tradition of China teaches that all reality springs from Tao, the "Mysterious Female, "Mother of All-Under-Heaven." The whole of the created world emerges from her womb and depends on her for its ongoing existence.

The creation hymns of the *Rg Veda* refer to a primal act of incest between a father and daughter as the origin of earthly existence; other ancient Vedic hymns speak of a sacrificial dismemberment of the primeval Man, with his severed limbs becoming the various elements of the newly created world. Later Hindu texts expand this cosmogonic story to include a cyclical process of creation and recreation: "At the end of each aeon (*kalpa*), the universe is destroyed by fire to remain submerged in the cosmic waters while Brahma sleeps, until the time when all is to be created anew."[21]

Hesiod's *Theogony* provides the classic Greek view of creation, by which primordial Chaos is interrupted by the spontaneous generation of Gaia (Earth), Tartarus (the deepest underworld), and Eros (Love). Chaos gives birth to Erebos (another underworld realm) and Night, and after multiple rounds of busy, often incestuous, and frequently violent sexual coupling the Titans are born, then the Olympians, and then a huge proliferation of gods, goddesses, monsters, nymphs, and heavenly bodies.

The Book of Genesis in the Hebrew Bible provides the central creation story for the traditions of Judaism and Christianity: "In the beginning God created the heavens and the earth. The earth was without form and void, and darkness was upon the face of the deep; and the Spirit of God was moving over the face of the waters." Using the power of words, God makes the world and all its living inhabitants. The two different versions of how humans first appeared — in one, man and woman are created equally in God's own image (Genesis 1:27); in the other, man is created first and then woman from one of his ribs (Genesis 2:4–23) — has made for a lasting ambiguity in Jewish and Christian attitudes toward women.

Islam draws on the Biblical tradition of God as the supreme Creator of all life, as indicated by several verses of the *Qur'an*: "Allah created you from dust, then from a little germ. Into two sexes He divided you. No female conceives or is delivered without His knowledge. No man grows old or has his life cut short but in accordance with His decree. All this is easy for Him" (sur. 35:11). And this, from the first revelatory decree of the *Qur'an* delivered to Muhammad by the Angel Gabriel: "Recite in the name of your Lord who created, created man from clots of blood!" (sur. 96:1)

The list of such stories could go on and on, right into our present-day context with the speculative theories of modern cosmology and their astonishing (and sexually suggestive) accounts of the Big Bang, black holes, dark matter, multiple universes, and the uncertain future of our universe — will it keep expanding or will it someday stop growing and shrink back into nothing? These creation stories are no less wonderful for being scientific; indeed, they give us free license to wonder precisely because they push our cognitive systems to the very edge of their capacity for understanding. When Carl Sagan invited us to join him in rapturously contemplating the "billions and billions" of stars in the universe (Figure 3.2) and when Stephen Hawking concluded *A Brief History of Time* with the hope that theoretical physics will someday

Figure 3.2 Based on current telescope technology, astronomers estimate the visible universe contains at least 70 sextillion stars (a 7 followed by 22 zeros).

enable us to "know the mind of God," they were expressing a deep faith that the scientific study of Creation can lead us to discoveries every bit as awesome and revelatory as the sacred myths of ancient religious traditions. From the mysteries of neurogenesis to the mysteries of cosmogenesis: Contemporary science has given us cause to wonder from one end of the physical spectrum to the other, and standing between the two, drawing energy and inspiration from both, are the mad glories of human creativity.

In the interest of space and as a way of focusing our discussion more precisely, I want to consider just one form of creative expression, namely music. Although this means we will not consider several other important types of art, we will be able to investigate this one in somewhat greater detail to provide a model for future studies of the other types we have neglected.

In the late 1980s, the French archaeologists Iegor Reznikoff and Michel Dauvois made a remarkable discovery about the painted caves of Paleolithic Europe, which have long been celebrated as supreme expressions of the "creative explosion" that occurred in that part of the world some 40,000 years ago. Reznikoff and Dauvois investigated three caves (in the Ariege region near the French Pyrenees) in terms of their acoustical dynamics, systematically testing each spot in the caves for possible resonance with a series of musical notes spanning several octaves (Figure 3.3). The two researchers then drew up a "resonance map" of each cave and compared it with the locations of the various paintings. It turned out that most of the cave paintings are at or within one meter of specific resonance points, and that places in the caves with no

Figure 3.3 The first amplifiers.

resonance had fewer paintings. Most significantly, the spots with the strongest musical resonance were always marked with some kind of painting or pigmentation, even when the physical features of the cave wall made it difficult to create any full-sized figures. These observations strongly suggest that Palaeolithic cave paintings may in fact have been just one element in a far more complex and musically oriented practice of cultural creativity. On the question of how these early human communities made the sounds that provoked such distinctive acoustic resonances, archaeologist Chris Scarre comments: "Drums, flutes and whistles may have been used in cave rituals — bone flutes have been found at several Palaeolithic sites in Europe of roughly the same age as the paintings. The potential of cave resonance would, however, be elicited only by the much greater range of the human voice. The image of the cave artists chanting incantations in front of their paintings may not be too fanciful."[22]

The history of music as an element of ritual and a source of inspiration thus extends at least 40,000 years into the past. Future archaeological research may well push that date back even further. The long temporal duration of human musicality is matched by its tremendous breadth of geographic diffusion — traditions of musical expression are found in every culture on the planet, and these traditions are nearly always related to the given culture's religious beliefs and philosophical world views. For vast numbers of humans throughout history, music has offered a means of harmonizing the anxious, uncertain rhythms of human life with the more perfect rhythms of divine power and ultimate reality. This was certainly true for the ancient Greeks and particularly for the philosophical schools of Pythagoras and Plato, who made explicit connections between musical and mathematical education and who taught that music helps to create a well-ordered human soul that mirrors the transcendental soul of the universe.[23] Indeed, the English word "music" derives from the Greek myth of the *Muses*, the nine daughters of Zeus and Mnemosyne (Memory) who were born following nine consecutive nights of lovemaking and who were worshipped by the Greeks and then by the Romans as the source of poetry, song, dance, and other forms of creative inspiration.[24]

Among the Australian Aborigines, the ancient traditions of the "songlines" provide elaborately detailed maps of the landscape that harken back to the primal Dreamtime, musically weaving together personal visions, mythic events, ancestral teachings, and the fundamental structures of the created world. Hinduism has long taught that special sounds in the form of chants, songs, *mantras*, and prayers echo the sacred music that permeates the cosmos, and this fundamental belief sonically unites the tradition's colorfully pluralistic pantheon of gods and goddesses.[25] Medieval Islamic philosophers such as al-Kindi and Renaissance European Neoplatonists such as Marsilio Ficino argued that "all realities emit vibrating rays which together compose the harmonious chorus of the universe. The well-tempered human spirit ... recognizes that each sonic emission is attuned to other resonances which reverberate in accord with the first sound because they resemble it in some measure."[26] Similar insights inspired the musico-theological speculations of early modern European scientists such as Johannes Kepler and Isaac Newton. Although James Gleick's recent biography of Newton downplays the significance of religion in his life,[27] it remains a fact that Newton, one of the giants of Enlightenment physics and mathematics, devoted himself to extensive reflection on the ultimate spiritual consequences of his scientific discoveries: "The soul of the world, which propels into movement this body of the universe visible to us, being constructed of ratios which created from themselves a musical concord, must of necessity produce musical sounds from the movement which it provides by its proper impulse, having found the origin of them in the craftsmanship of its own composition."[28]

Closely aligned with these views is the widespread religious use of music as a means of stimulating trance, ecstasy, divine union, and a variety of other modes of extraordinary consciousness. In *The Varieties of Religious Experience*, James says, "[N]ot conceptual speech, but music rather, is the element through which we are best spoken to by mystical truth. Many mystical scriptures are indeed little more than musical compositions."[29] To the extent that music reflects and recreates cosmic harmonies, it can be cultivated as a technique for greater human knowledge of and communion with the realm of the sacred. For example, the Tantric Buddhists and Saiva worshippers of Java have a long tradition of musical performance that is aimed at providing listeners with a vehicle to mystic union with the gods: "He [the listener] follows every single step, imagining the dissolution of each element into its preceding cause, until in the end he is ultimately dissolved or immersed in his cosmic source."[30] The Hebrew

Bible is filled with references to music as a means of communicating with God and becoming infused with divine power. The Psalms are the clearest instances of this: "Make a joyful noise to God, all the earth; sing the glory of his name; give to him glorious praise!" (Ps. 66:2). Also, "Praise the Lord with the lyre, make melody to him with the harp of ten strings! Sing to him a new song, play skillfully on the strings, with loud shouts" (Ps. 33).

The great King David was renowned for the power and beauty of his voice and harp playing, and the Prophet Elisha explicitly used music to stimulate an oracular trance. Speaking before the Moabites, Elisha said, "'Now bring me a minstrel.' And when the minstrel played, the power of the Lord came upon him. And he said, 'Thus says the Lord…'" (2 Kings 3:15–16). A particularly striking passage in this regard comes in 1 Samuel 10:5–7, when the aged Samuel anoints the new prophet Saul and tells the youth of the journey he must make: "'You shall come to Gibeathelohim, where there is a garrison of the Philistines; and there, as you come to the city, you will meet a band of prophets coming down from the high place with harp, tambourine, flute, and lyre before them, prophesying. Then the spirit of the Lord will come mightily upon you, and you shall prophesy with them and be turned into another man. Now when these signs meet you, do whatever your hand finds to do, for God is with you." According to these passages, musical creativity is to be embraced both as a means of calling God and as a tangible indication of the presence of the divine.

Even better known are the ecstatic musical performances and highly energetic dances of the Sufis of Islam, which are explicitly intended to provoke a transcendent experience of intimacy with Allah and an anticipation of the Paradise to come. Musicians called *qawwal* lead an assembly of worshippers into a fast-moving aural current of beating drums, clapping hands, and chanting voices that carries them to a point of total, blissful concentration on God. The writings of the eleventh-century Persian Sufi mystic al Ghazzali regarding the religious power of music remain highly influential today in Iran, Afghanistan, Pakistan, Northern India, and other parts of the Muslim world: "The heart of man has been so constituted by the Almighty that, like a flint, it contains a hidden fire which is evoked by music and harmony and renders man beside himself with ecstasy. These harmonies are echoes of that higher world of beauty which we call the world of spirits; they remind man of his relationship to that world and produce in him an emotion so deep and strange that he himself is powerless to explain it."[31]

As anyone familiar with religion in contemporary America well knows, Pentecostal Christian worship services are remarkably similar to the Sufi practices with their nonstop musical performances using pianos, organs, guitars, drums, and a variety of cries, shouts, and vocalizations to generate intense emotional reactions among the church members, prompting them to "testify" to God in a passionate frenzy of piety. "Pentecostal musical offerings shape a musical/emotional/religious arc that carries the congregation along with it. A service will begin with quiet, slow, soothing music…. As the music becomes louder, more rhythmic, and more repetitive, its driving quality supports, propels, and sustains the hand-waving, hand-clapping, foot-stomping choruses of 'Amen!' as the emotional temperature of the congregation gradually rises. High on the trajectory of the musical arc, worshippers may come forward to the alter to pray, and some may dance or trance."[32]

An obvious effect of these widespread musical practices is a stronger sense of community bonding among the participants. In this regard, religious music beautifully illustrates Emile Durkheim's thesis in *The Elementary Forms of Religious Life* that religious rituals serve to connect people with a power that is truly greater than themselves, a power that has created and sustained them and merits their eternal worship and gratitude — the power of society, the human community to which each of us belongs.[33] The "creative effervescence" that for Durkheim marks an effective religious ritual is found in abundance in musical performances, where group members are lifted "out of themselves" and subsumed into a harmonious, well-integrated social whole. From the ballgame chants of the Choctaw people of North America to the grand choral arrangements of the Mormon Tabernacle Choir, from the even-paced melodies of the Confucian Sacrificial Ceremony in China to the history-laden drumming of the Dagbamba people of northern Ghana, music has always promoted greater social cohesion, moral consensus, and religious identification.

The tremendous power of music can also be dangerous, as social and religious authorities have long recognized. Euripides' play *The Bacchae*, in addition to offering a morality tale about the grave consequences of disrespect to the gods, also illustrates the potentially violent dangers posed by groups of people who whip themselves into an intoxicated frenzy of music and dance. It is perhaps with this mythic story in mind that Plato warned against excessive self-surrender to music as a threat to martial vigor. Some musical education is necessary, he said, but too much indulgence in sonic ecstasy is a problem: "When [a man] continues the practice [of music] without remission and is spellbound, the effect begins to be that he melts and liquefies till he completely dissolves away his spirit, cuts out as it were the very sinews of his soul and makes of himself a 'feeble warrior.'"[34]

The contrast between efforts to promote the positive religious dimensions of music while controlling or prohibiting the negative ones is particularly vivid in the case of Islam. Chanting verses of the *Qur'an* is an essential element of Muslim worship, and in some communities the first sound a newborn child hears is a recitation of the *kalma*, the Islamic creed. Musical expression is actively encouraged in the contexts of prayer, pilgrimage, family celebrations, occupational work, and military training (the elaborate military music of the Janissaries is rooted in the marching practices of Muhammad and his early Medinan followers); however, over the tradition's long history many types of musical expression have been restricted or even banned for their distracting effects on religious piety. Music that involves vocal and/or instrumental improvisation has been questioned for its deviation from established Qur'anic references, and music that relates to pre-Islamic or non-Islamic cultures is automatically suspect (though some degree of rapprochement is possible). Nearly all Muslim clerics and authorities agree that "sensuous music" (i.e., music that arouses sexual desires and the "lower passions") is to be condemned as illegitimate, unlawful, and a threat to the Islamic community.[35] In the words of Islamic Studies scholar Seyyed Hossein Nasr, the contrasting Muslim teachings all derive from a fundamental recognition of and respect for the overwhelming power of music:

> [F]or a person whose soul is ready to move in the direction of the Divine, that is, for one for whom there is already this attraction for the Divine, music has the power of accelerating this attraction and, in a sense, helping the person achieve what is very difficult to do otherwise. Music for such a person becomes a vehicle for the journey of the soul to God, whereas for a person who does not have that inclination music simply increases the passions. There is a very famous saying in Persian that music causes whatever is within the soul to become more intense. If the soul has an inclination to sink like a rock, it will sink faster, toward the world of passions; but, if it has the inclination to fly like a bird, music will strengthen the soul's wings.[36]

The religious dimensions of musical creativity we have been discussing — echoing the divine harmonies of the cosmos, transporting us via ecstatic trance to communion with those divine harmonies, bonding large groups of people into well-integrated social wholes — are found in so many different cultures and different periods of history that anyone who claims to have a comprehensive theory of human nature must find some way to account for them.[37] CN researchers make exactly those kinds of broad theoretical claims, yet so far their efforts to explain music, religion, and many other forms of cultural creativity are problematic at best. Here, again, Steven Pinker provides the most excessively phrased and combatively toned version of authoritative, mainstream CN thinking: "As far as biological cause and effect are concerned, music is useless."[38] The various types of musical expression around the world can all be reduced to "an abstract Universal Musical Grammar," analogous to the universal grammar for spoken language studied by Noam Chomsky, Pinker himself, and many others. Music may have some physical and emotional effects on people, but this does not mean musical ability has been selected by evolutionary pressures to serve any specific beneficial purpose. Pinker says, "I suspect music is auditory cheesecake, an exquisite confection crafted to tickle the sensitive spots" of our authentically adaptive mental faculties for language, auditory perception, and motor control.[39] Music may be many things, but according to Pinker it is emphatically not an evolutionary adaptation.

A less partisan reading of the evidence, however, leads to a different conclusion. Despite Pinker's categorical rejection, many research findings are pointing to a number of adaptive effects of musical creativity. These evolutionary benefits have intriguing parallels to the religious dimensions of music we just finished surveying. Indeed, the many religious traditions around the world in which music plays an integral role appear, in light of current CN research, to be drawing rather wisely upon a highly refined brain–mind capacity that evolved to support the survival and procreative flourishing of humankind.

Humans are not, of course, the only species to create music. Whales, birds, and nonhuman primates make vocalizations to each other that employ structured variations in pitch, tone, rhythm, and melody. Darwin was the first to suggest that music evolved in humans and in these other animal species as an aid to courtship. He pointed to the unusually large difference in the frequency range of human male and female voices, much larger than can be accounted for by body size alone, as one possible sign of physiological adaptation in the direction of greater singing ability for women: "[M]usical tones and rhythms were used by our half-human ancestors, during the season of courtship, when animals of all kinds are excited not only by love, but by the strong passions of jealousy, rivalry, and triumph.... Women are generally thought to possess sweeter voices than men, and as far as this serves as any guide we may infer that they first acquired musical powers in order to attract the other sex."[40] Darwin's general idea about music and mate selection certainly accords with the prominence of music in human courtship rituals, and it conforms with a cardinal principle of evolutionary psychology (EP) reasoning: Anything that improves an individual's ability to attract a better sexual partner is sure to be favored by evolutionary selection pressures. By this standard, musical ability has the definite markings of an evolutionary adaptation.

Here, also, from the RS perspective, appears a prime reason for the tension that often develops between music and religion. Music most definitely has the power to arouse the "lower passions" and prompt people to seek reproductive opportunities at the earliest possible moment regardless of the consequences for social stability and moral standards. Many if not most of the world's religious traditions prohibit and actively suppress certain types of music that authorities have deemed too lascivious, sexually suggestive, and morally subversive.

In some traditions the power of music is actually transformed into a means of resisting and controlling the violent pressures of sexual desire. Legends surrounding the third-century C.E. Christian martyr Saint Cecilia tell of her forced marriage to an aristocratic young pagan. While glorious ceremonial music played at the wedding, Cecilia inwardly prayed for help in defending her vow of chastity later that night. Her prayers were answered — in fact, she not only preserved her virginity but also succeeded in converting her husband to Christianity. Unfortunately, Cecilia and her husband were soon imprisoned and quite viciously martyred, but the hagiographic story of Cecilia's miraculous musical power grew over the subsequent centuries until by the time of the early Renaissance she had become the patron saint of musicians and the subject of popular songs, odes, and poems. John Dryden's "From harmony, from heav'nly harmony" (1687) includes these lines: "Orpheus could lead the savage race/And trees uprooted left their place/Sequacious of the lyre/But bright Cecilia rais'd the wonder high'r/When to her organ vocal breath was giv'n/An angel heard, and straight appear'd/Mistaking earth for heaven."[41]

Another body of scientific research has identified a second evolutionary value to music, one that also ties in with the relatively greater vocal abilities of women. The global ubiquity of mother–infant singing reflects the innate vulnerability of newborn humans to painful bursts of emotional hyperarousal. The cooing, melodic babbling, and lullaby singing of mothers have a demonstrable effect in modulating such arousal and helping infants restore emotional homeostasis. Responsiveness to music begins *in utero*, and newborn humans are precociously attuned to their mother's voices and to musical patterns in general (five-month-old infants can discriminate between the smallest interval used in Western music, a semitone), all of which indicates a well-developed "fit" between maternal singing and neonate listening. Here is EP researcher Anne Ferand's account of the beneficial effects of mothers' vocalizations to their infants:

> The exaggerated melodies of mothers' speeches to infants serve many different functions in early development, prior to the acquisition of language. The distinctive prosodic patterns of maternal speech are prepotent signals for the infant at birth and are effective in the early months in eliciting and maintaining attention and in modulating arousal. Prior to the time when the mother's speech sounds can influence her child's behavior symbolically through their referential power, her intonation affects the child directly. When her intention is to arouse and delight the infant, she uses smooth, wide-range pitch contours, often with rising intonations; when her goal is to soothe, she rocks the infant and speaks with low, falling pitch. And just at the vestibular rhythms of rocking have a direct calming effect on the child, the acoustic features of the mother's soothing melodies also function directly to decrease arousal and calm the infant. Thus in the first year of the infant's life, the communicative force of the mother's vocalizations derive not from their arbitrary meanings in a linguistic code but more from their immediate musical power to arouse and alert, to calm, and to delight.[42]

It seems reasonable to connect this research on mother–infant singing with experimental findings about the power of music to affect mood regulation and emotional control in adults. A moment's reflection provides multiple examples of this power in everyday life — becoming happier when listening to a favorite song, feeling calmer when listening to the stately grace of a classical symphony, becoming aroused by a military march or a patriotic anthem, feeling annoyed by the bland Muzak® permeating a shopping mall. The emotional responsiveness of human adults to various types of music can thus be seen as a developmental outgrowth from early life experiences within the sonic context of mother–infant communication. This in turn provides new insight into the effectiveness of music in promoting social bonding. The roots of the emotional power of music reach all the way back to the original formation of our basic feelings toward ourselves and the world and to our earliest experiences of safety, pleasure, and caring. By allowing us to communicate those primal feelings to other people, music provides an excellent means of deepening trust, loyalty, empathy, and other virtues essential to social cooperation. And, as we have seen, the religious traditions of the world have made ample use of music for exactly these purposes. These traditions do not, as I understand them, have any reason to disagree with EP researchers who focus on the contribution of music to survival and procreation, nor for that matter need they dispute Durkheimian sociologists who point to the community benefits of musical rituals. Religiously inspired and inspiring music may serve all of these functions and serve them well. Yet, in the experience of the listening faithful, music can also become something *more* than that, something that lifts one above the frailties and imperfections of ordinary life, something that brings one closer to the divine.

Additional CN insights on the nature of human musical abilities have come from the use of neuroimaging techniques and lesion studies.[43] The earliest investigations suggested that perhaps music was primarily a right hemispheric phenomenon, subserved by neural systems opposite to those used in the language centers of the left hemisphere. Later studies have not supported this notion, however, and have shown instead that musical perception involves the activation of many different regions in both hemispheres of the brain. The left hemisphere seems especially active in processing rhythm, with its sequence and beat, while the right hemisphere is selectively activated in the response to timbre (the distinctive overtone patterns of instruments and voices). Perception of melody stirs heightened neural activity in both hemispheres, while familiar music activates Broca's area in the left hemisphere, the neural region best known for its centrality in processing spoken language. Research on the differences between musicians and nonmusicians have produced the intriguing result that musical novices have relatively greater right hemispheric activation and less limbic system stimulation while listening to music, while trained musicians have relatively greater left hemispheric activation and more limbic system stimulation while listening to the same music. The musicians are evidently experiencing a greater emotional response to the music while simultaneously processing the music's more familiar, language-like qualities. The novices, on the other hand, seem less likely to be emotionally moved by the music, less capable of putting their responses into words, and more reliant upon the right hemisphere's capacity for processing strange, anomalous phenomena.

Neuroanatomical studies have shown that the brains of musicians are characterized by a larger than average cerebellum, the large region near the brainstem responsible for coordinating complex rhythmic motor movements, and also by a wider than average corpus callosum, the centrally located fiber tract that connects the two cerebral hemispheres. A bigger cerebellum makes good sense for musicians such as pianists and string players who must perform fast, precise, carefully timed movements with their hands and fingers, and an expanded corpus callosum for musicians may well indicate a greater need to engage in cross-hemispheric processing. This area of research is still at a very early stage, but the findings so far indicate that musical education has a discernibly physiological impact on the structural development of the brain.

Much ado has been made over the "Mozart effect," first documented in 1993 by researchers who had 36 subjects first listen to relaxation music, Mozart's sonata for two pianos in D major, or silence for ten minutes and then take three sets of standard IQ spatial reasoning tasks.[44] The researchers reported that the Mozart listeners demonstrated markedly greater skills on these tests, on the order of eight to nine IQ points better than the subjects in the other two conditions. Although the original study focused specifically on the effects of Mozart's music on spatiotemporal tasks involving mental imagery and temporal ordering, these findings were quickly assumed to mean that music has a general effect in promoting intelligence. Numerous books and audiotapes appeared to trumpet the IQ-boosting power of Mozart, and Georgia Governor Zell Miller felt so inspired by the research that he created a government program by which every newborn child in his state would be given a classical music CD or tape: "I believe it can help Georgia children to excel." Unfortunately, subsequent experimental research has offered only mixed support for these claims, and indeed a heated debate continues over whether any genuine Mozart effect exists at all, at least of any statistical significance.

Here is the place to note a basic limitation in the research methodology of these experiments. They all depend on the subjects remaining in a calm, motionless physical posture while listening passively to the music. This condition bears little resemblance to the actual experience of musical perception in most of the world's cultural traditions, where music regularly produces strong bodily changes in people, with heightened emotional arousal and active, spontaneous physical responsiveness to what they are hearing. *Music makes the body move* — just ask Odysseus as he listened to the Sirens. This fact poses a serious obstacle for any research method that depends on limiting and controlling the subject's physical and emotional reactions (e.g., neuroimaging techniques such as PET and fMRI that require subjects to remain motionless, or psychological tests that are administered in school settings). Whatever CN researchers may or may not be able to say about the Mozart effect, the more important point to realize is how little CN can tell us about all the music that comes from *outside* the sphere of the Western classical concert culture, a culture in which "audiences are taught to listen silently and respectfully with minimum bodily movement or emotional expression (until the end)."[45] This Western concert culture may provide a good pool of compliant research subjects, but it cannot automatically be assumed to represent all possible emotional and physical responses to all types of musical expression. Is there a distinctive "*Qawaddi* effect?" A "Songlines effect?" A "Gospel effect?" A "Rap effect?" A "Punk effect?" Probably yes. But, if we want to study more closely what makes for these different musical effects, we cannot rely exclusively on CN, because its primary research methods are incapable of directly investigating musical experiences that involve energetic bodily movement and extraordinary, unpredictable emotional displays.

What this means is that CN is best understood not as an authoritative guide but as a helpful resource in the study of musical creativity. CN provides a naturalistic basis for understanding the prominent role of music in religion, particularly the effectiveness of music in nurturing and sustaining a cooperative human community. CN also adds to our understanding of the individual impact of music by documenting the neuroanatomical changes produced by musical training and education. CN cannot, however, tell us anything definitive about religiously charged experiences of extreme musical arousal nor about religious beliefs that music echoes the divine harmonies of the cosmos. For now, the best scientific method to study these types of extraordinary musical experience is to explore recurrent themes and patterns in large numbers of narrative self-reports (a method used with great effectiveness in the works of Alf Gabrielssen and his colleagues). This line of research has produced findings that correlate very closely to the RS material discussed earlier. Gabrielssen has found that strong experiences with music (SEM) regularly involve physical responses such as "thrills, shivers, and changes in heart rate" and often lead to transcendent states that are explicitly likened to religious or spiritual revelation: "Positive emotions dominate in SEM reports. The by far most frequently mentioned feelings, singly or in various combinations, are happiness, joy, elation, and bliss. In many cases, the feelings are described in even stronger terms, such as a kind of intoxication, rapture, or euphoria bordering on ecstasy."[46] Of particular significance for our interests are the reports gathered by Gabrielsson that frequently mention a sensation of communion, perfection, and harmony with the divine — exactly the experiential qualities that religious music in all its historical and cross-cultural variety has sought to recreate.

This raises a question that unexpectedly goes right to the heart of CN: Does music make us more conscious? In their quest for an ultimate explanation of human consciousness, CN researchers have rejected the phrenological hunt for a specific neuroanatomical location, and they are now more persuaded by the idea that consciousness is the product of highly synchronized firings throughout the brain, a kind of harmonization of neural timing.[47] If this is so, and if current research is correct in that music has a powerful effect in stimulating synchronous neural and physiological activation, then it seems plausible to suggest that music is indeed a creator and sustainer of human consciousness. The harmonies of music entrain the harmonies of neural networks, carrying consciousness to higher levels of resolution and wholeness — this is why

Persians say that "music causes whatever is in the soul to become more intense," why folk tales around the world speak so often of music soothing the savage beast, why music is so widely accorded healing powers, and why music is believed to connect people to the transcendent harmonies of Creation. The religious power of music is the power to align the rhythmic patterns of human consciousness with the greater rhythmic patterns of divinely created reality.[48]

I have waited until now to discuss one final aspect of religious music because it helps introduce a new voice into our discussion of creativity, madness, and wonder. This last aspect of religious music involves its relationship with death, and the new theoretical voice is that of Peter Homans, a psychologist and sociologist of religion who has carefully studied mourning, the dynamic process by which experiences of loss, disappointment, and disillusionment lead to the creation of new cultural meanings and psychological structures. Music has always played a key role in human mourning practices. Special types of sound making — dirges, lamentations, ululations, weeping, howling, keening — regularly accompany funeral rites in cultures all over the world. Women often serve as the chief vocal mourners at these rites both because of the higher range of their voices and because of their gender's traditional association with death, body, and pollution. Early Western examples of this appear in ancient Greek and Jewish texts, with the fair Briseis ("in the likeness of golden Aphrodite") and the other Achaean women crying over the body of Patroklos in *The Iliad* (19.282–303) and the prophet Jeremiah, calling for "the mourning women to come" and "raise a wailing over us" in lament over Zion's divine punishment (Jer. 9:17–18). In the Islamic world, an especially vivid example of religious music serving to express feelings of collective mourning is the *majli*, the central religious practice of Shi'a Muslims. *Majlis* are elaborate musical and recitational rituals that commemorate the martyrdom of Imam Husain, the Prophet Muhammad's beloved grandson who was hunted down and brutally killed along with his family by an army of religious rivals at the town of Karbala in 680 C.E. *Majli* performances are most intense during the month of Muharram, when they mark each of the ten days that Husain and his small band of followers resisted the attacking army before their ultimate defeat and martyrdom: "Diverse hymns that express all spiritual and emotional facets of mourning, devotion, and remembrance are gathered together in a sequence that takes the listener from hymns expressing introspective personal grief, through dramatic narrative poetry and a sermon, to fervent communal mourning which is marked by intense participation through *matam*, the beating of the chest in mourning."[49]

So, here is another vital role that music plays in the human life cycle: commemorating the deaths of loved ones and giving voice to overwhelming feelings of pain, sorrow, and despair. At one level, this relates to the general capacity of music to promote social bonding. When a person dies, a hole is torn in the shared emotional fabric of the community. Music helps in the process of weaving the fabric back together after the death, restoring a sense of ongoing community among those who are still living. At another level, however, the music of mourning points to a more transformative process at work, a process that does not simply return to a pre-loss condition but which propels the mourners forward, *through* the loss, into a new condition of strength and vitality.

The American tradition of the Blues illustrates this quality particularly well. Originating in the "field hollers" of African slaves in the antebellum South, Blues music expressed the suffering, privation, and despair of black people working on plantations, in prison road crews, and later in northern city factories. Over time, a distinctive musical style emerged, with a free use of bent pitches to mimic emotionally inflected vocal sounds; a characteristic twelve-bar progression of I, IV, and V chords; and a simple verse structure of two repeated lines and a third rhyming line. Although steeped in the religious beliefs of both their African ancestors and their Christian masters, Blues musicians were not singing for church — their lyrics were unsparingly honest about their quite earthly feelings of lust, jealousy, betrayal, anger, fear, and alienation. They did not shy away from arousing the "lower passions" and singing of their personal experiences in the darkest realms of human emotion. On the contrary, they made this intimate familiarity with darkness their strength, and using that strength they created something original, beautiful, and true.

Mourning, I want to suggest, is a consequence of *violent* wonder, wonder born of suffering, destruction, and death. It follows the shock of violation, the traumatic decentering of the self, the abrupt annihilation of a basic capacity for comfort and joy. Mourning is the process by which the painful experience of loss leads to a recentering of the self and thus to a revitalized potential for future growth. We have touched on this earlier, but now is the time to state it more directly: Moments of wonder can be *terrible*. They are not always happy, uplifting experiences; sometimes they are absolutely horrifying, intensely painful, and suffused with feelings of loss, despair, and alienation. A study of wonder cannot ignore these negative qualities in favor of the more cheerfully positive ones. Indeed, *every* experience of wonder involves loss — the loss of one's previous center, the shedding of old ideas, the overthrow of one's previous sense of self and world. What makes an experience of violent wonder different is the abruptness of the change, the extreme painfulness of the loss, and the seeming impossibility of hope for the future. To suddenly lose a loved one, a relationship, a home, a time of life, or a cherished ideal can be a genuine occasion for wonder in the sense of an unexpected revelation of a new truth or reality — the truth of human frailty, the reality of a hostile world. The old center is most definitely gone, but a new one is nowhere to be seen.

Mourning, as I understand the term, corresponds to the recentering process we have been discussing throughout this book. The value of Homans' work is that it enables us to understand and appreciate better the complex interplay of psychological, sociological, and religious forces that recenter the self following an experience of violent wonder. Three of his ideas are especially helpful. First is the aphorism that "analytic access always exists at the margins of a common culture." The ability to introspect and reflect critically on one's own life stands in an inverse relationship to one's immersion in the shared symbolic world of one's family and extended community. The closer people are to the common culture, the less likely they are to think psychologically — the less they *can* think psychologically and the less they *need* to think psychologically. By contrast, the farther people are away from the common culture the more likely they are to engage in deep, sustained introspection; they can do so, and oftentimes they must. Homans shows how this tension between analytic access and common culture played out in the lives of Freud, Jung, and other creative social scientists, and what I want to do is extend that framework to the study of wonder, particularly to those experiences of wonder that involve a sudden, violent break with traditional emotional attachments. In this regard, we can say that violent wonder forces analytic insight on people by virtue of a brutally painful rupture with their common culture. This is not, however, to say that all experiences of wonder necessarily provoke analytic insight in just this way. Many moments of wonder occur *within* a common culture context, within large gatherings of people, and these experiences naturally stimulate greater emotional attachment to the community.

The second idea to draw from Homans is his view of the "culture of fantasy" that has emerged in the more recent history of the West. The pace of scientific discovery and technological innovation has accelerated so quickly in just the past few decades that maintaining social and psychological stability has become a nearly impossible task. Modern Western society has reached a point where it suffers from a "unique and peculiar kind of instability: it is constantly breaking itself down and building itself up, virtually before our very eyes."[50] As a response to this instability and as a way of mourning the continually fresh losses and dislocations, members of this society have used the new technologies to facilitate the expression of fantasy, symbol, and dreaming. Homans takes special interest in films as instances of collective mourning and meaning making. He cites with approval Eberwein's concept of the "dream screen"[51] to describe the psychological and cultural dynamics of cinematic experience, and he says, "It is this socially shared screen which today has come to mediate between the contents of the individual person's unconscious inner world and the myriad productions of the various social orders of modern society, for these productions are more and more likely to reach individuals in the form of fantasy structures.... The screen is, in this sense, the generative source of a new 'common culture.'"[52] Naturally, I agree with Homans on the cultural significance of film, and I would simply extend that analysis to other forms of cultural expression — particularly music — that have been radically transformed by the powerful new technologies of fantasy.[53]

Third, Homans provides a helpful analysis of what he calls Freud's "three blows" theory of Western history. Coming in his 1917 essay "A Difficulty in the Path of Psychoanalysis" and also in Lecture 18 of the *Introductory Lectures on*

Psychoanalysis, Freud explains the major transformations of the West in terms of three scientific revolutions that have painfully displaced humans from their previously grandiose (and religiously legitimated) self-regard. First, the discoveries of Copernicus in astronomy revealed that humans do not dwell at the center of the universe. Then the discoveries of Darwin in evolutionary biology revealed that humans are not uniquely created but have evolved from other forms of animal life. And, now, Freud says, his own discoveries in psychoanalysis have revealed that the human ego is pitifully unaware of its own primal wishes and desires — the I does not know who It is. These three catastrophic blows to human narcissism have also, in Freud's view, been severe blows to the authority of religion. The last of them, Freud's psychoanalytic investigation of the hitherto sacred sanctuary of the "soul," has left religion with no place to hide, and Freud clearly intends his blow to be the fatal one. In the final years of his life (before he committed suicide at the age of 78) he devoted great energy to arguing against religion and for the necessity of developing new structures, both psychological and social, to advance humankind beyond its infantile consolations.

What I want to draw from this "three blows" theory is a question: Does a revolutionary new advance in scientific knowledge necessarily destroy the legitimacy and viability of a religious world view? Freud assumed it does, but I would suggest the answer is not so simple. In Western history scientific advances have certainly had the effect of destabilizing traditional religious beliefs and caused feelings of loss, disappointment, and disillusionment. But, in looking at people's responses to such experiences, it should not be forgotten that the process of mourning, as Freud himself said, works toward a creative restructuring of the relationships among self, community, and world. No special psychological reason exists as to why this creative restructuring cannot include elements of the previous religious world view and/or authentically new religious elements. Sometimes the mourning process results in diminished engagement with religion, and sometimes the result is an increased religiosity. Losing a traditional religious world view sets in motion a process far more complex than Freud realized.

Religion and Psychology Interlude II: How Jung Fares

Freud may be regularly maligned by CN researchers, but Jung is more or less ignored by them. The preeminent textbook in the field, *Principles of Neuroscience* by Kandel et al., includes four references to Freud, none to Jung. The lack of CN interest in Jung is due in some degree to the less systematic nature of his theories. Freud's two tripartite models of the mind (unconscious/preconscious/consciousness, id/ego/superego) are much simpler in structure than the open-ended polytheism of Jung's archetypes. Freud's resolute hostility to religion is also more agreeable to mainstream CN than Jung's wild mystical blend of Neoplatonism, Gnosticism, alchemy, Christianity, and Oriental religion. From a CN perspective Freud remains the more accessible thinker —

almost totally wrong, but at least comprehensible. The CN disregard of Jung may also be due, ironically, to an insufficiently critical acceptance of Freud's explanation for his split with Jung (according to Freud, Jung was excessively grandiose in his ambitions and wanted to turn psychoanalysis into a new religion). The attitude seems to be that nothing Freud says can be trusted, except when he is giving his side of a bitter emotional conflict.

One of the few exceptions to this pattern of neglect is J. Allan Hobson, who makes a point in *The Dreaming Brain* of defending Jung's scientific credentials and affirming Jung's notion of dreams as "transparently meaningful" rather than censored and symbolically disguised, as Freud claimed.[54] But, even in Hobson's work, the key concepts of Jungian psychology (i.e., the collective unconscious, the archetypes, individuation) play no substantive role, and little effort is made to reevaluate Jung in the light of present-day CN research. I regard this as a serious issue for a project such as ours, because for the past several decades Jung's archetypal theory has played a major role in guiding scholarly conversations between religion and psychology. According to David Wulff, "No psychologist has received more attention from contemporary scholars of comparative religion than Jung."[55] So now we must ask, how does Jung's theory stand up to the latest scientific findings on the psychology side of that conversation? How, for that matter, does his thought fare in relation to recent developments in RS? Does archetypal psychology have any relevance to the contemporary CN/RS dialogue about wonder, or about any other topic?

Let us start with the main charges against Jung, which are well summarized by G. William Domhoff in *The Scientific Study of Dreams* and by Wulff in *Psychology of Religion*.[56] First, the notion of the collective unconscious, a deep stratum of the human mind that is the repository for inherited psychological predispositions and patterns of behavior, is fatally flawed by the Lamarckian assumption that acquired characteristics can be inherited. The seemingly universal symbols and myths that Jung says emerge from the collective unconscious are more plausibly explained by reference to ordinary human experiences and situations that naturally recur in most people's lives. Second, Jung's characterization of the major archetypes (e.g., the persona, shadow, anima/animus, trickster, divine child, Self), which supposedly reflect a transcendent human wisdom, seem to include more of Jung's own cultural and religious predilections than he is willing to admit. As Frederick Crews mockingly asks, "If the Jungian unconscious is universal, how come it proves to be so very Germanic?"[57] All the different archetypal symbols of Jungian psychology (he identified dozens, and his followers have found many others besides) can be more parsimoniously explained in terms of the basic workings of conceptual metaphor as described by George Lakoff and other cognitive linguists. Normal human development involves "a gradual linguistic socialization into the huge treasure trove of conceptual metaphors that are part of a group's cultural heritage," and this comparatively straightforward socialization process obviates the need to postulate any transcendent psycho-spiritual agencies working behind the scenes of our symbolic expressions.[58] Regarding the notion that archetypal dreams function to provide unconscious compensation for the developmental imbalances of consciousness, little scientific evidence supports such a claim. While Jung confidently asserts, "We can take the theory of compensation as a basic law of psychic behavior,"[59] current research on dream content has emphasized the *continuities* rather than the discontinuities between dreaming and waking life. People tend to dream about the same people, places, and situations that most concern them in their waking lives, and these patterns of continuity usually remain consistent across the lifespan. Not only do these findings undermine Jung's compensatory function of dreaming, but they also call into question the idea that human life unfolds according to a process of individuation by which people, particularly in the second half of life, undergo major psychological changes. The data from long-term dream series show no evidence of such changes across the life span.

Another set of charges against Jung relates not to his theories *per se* but to various controversial features of his personal life. As recounted by biographers such as Paul Stern and Richard Noll, Jung was a serial womanizer who repeatedly had affairs with his patients, who openly kept the adoring Toni Wolff as a mistress for forty years, and who justified his behavior to his wife Emma as irrepressible manifestations of the "polygamous components" of his psyche. Even more troubling, Jung was slow to recognize the gathering danger of National Socialism in Germany in the early 1930s, and it appears he was seduced for a time by the Nazi claim to represent a spiritual revitalization of the German peoples against the softening, decadent influences of modernity.

It might seem unfair to raise these moral and behavioral issues in the context of evaluating Jung's psychological theories, except for the fact that Jung so frequently appealed to his own personal experiences as the generative source for his theoretical insights. He has invited us to connect his work to his life, and I think it necessary to accept his invitation and follow the path where it leads, even into areas where Jung might not have wanted us to go.

These multiple points of criticism make it clear that any future effort to use archetypal psychology as a scholarly resource must be preceded by an extensive reevaluation and reworking of Jung's basic concepts and principles. I do not agree with those who would dispense with Jungian psychology entirely, such as Crews, for example: "The beginning of wisdom is to stop reading Jung."[60] Nor do I agree with those in the RS field who dismiss Jung as just another outdated grand theorist who made the same mistake James Frazer, Mircea Eliade, and (most egregiously) Joseph Campbell did of trying to impose a universalistic, antihistorical, pseudo-scientific system of meaning on the diverse phenomenology of human religious, mythic, and symbolic expression. This is one of the few places where I question the judgment of Wendy Doniger; her distaste for Jung is apparent throughout her writings, yet she never develops an argument against him that moves beyond the basic charge of misguided universalism and "top-down" theorizing.[61]

If Jung were simply wrong, that would be the end of it; his theories would become just another chapter in the history of psychology, and no further effort would have to be spent trying to understand his ideas. But, on closer inspection, the charges against Jung turn out to be less damaging than his critics proclaim. In fact, some CN researchers have recently developed ideas that support central features of Jung's thinking. Let me be clear: I have no desire to get involved in the acrimonious battle between Jung's attackers and defenders, all of whom I think need to take several deep, calming breaths. Rather, I want to reevaluate, critically but fairly, a theoretical framework (Jungian archetypal psychology) that has for many years promoted fruitful scholarship in the study of religion and psychology and that may, in a revised form, continue to be a valuable resource for future research in that area.

To the personal life charges first: Was Jung a cad to his wife and a proto-Nazi? Absolutely yes and not really. His unwillingness to consider the harmful effects on other people of freely expressing the "polygamous components" of his psyche is reprehensible, and if he were a practicing psychiatrist today his sexual dalliances with his patients would likely land him in jail. In a perverse historical twist, Jung's basic attitude toward his wife and anyone else who questioned his behavior ("Sorry, honey, the archetypes made me do it") anticipates the troubling moral implications of EP research in its finding that male humans have instinctive inclinations to seek multiple sexual partners ("Sorry, honey, my genes made me do it"). In both cases, talking about the allegedly natural impulses is taken as the *end* rather than the *beginning* of moral reflection. To the extent that Jung failed to engage in this kind of sustained moral reflection, to the extent that he violated people's trust in him and carelessly caused emotional pain in others, his life and his work are indeed tarnished.

On the proto-Nazi charge, no doubt Jung traveled frequently to Germany in the early 1930s and talked with psychologists who were members of the National Socialist party and who were very excited by Jung's ideas about mythology, racial differences, and spiritual renewal. Jung, however, was hardly a virulent anti-Semite, and by 1936 he had seen enough of Nazism to write the prophetic essay "Wotan," in which he says the German people had become possessed by the hunter-god Wotan and were in danger of succumbing to his blindly destructive fury: "It has always been terrible to fall into the hands of a living god.... We who stand outside judge the Germans far too much as if they were responsible agents, but perhaps it would be nearer the truth to regard them also as *victims*."[62] The "Wotan" essay may not mollify his critics (Noll says that "again, Jung simply psychologizes the political problem"[63]), but I think it shows rather clearly that, whatever earlier affinities he may have felt, Jung explicitly rejected Nazism by 1936. More than that, his analysis of the psychological dynamics of nationalistic ideologies, zealous patriotism, and righteous war making is more acute (and of greater contemporary relevance) than he is usually given credit for.

Looking carefully at these personal charges against Jung also has the benefit of revealing, in a negative light, the role of wonder in his psychological theory. Although he rarely employs the term "wonder" itself, Jung frequently described people's reactions to archetypal manifestations in dreams, myths, art, etc., in terms that very closely match our notion of wonder as a surprising encounter with something extraordinarily true, real, powerful, and/or beautiful. Jung seemed to feel something similar in his own life with respect to his "polygamous components" and his initial interaction with Nazism — he was overwhelmed by forces and desires that brought him into contact with what he believed were transcendental life principles. When he wrote about how terrifying it can be "to fall into the hands of a living god," he was undoubtedly speaking from personal experience. Jung's life thus provides a cautionary tale of the potential *dangers* of wonder.

Now to the central features of archetypal psychology. Jung surely exaggerated when he claimed that compensation is the fundamental law of the psyche. The dream research data do, indeed, refute such a claim, at least in its strongest form, but elsewhere in writings Jung explicitly rejects the idea that dreams have only one function: "In putting forward a compensation theory I do not wish to assert that this is the only possible theory of dreams or that it completely explains *all* the phenomena of dream life."[64] Moreover, the dream research data may show that a majority of dream content is continuous with the ordinary features of waking life, but it also shows that a certain percentage of highly memorable dreams include content that is strikingly discontinuous with waking life. Such dreams by their very nature force new images, emotions, and ideas into waking consciousness. Jung's notion of psychic compensation is one good way to account for the impact of such dreams — not the *only* way, but a way that is helpful in making sense of them.

The claim that all human development follows a path of individuation, by which the psyche grows toward greater integration, balance, and wholeness, is in my view impossible either to prove or disprove. Individuation is a boundary concept, an over-belief, a gesture toward horizons that can be glimpsed but never reached. In religious terms, it is a confession of faith. As a creative vision of human ultimacy, the concept's validity depends less on its suitability for experimental research than on its general hermeneutic usefulness in clarifying the primary tendencies of human development. At the very least, nothing discovered by CN or RS research has given a decisive reason to reject Jung's notion of individuation as a framework for thinking about human development. To put the argument in stronger terms, individuation can become an even more valuable conceptual tool if it is refashioned along the lines of what Homans does in *The Ability to Mourn*. Homans strengthens Jung's basic idea by combining it with Freud's work on mourning, the sociological teachings of Durkheim, Weber, and Levi-Strauss, and the Western historical experience of secularization. Homans is thus able to show how individuation is driven by a complex interplay of personal and collective forces: "Individuation is the activity whereby the various conflicts which beset all persons — losses which are intra-psychical, interpsychical, and sociohistorical — are worked over, broken down, and built up.... [Individuation] is the creative outcome of mourning, and the outcome of individuation is in turn the creation of meaning, a building up of new structures of appreciation born of loss."[65] Homans' reformulation of this key Jungian idea holds the promise of more precise linkages between archetypal psychology and CN research on loss, fantasy, and creativity.

Support for the collective unconscious, the key innovation of Jung's model of the mind, comes from an unlikely source: E.O. Wilson. In *Consilience,* Wilson devotes a remarkable ten pages to the subject of snake dreams, arguing that the frequency of this particular type of dream is an especially clear example of how environmental pressures and biological processes give rise to psychological experience.[66] He notes that a "fear of snakes is deep and primordial among the Old World primates, the phylogenetic group to which *Homo sapiens* belongs."[67] He also points out that human children display a "prepared learning" response to snakes — that is, an inborn propensity to fear snakes that can, after just one or two bad encounters, produce a deep and permanent aversion to the creatures. Unlike most other childhood fears, the fear of snakes grows stronger during adolescence and continues through adulthood. These findings prompt Wilson to make what he admits is a bold claim: that the human fascination with snakes which pervades myths, religions, and dreams in cultures all over the world can ultimately be reduced to biological processes that obey the basic laws of evolution:

> Snakes and dream serpents provide an example of how agents of nature can be translated into the symbols of culture. For hundreds of thousands of years, time enough for genetic changes in the brain to program the algorithms of prepared learning, poisonous snakes have been a significant source of injury and death to human beings. The response to the threat is not simply to avoid it, in the way that certain berries are recognized as poisonous through painful trial and error, but to feel the kind of apprehension and morbid fascination displayed in the presence of snakes by the nonhuman primates. The snake image also attracts many extraneous details that are purely learned, and as a result the intense emotion it evokes enriches cultures around the world. The tendency of the serpent to appear suddenly in trances and dreams, its sinuous form, and its power and mystery are logical ingredients of myth and religion.[68]

Wilson is evidently satisfied that a propensity to create particular symbolic forms can be developed through Darwinian rather than Lamarckian mechanisms. What is required is (1) a recurrent phenomenon of human experience that directly relates to survival and procreation, and (2) a sufficient amount of time for prepared learning to take genetic root.[69] The resulting conceptual and behavioral predispositions would form part of the innate structure of the human mind, preceding the development of individual consciousness and manifesting themselves at certain crucial moments to promote adaptive responses to the environment. If we follow this line of thinking, it is far from crazy to continue using Jung's term "collective unconscious" to refer to our inborn storehouse of prepared learning. Much more work needs to be done by both CN researchers and archetypal psychologists to develop this area of integration, but the potential is definitely there, and for now Wilson's mix of hesitation and enthusiasm is the best attitude to emulate: "It is quite possible," he says, "that the brain is genetically predisposed to fabricate certain images and episodes more than others. These fragments may correspond in a loose way to Freud's instinctual drives and to the archetypes of Jungian psychoanalysis. Both theories can perhaps be made more concrete and verifiable by neurobiology." I fully agree, and I would add the corresponding possibility that perhaps CN thinking about human development can be enriched and refined by greater attention to Jung's detailed investigations of what he called the collective unconscious.

This opens the way to a more precise way of speaking about the archetypes. The challenge has always been to say something meaningful about these psychic constellations without being either overly specific or overly abstract; Too far to one side, and Crews will accuse it of sounding suspiciously Germanic; too far to the other side, and Doniger will reject it as empty and useless. Jung was aware of this problem, and he tried in his therapeutic practice to do justice to both the archetypal patterns and the personal life contexts of his patients: "It does not, of course, suffice simply to connect a dream about a snake with the mythological occurrence of snakes, for who is to guarantee that the functional meaning of the snake in the dream is the same as in the mythological setting? In order to draw a valid parallel, it is necessary to know the functional meaning of the individual symbol, and then to find out whether the apparently parallel mythological symbol has a similar context and therefore the same functional meaning."[70] In this passage, Jung shows a notable appreciation for the archetypes not as fixed entities but as patterns of dynamic interaction between individual and collective dimensions of psychological experience. To speak of the archetypes is to speak of tendencies to react and probabilities of response.

Jung was strongly encouraged in this direction by one of his patients, the pioneering quantum physicist Wolfgang Pauli. Pauli exchanged a series of letters with Jung about the parallels between archetypal psychology and the revolutionary new discoveries that Max Planck, Neils Bohr, Werner Heisenberg, and Pauli himself were making about the subatomic dimensions of reality, dimensions that extend far beyond the conceptual limits of Newtonian physics. In one letter, Pauli wrote, "The archetypal element in quantum physics is to be found in the (mathematical) concept of probability — i.e., in the actual correspondence between the expected result, worked out with the aid of this concept, and the empirically measured frequencies."[71] Jung replied, "Your idea that the probability concept in mathematics corresponds to the archetype was most illuminating. In fact, the archetype represents nothing else but the probability of psychic events. To a certain extent, it is the symbolically anticipated result of a psychic statistic."[72]

Here, again, is a question that deserves much more investigation in the future. Schwartz and Begley make a compelling argument in *The Mind and the Brain* that the classical physics of Newton are insufficient for a proper appreciation of complex brain–mind phenomena, and they say CN must do more in the future to include the insights of quantum physics in its theoretical models. Similar arguments have been made by neuroscientists Walter J. Freeman and David Kahn.[73] Both claim the probabilistic approach of quantum physics explains the neuropsychological processes underlying human experience better than the deterministic framework of Newtonian physics. It is too early to say for sure, but if Pauli was right about the close affinity between quantum physics and archetypal psychology, then perhaps Jung's ideas will turn out to be a surprisingly helpful resource in revising both CN and RS thinking about the brain–mind system in light of new developments in physics. Such an outcome would have no small measure of poetic justice — the psychologist long reviled for his mystical irrationality is able in the end to "out-science" his detractors, many of whom have themselves been clinging to a historically outmoded view of how the physical world works.

IV. No Recess

To bring this chapter to a close I want to descend from the speculations of natural philosophy and return to the realm of the body, to the complex, messy details of an individual human life. The life I want to explore, Kurt Cobain's, is chosen not because it represents an artistic model or creative ideal, but rather because it provides a vivid example of how everything we have been discussing in this chapter (mourning, music, religion, mental illness, drugs, death) may come together in a tremendous collision of force that can be both violently destructive and beautifully creative. The wonder Cobain experienced and the wonder he provoked are worth our attention because they illuminate the primal powers that swirl within all of us. We may or may not admire how he handled his demons, but we can learn something from his creative efforts to name them and give them a voice.

He was born on February 20, 1967, in the town of Aberdeen, on the rainy, densely wooded coast of Washington state. He was the first child of his parents Don, a twenty-one-year-old auto mechanic, and Wendy, who got pregnant at nineteen just after graduating from high school and who married Don a few months later. Kurt was the first grandchild on both sides of the family tree, and his birth was a cause of great celebration among the numerous relatives living in the Aberdeen area. His mother's family included several musicians, and from the age of two Kurt eagerly joined in with the family jam sessions and took the lead in singing songs by the Beatles, the Monkees, and Arlo Guthrie. His first instrument was a Mickey Mouse drum set, and at age seven he was given his first guitar. Along with his musical talents he also showed early skill in painting and drawing, and his proud family and relatives encouraged him by giving him art supplies at every birthday or holiday. Writing in his journal many years later, he looked back at this time of life with delight: "The first seven years of my life were amazing, incredible, realistic and an absolute grateful joy."[74]

At a certain point, Cobain's seemingly endless physical energy and noisiness became a concern to his parents and teachers, and in second grade he was finally taken to a medical doctor, who prescribed Ritalin® to control the hyperactivity. Then, in 1976, when Kurt was nine and his sister, Kim, was six, their parents abruptly got divorced. Wendy left the house and moved in with a new boyfriend, a longshoreman with a violent streak who fanned the flames of her increasingly bitter feud with Don. Kurt, his family disintegrating before his eyes and his parents locked in an ugly, venomous, and very public battle, reacted by withdrawing in every way possible — emotionally, socially, even physically. For a time he was hospitalized with stomach problems and malnutrition, which was all the more alarming given that he was already relatively slender for his age.

He lived for a time with his mother, then his dad, and then with various relatives and family friends, never staying long with any of them. In eighth grade, he began smoking marijuana and using LSD, and within a year was smoking pot daily. The physical changes (or lack of them) of adolescence brought new cause for despair. His small physical size prevented him from competing successfully in athletics, and this both disappointed his extremely sports-oriented dad and made him an object of ridicule by the jocks in high school. In a town that was totally dependent on the muscular labors of brawny men working in the lumber industry, Kurt's slight build, blond hair, and fair skin most definitely did not fit the traditional masculine ideal.

Although he was cutting school more and more frequently, he still found some enjoyment in art classes. He gained a small but precious measure of social esteem for his drawing and cartooning skills, and this introduced him to a new pleasure — shocking other people with his dark humor and taboo fantasies. One day the class was asked to portray an object as it developed, and to everyone's amazement Kurt drew a beautifully rendered picture of a sperm fertilizing an egg and turning into an embryo. One of his classmates later recalled, "That sperm was a shock to all of us. It was such a different mental attitude. People began to talk about him, wondering, 'What does he think of?'"[75]

Music became his refuge, and his liberation. He played his electric guitar for hours on end in whatever bedroom he happened to be staying, teaching himself popular songs by Led Zeppelin, AC/DC, and other heavy-metal bands. Then he had an experience that changed his whole understanding of what music could be, and by extension what *he* could be. It happened in the summer of 1983, when he was sixteen years old. He described it in his journal with only partial self-mockery as a kind of religious conversion:

> I remember hanging out at a Montesano Thriftway when this short-haired employee box-boy, who kind [of] looked like the guy in Air Supply, handed me a flyer that read: "The Them Festival. Tomorrow night in the parking lot behind Thriftway. Free live rock music." Monte was a place not accustomed to having live rock acts in their little village, a population of a few thousand loggers and their subservient wives. I showed up with stoner friends in a van. And there stood the Air Supply box-boy holding a Les Paul with a picture from a magazine of Kool cigarettes on it. They played faster than I ever imagined music could be played and with more energy than my Iron Maiden records could provide. This was what I was looking for. Ah, punk rock. The other stoners were bored and kept shouting, "Play some Def Leppard." God, I hated those fucks more than ever. I came to the promised land of a grocery store parking lot and I found my special purpose.[76]

The guitar-slinging box-boy was Buzz Osborne, front man for the band The Melvins and a local underground authority on all things punk. Kurt joined the small group of teenage boys who hung around The Melvins' practice sessions and came to all their shows, despite being ridiculed and heckled by pretty much everyone else in the area. "Punk Rock is Freedom" was a phrase that began appearing frequently in Kurt's journals.

The story of his punk rock conversion has become a well-known part of Cobain's hagiography. What is not so widely known or appreciated is the fact that after the Melvins concert he experienced another conversion, one that was much more traditional in form. He became a born-again Christian. It happened a year after his Thriftway parking lot revelation, when he was seventeen. His dad had remarried and started a new family, and his mother had angrily kicked him out of her house for the last time. Failing most of his classes, with no job or money and all his possessions in four green garbage bags, he spent four months sleeping on friends' couches, in the hallways of old apartment buildings, and in the waiting room of the local hospital where he had been born. During this bleak time (later mythologized in the song "Something in the Way"), one of his best friends, Jesse Reed, persuaded him to start coming with him to the Sunday services of the Central Park Baptist Church. Jesse's parents were born-again Christians, and as they got to know Kurt they decided to try helping him by offering to let him live with them. The appeal of this offer of basic shelter and food was all the greater because Jesse's father was an avid rock musician with numerous albums, guitars, and amps in the house that Jesse and Kurt were free to play. Kurt agreed and moved in. Within a couple months he became baptized in the church and regularly attended the Sunday services as well as the Wednesday night Christian Youth Group meetings.

He stopped doing drugs, took up reading the Bible, and embraced an evangelical Christian outlook. Jesse recounts one of their conversations: "One night we were walking over the Chehalis River bridge and he stopped, and said he accepted Jesus Christ into his life. He asked God to 'come into his life.' I remember him distinctly talking about the revelations and the calmness that everybody talks about when they accept Christ."[77] When Kurt turned eighteen, the Reeds held a birthday party for him, which he described in a thank-you letter to one of his aunts who had sent him a present: "All the kids from the church Youth Group came over, brought cake for me and Jesse, then we played stupid games and Pastor Lloyd sang some songs (he looks exactly like Mr. Rogers). But it was nice to know people care about ya."[78]

Just two months later it was over. Kurt had badly cut his finger at his dishwashing job and quit on the spot, terrified that he might not be able to play guitar again. Jobless once more and without even the consolation of playing guitar, he went back to doing drugs, skipping school, and holing up in the Reeds' house by himself. The Reeds decided they could do nothing more for him and asked him to leave their house. His relationship with the church ended.

It is tempting to agree with Charles Cross that "Kurt discarded his faith like a pair of pants he'd outgrown,"[79] but that is too simplistic. Images of Jesus, Christianity, and religion recur throughout his later life in his music, journal writing, and graphic art. To be sure, he gave up the born-again faith of the Reeds, and later he would harshly condemn the moral hypocrisy of right-wing Christians, but he always maintained a sympathetic view of the human desire for religion, and he clearly remained fascinated by the story of Jesus and its relevance to his own sufferings. More than that, he felt, despite everything that had happened to him, a genuine sense of the sacred in the world, and he held onto this feeling in the face of explicit skepticism from his new musical community: "The only problem I've had with … punk rock is that absolute denial of the sacred. I find a few things sacred such as the superiority of women and the Negro contributions to art. I guess what I'm saying is that art is sacred. Punk rock is freedom. Expression and right to express is vital. Anyone can be artistic."[80]

The best that can be said about the religious teachings of the Reeds and the Central Park Baptist Church is that they provided Cobain with a period of relative calm and quiet, an Eriksonian social moratorium in which he could gather his energies and focus them toward a self-chosen goal. His conviction about the sacred quality of art became a core element in the plan he carefully nurtured in those pious months with the Reeds: He was going to become a professional musician. He became friends with Krist Novoselic, another Christian Youth Group member who experienced a similar transformation after hearing the music of The Melvins. The two began practicing together, and soon they were looking for a drummer so they could form a real band. After trying several different names ("Fecal Matter," "Throat Oyster," "Ted, Ed, Fred"), they finally settled on "Nirvana." Kurt had once watched a late-night

TV show on Buddhism, and he liked the absurdity of calling their band by a strange religious term that means enlightenment, release, and self-annihilation — "oooh, eerie, mystical doom," he comments in his journal.[80]

The band's first performances did not go over well with the local audiences, especially with the "rednecks" whom Kurt and Krist so openly despised, but the band drew energy from outrage they provoked, and their shows began to cultivate a deliberate sense of mayhem and anarchy. Their musical skills improved to the point where they recorded a demo tape, put out a single with a local label, and started to receive some favorable attention from punk rock fans all along the Washington coast.

A breakthrough came when they played a short but wild set at a pre-Halloween party at Evergreen University in Olympia. Nirvana gave by all accounts their most intense performance yet, and at the end of the last song Kurt lifted his guitar in the air and, without any warning, suddenly smashed it on the ground. Shattered pieces flew everywhere; the band stopped playing, and a wailing, ear-splitting feedback filled the room. He held aloft what was left of his guitar for a few seconds before the awestruck crowd, then smashed it down again and walked away. A friend of Kurt's who was at the party said, "He never explained why he freaked out, but he was smiling. There was a finality to it — it was like his own little private celebration. No one got hurt, but when he smashed that guitar, it was as if he didn't really care if he hurt anyone. It was completely out of the blue. I was talking to him after the show and the guitar was laying there on the floor, and people kept grabbing pieces of it."[81] Word quickly spread through the local college circuit: A Nirvana show was a *wonder*. When the band graduated to playing on formal stages (instead of the corner of someone's living room), the scene only became more chaotic. Hundreds of people threw themselves into a slam-dancing frenzy in front of the stage, with fans who felt especially inspired climbing onto the stage, thrashing around with the band, then diving headlong back into the crowd. Kurt usually played on, oblivious to the hurricane of bodies around him, but then he would suddenly take a leap of his own — "He was the first person I ever saw fling himself into the crowd with his guitar and not give a rat's ass," said a member of another local band.

His energy turned increasingly to various kinds of physical art, including collages, paintings, and three-dimensional constructions. The walls of his apartment were soon covered with free-form creations made of paint, magazine clippings, broken dolls, various bodily fluids, and religious artifacts such as crosses and sculptures of the Virgin Mary (which he stole from the local cemetery). His girlfriend said he rarely spoke about religion, but when he did it was to deny the presence of any benevolent deity in the world: "I think he believed in God, but more in the devil than actually in God."[82]

All the darkness, rage, and self-loathing he had felt since his parents' divorce came into the open during this time, as he repeatedly wrote about suicide, his fantasies of violence, and the disgusting nature of his pathetic, feeble body. Much of his artwork focused on switching the sexual organs of men and women, so a man might have a vagina for a head and a woman a penis as well as breasts, and his collages included gruesome pictures of diseased vaginas from medical pathology books. Similarly uncanny themes haunted him in his dreams, too. His girlfriend, Tracy Marander, was the first person to observe his post-childhood sleep behavior over a lengthy period of time, and she did what she could to help him with his terrible recurrent nightmares. "Ever since he could remember, he had dreams about people trying to kill him. In the dreams, he'd be trying to fight people off with a baseball bat, or people with knives coming after him, or vampires.... He had those dreams all the time."[83]

His primary focus in these intensely creative months was putting together a new album. The working title, *Sheep*, was an admission the band was seeking to attract as large a herd of commercially compliant, CD-buying, concert-attending, T-shirt-wearing fans as possible. Even his most grandiose fantasies of success, however, could not have anticipated what would happen when the album was finally released in September of 1991 (with the title *Nevermind*). The band's concerts during a promotional tour for the album quickly gained a national reputation as marvels of slam-dancing, stage-diving madness. The newly fledged MTV network, flexing its muscles as a musical tastemaker, gave constant play to a video of the first single from the album, "Smells Like Teen Spirit," a song that combined a simple guitar riff and verse–chorus–verse structure with monstrous distortion, emotionally intense but only partially coherent lyrics, and Cobain's arresting vocals. Despite a small first printing and little prerelease promotion or advertising, *Nevermind* sold so quickly that by December it had risen to the number one spot on the U.S. pop music charts.

What makes this tale of rock stardom relevant to our interests is its illustration of the power of music to provoke wonder. If ever an album of rock 'n roll can be said to have provoked genuine wonder among a broad public, it was *Nevermind*. Besides "Smells Like Teen Spirit," the album contained two other songs that had an especially jarring effect on listeners. "Lithium" displayed the band's skill at creating striking contrasts of musical dynamics, moving from a first-person confession of the brain-addled happiness of believing in God, sung softly to a pleasantly strummed guitar, to a sudden eruption of distortion and wordless screaming, followed by a shifting of chords and Kurt letting loose with primal cries of love, hate, and murder. The song's title makes it as clear as possible — religion is a drug, just another narcotic to deaden life's pain and control the seething, crazy, self-contradictory desires within, but the view is not that of an outsider criticizing religion; the song invites listeners into the world of a person for whom lighting candles in a daze is a good and meaningful thing to do, even if those darker forces of murder and mayhem never really go away. Similarly, "Polly" adopts a strange and extremely unsettling point of view — that of a rapist. Based on a local newspaper story of a girl who had been abducted and horribly abused by a Tacoma man, the song turns Cobain's fervent hatred of macho sexual aggressiveness inside out and confronts listeners with one of Nirvana's very few purely acoustic songs, with a slow tempo, soft vocals, and a final verse that discovers wonder in the defiance of the victim — "it amazes me the will of instinct."

The massive burst of attention the band received for *Nevermind* was everything Kurt had dreamed of, in all senses of that term. In public, he responded to the pressures of the rock-star persona with a tricksterish defiance of traditional gender stereotypes, aiming his wonder-working power against the rednecks of the world. He wore thrift-store dresses and colorful ball gowns to interviews, he repeatedly denounced the hypermasculinity of American society, and he performed at benefit concerts for female victims of sexual abuse. In his journal, he wrote that "our band (Nirvana) has consciously decided that it is our devout crusade, as a band, to teach men not to rape," and he cast this crusade as nothing less than a radical split with past generations: "For boys, step one: remember that your older brothers, cousins, uncles, and your fathers are not your role models. This means you do not do what they do, you do not do what they say. They come from a time when their role models told their sons to be mean to girls, to think of yourself as better and stronger and smarter than them."[84]

In private, however, he took increasing advantage of another response to the pressures of fame — heroin, inscribed in his journal as "heroine." His use of the drug intensified from scattered experimentations before the release of *Nevermind* to full-blown addiction in the months after its skyrocketing success. This was also the time when his relationship with Courtney Love, whom he had met the previous year, grew into a permanent bond. They were married in early 1992 and had a daughter later that summer. The genuine happiness he found in his new family was darkened, however, by his and Courtney's misadventures with drugs and parenting, which made them the target of relentless tabloid coverage, police intervention, and *schadenfreudliche* gossip. Just as quickly as Nirvana's popularity had come, it started to turn against them, with critics who had initially gushed over the brilliance of their music now asking if the band was nothing but a one-hit wonder.

Kurt's morbid working title for the next album was *I Hate Myself and I Want To Die*; however, he was persuaded that such a title could make the band vulnerable to lawsuits so he switched the title to *Verse, Chorus, Verse* and finally to *In Utero*. The cover of the album was a disturbing tribute to the uncanny, featuring his favorite "visible woman" anatomical model on the front and a three-dimensional collage of fetal medical models, orchids, and umbilical cords on the back. The first single released was "Heart-Shaped Box," and the video involved a wild religious tableau with images that Kurt said came directly from his dreams: "The video centers around a junkie-looking elderly Jesus dressed as the Pope, wearing a Santa hat while being crucified in a field of poppies. A fetus hangs from a tree, and reappears crammed inside an IV bottle being fed into Jesus, who has moved to a hospital room. Krist, Dave

[Grohl, the drummer], and Kurt are shown in a hospital room waiting for Jesus to recover. A giant heart with a crossword puzzle inside it appears, as does an Aryan girl, whose white KKK hat turns to black. And throughout these images, Kurt's face continues to charge the camera."[85]

This twisted assault on Christian iconography, in a video that was guaranteed to receive immediate international airtime, was outrageous enough, but by far the most controversial song from the new album was titled "Rape Me." Using what had become the band's trademark musical structure of soft lyrics alternating with crashing choruses, the song expressed in just a few stark lines a raging defiance against the public's needy expectations, against the coercive pressures of the music business, against the power of addiction to heroin, and more generally against anyone who subjects other people to sexual aggression and domination. The mere title of the song prompted the Wal-Mart and K-Mart retail store chains to refuse to stock *In Utero*, although their spokespeople claimed the reason was because of "little consumer interest" for the album (which debuted at number one on the national charts).

His rising success as a musician and his enjoyment of a loving family life coincided with a further worsening of his heroin habit. He wrote in his journal that the drug helped him with his stomach pains, although its capacity to eliminate ordinary consciousness and detach a person from external sensory stimulation clearly had an appeal to someone who felt overwhelmed by public attention. Sometimes he fought the slide into addiction, heeding his increasingly desperate family and bandmates and checking himself into professional detox treatment centers. But most of the time he embraced it, sliding farther and farther into opiated indifference. His appetite for the drug grew to the point where even his junkie friends became alarmed. "It amazed me," said one such friend, "for such a small person, and such a slight guy, how much he could do. You couldn't fit enough in the syringe for him."[86] He had his first near-death overdose in January of 1992, just hours after a much-heralded performance on the "Saturday Night Live" television show. By the middle of 1993, he was using heroin daily and suffering one overdose after another, each one bringing him for a moment to what was, in both medical and legal terms, a state of death.

In the dwindling amount of time he spent in a conscious and conventionally functional condition, he continued to make music. Nirvana performed a mostly acoustic set for the MTV "Unplugged" series, on a stage that Kurt had ordered decorated in funereal style with lilies, black candles, and a crystal chandelier. The band played eight of its own songs and six covers of songs from other bands, with five of those covers dealing in some way or other with death. The final song was "Where Did You Sleep Last Night?" by the early Blues musician Leadbelly. Cobain introduced it by saying Leadbelly was his favorite performer, explicitly affirming his feeling of spiritual kinship with, and historical indebtedness to, an earlier American tradition of musical protest, mourning, and liberation.

In March of 1994, while on tour in Rome, Cobain experienced an overdose so severe that he fell into a coma for 20 hours (CNN broke into its regular broadcast with the not entirely mistaken news that he had died). When he returned to Seattle, he shocked the junkie crowd at a local dealer's house by shooting a gargantuan amount of heroin; panic-stricken, his "friends" dragged his inert body outside, dumped him in the backseat of his car, and fled. He survived, but a few days later, after one last try at a detox center, he evidently decided his time had come. He wrote two letters, one to his wife and daughter, which included an entire page filled with the words "I'm sorry," and the other to his imaginary friend Boddah. Then he injected an inescapably fatal dose of heroin into his arm and put a shotgun into his mouth.

This time CNN was more cautious. For almost 24 hours the network reported that a dead body had been found at Cobain's Seattle home, the victim of a suicide, but the police would not confirm the person's identity. When the news was finally released, the reactions were, as we noted earlier, intensely emotional and surprisingly widespread. A representative fan eulogy was printed in the Seattle *Post-Intelligencer*: "I won't judge the circumstances or the pain of Kurt's leaving, though that pain must have been incomprehensible. Beautiful and gifted as he was, maybe there was no one who could have made him recognize it in himself, or bring him back from his despair. I will not judge, nor tolerate those who will. Rather, I stand with those who adored the poet, the sage, the wondrous minstrel that Kurt Cobain was. I stand in celebration of a bright and fleeting star who graced the planet with the song of angels."[87]

At the same time as people like this fan were publicly mourning their loss, several leading media commentators took the occasion of Cobain's suicide to fire back at his anarchic musical creativity and at anyone who took guidance or inspiration from his work. In a way, these hypermoralistic attacks are the best possible tribute to the influence of Cobain's music, the strongest evidence of his dark wonder-working abilities. Syndicated radio talkshow host Rush Limbaugh expressed his opinion with characteristic delicacy: "Kurt Cobain was, ladies and gentlemen, a worthless shred of human debris."[88] (Cobain himself would probably not have argued.) In the British newspaper *The Times,* Bernard Levin sharply questioned the moral judgment of those people who found any interest in Cobain's music: "We all need idols, and some of us find them in the most extraordinary situations. Why should not ten million youths find theirs in a foul-mouthed, brutish, violent singer-guitarist, drugged to the eyebrows and hating himself and his way of life?"[89] Nothing, however, could surpass Andy Rooney's diatribe on the CBS news magazine "60 Minutes" the Sunday evening following the suicide: "No one's art is better than the person who creates it. If Kurt Cobain applied the same brain to his music that he applied to his drug-infested life, it's reasonable to think that his music may not have made much sense either.... When the spokesman for his generation blows his head off, what is the generation supposed to think?"[90]

Exactly so.

4

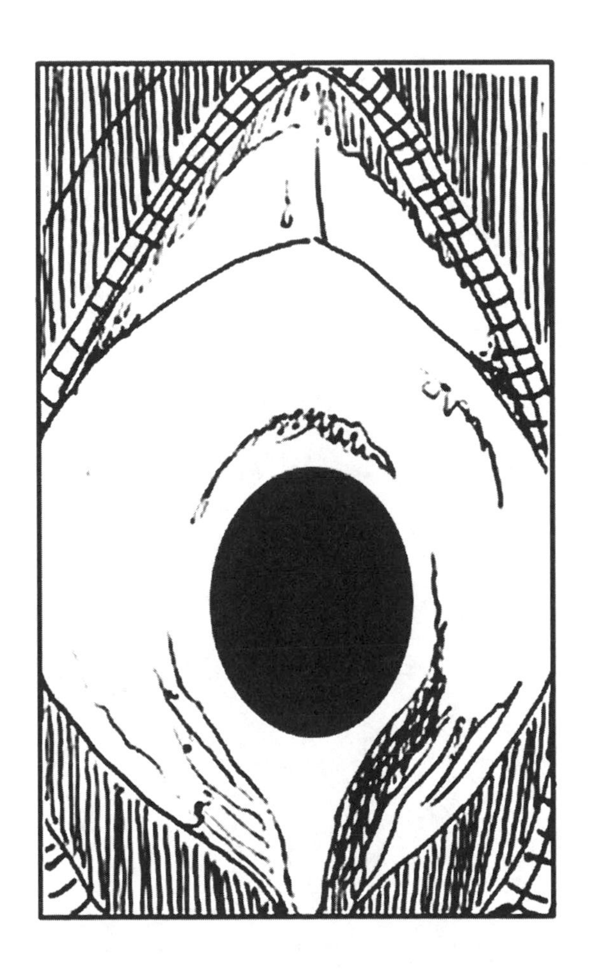

Contemplative Practice

4
Contemplative Practice

I. "Recite!"

The angel Gabriel first came to Muhammad in a cave on Mount Hira during the holy month of Ramadan in 610 C.E. Muhammad was forty years old at the time, married to a deeply devoted wife named Khadija, and father to several children, stepchildren, and foster children. He was a well-respected merchant in the city of Mecca, and although he had started life as an orphan he made up for that familial deficit with his trustworthy behavior and fair-minded dealings with others, earning the nickname "the reliable one." He was also observant of the traditional religious practices of his people. He gave alms to the poor, participated in public ceremonies, and made frequent circumambulations (*tawaf*) of the Ka'ba, the holiest shrine in all Arabia. Inside the Ka'ba, embedded in its southeast wall, resided the Black Stone (*al-hajar al-aswad*), an object about a foot across that, according to tradition, fell from the heavens many ages ago. Worshippers at the Ka'ba would walk around the temple to the right, counter-sun-wise, time after time after time, periodically stopping to kiss and bow to the Black Stone. Throughout his life Muhammad regularly practiced the *tawaf*, and he also participated in the rituals devoted to the various divinities associated with the Ka'ba (one of whom was the creator god Allah). Muhammad may have been poor and fatherless, but no one could deny that he was as pious, faithful, and god-fearing as any of the wealthier tribal leaders of the city.

In addition to those public religious performances, Muhammad practiced various forms of personal devotion, most often in the cool, dark caves that dotted the Arabian wilderness. Here he would pray, think, sleep, and imagine. He began to have dreams, marvelous visions of hope and promise so filled with brilliance they struck him "like the dawn of the morning." Then, one night during a month-long retreat in the caves of Mount Hira, he had an experience that changed him forever. Muhammad was suddenly awakened by the powerful presence of Gabriel, who appeared beside him and gave him a simple order: "Recite (*Iqra*)!" Terrified, Muhammad initially resisted the call, but Gabriel's numinous intensity overwhelmed him and compelled his complete and total assent. Muhammad humbly asked what he should recite, and Gabriel revealed to him the first words of the *Qur'an*, which we have heard once before: "Recite in the name of thy Lord who created! He createth man from a clot of blood. Recite: and thy Lord is the Most Bountiful, He who hath taught by the pen, taught man what he knew not."[1]

Muhammad woke up with these words still sharp and vivid in his memory, "as if they had written a message in my heart." He walked outside, and a second time he was struck by the divine: "When I was midway on the mountain, I heard a voice from heaven saying: 'O Muhammad! Thou art the apostle of God and I am Gabriel.' I raised my head toward heaven to see who was speaking, and lo, Gabriel in the form of a man with feet astride the horizon.... I stood gazing at him moving neither backward or forward; then I began to turn my face away from him, but towards whatever region of the sky I looked, I saw him as before."[2] Gabriel was everywhere. All directions led to the same divine reality, the same cosmic epiphany, the same transcendent truth. Muhammad's old center of selfhood had been obliterated, and he found himself thrust into a radically new center, a center totally enveloped by the awesome omnipresence of God.

Deeply shaken by the physical intensity of this revelation, Muhammad staggered back down the mountain to his family. He feared he had become possessed by the *jinn*, fiery spirits from the desert wilds who caused endless mischief in human life. All Arabians were familiar with these supernatural beings, and professional soothsayers (*kahin*) claimed to receive help from the *jinn* in finding lost objects and foreseeing the future. Muhammad had no desire to join the ranks of the *kahin* — he regarded their obscure oracles and mad prophecies as worthless distractions from the true worship of the divine. But, if he was not a *kahin*, what exactly had he become? Khadija reassured him that no malevolent *jinn* could be involved in his revelatory experience, as God would not allow such a good and honest man to be misled like that. She urged him to do whatever he could to better understand the full import of Gabriel's call.

Heartened by his wife's encouragement, Muhammad continued with his devotional practices, and he was rewarded with a number of additional revelations. Some were primarily visual, involving lights as bright as the breaking dawn. Others were entirely auditory, with distinctly spoken messages and teachings. Still others were bodily perceptions of titanic waves of power, "like the reverberations of a bell, and that is the hardest on me." All of these experiences strained his physical being to its limit: "Never once did I receive a revelation without thinking that my soul had been torn away from me."

Muhammad came to understand himself as a "warner" sent by Allah to teach people the proper worship of the one God, which was in fact nothing more than a purified version of the traditional worship of Allah at his shrine in Mecca. Muhammad soon attracted a fair-sized group of followers, most of them (not surprisingly) from the city's growing population of poor, outcast, and enslaved people, but some of his followers came from socially prominent clans, defying their families to join him, and this finally provoked a reaction from Mecca's tribal leadership. Who was he, they demanded of Muhammad, to claim to speak on behalf of Allah himself? How did he know he was not being deceived by the *jinn*? Why should anyone follow his supposed revelations, which, despite his denials, were clearly subversive of Mecca's traditional religious practices? Was he not simply trying to gain greater power and authority for himself, at the cost of family dissension throughout the city?

In reply, Muhammad stressed the absolute purity of his message. He did not expect it, did not fabricate it, did not wish for it — his prophecies were an unbidden miracle, a divine gift to humankind for which Muhammad, an unlettered man of no special distinction, was only the humble bearer. Still, Muhammad knew from the growing controversy surrounding him that he had to respond to the question of how exactly his teachings about Allah would affect worship of the other gods traditionally recognized in Mecca. Many of these deities had been objects of deep veneration for centuries beyond counting, and people were understandably reluctant to accept Muhammad's claim that Allah was ordering them to abandon these ancient practices.

According to one of his earliest biographers, Muhammad experienced at this tense political moment a new revelation, the verses of which he recited at the Ka'ba in front of a crowd of startled Meccans: "Have you considered al-Lat and al-Uzza and Manat, the third, the other? These are the exalted birds whose intercession is approved." Muhammad was referring to three goddesses, known together as "the daughters of Allah" (*banat al-Llah*), whose cult was of the greatest antiquity and who were worshipped at special temples in Mecca and other cities around Arabia. Muhammad's words were enthusiastically welcomed by the people of Mecca as a clear sign that he was acknowledging a harmonious continuity between his new religious teachings and traditional Arabian worship practices. Allah was indeed the supreme creator, to be revered as such, and the goddesses al-Lat, al-Uzza, and Manat were acknowledged to be divine intermediaries between God and the human realm and thus deserving of devotion in their own right.

Muhammad then had another revelation, perhaps his most startling one yet. Gabriel spoke to him by night and severely chastised him for reciting words that came not from God but from Satan (*shaitan*). The earlier verses about the three goddesses must be removed from the *Qur'an*, Gabriel commanded, and new verses inserted in their place. These new verses categorically rejected the goddesses as legitimate deities worthy of any attention, dismissing them as mere projections of human fantasy: "They are naught but names yourselves have named, and your fathers; God has sent down no authority touching them. They follow only surmise and what their whims desire."[3]

When Muhammad announced this abrupt reversal in his recitation of the *Qur'an*, his followers, who had been troubled by his apparent concession to the Meccan authorities, responded with joy at the uncompromising monotheistic purity of his message. The tribal leaders of Mecca, however, were outraged, and they now realized that violent conflict with Muhammad was inevitable.

Muhammad experienced several other divine revelations in the twenty-three years between his initial encounter with Gabriel at Mount Hira and his death in 632 C.E. His life and mission as God's ultimate messenger, the "Seal of the Prophets," represents one of history's most momentous explosions of visionary experience and wonder-working influence. By the end of his life he had conquered his opponents in Mecca, converted virtually the whole of Arabia to his religious cause, and started a spiritual revolution that would grow over the century following his death to a movement of sweeping geographic proportions. He bequeathed to his followers a set of contemplative techniques to help them concentrate their thoughts, purify their minds, and focus all their energies on devotion to God and God alone. As the *Qur'an* testifies, these methods prepared Muhammad for the gift of divine revelation, and over the many subsequent centuries his followers used the same methods to cultivate a greater receptivity to the living power of God's presence.

The nature and effectiveness of such techniques is the subject of this chapter. "Contemplative practice" is the term I will use to refer to a variety of methods of intentionally transforming ordinary consciousness in order to open oneself to an experience of revelation and wonder. Muhammad developed a powerful set of methods for accomplishing this. Other methods, some quite similar to Muhammad's, some extremely different, have been developed and practiced in the world's other religious traditions. Although I will not go so far as to say that contemplative practices constitute the essential core or highest expression of all religion, I do believe the study of these practices can tell us something very important about the meaning and value of religion in people's lives. Religious studies (RS) scholars have already spent considerable energy on the investigation of cross-cultural phenomena such as meditation, prayer, trance, and spirit travel. The landmark book in this area is, of course, William James' *The Varieties of Religious Experience*, in which he lays out a comparative analysis using the resources of religious history, personal introspection, and the latest findings of psychological science. In the century since James' pioneering work, researchers from both RS and cognitive neuroscience (CN) have followed his lead in exploring the various means by which extraordinary states of consciousness are produced and unusual/transcendent/revelatory types of knowledge are gained. This topic is without question the most fertile area of current RS/CN dialogue, and one that has attracted a surprisingly large public response. With our preceding discussions of dreams, sexuality, and creative madness as a background, we are in a good position to add something new to this interdisciplinary conversation.

II. Cognitive Neuroscience on Reality, Consciousness, and Meditation

To understand experiences of extraordinary consciousness it helps to have a good grounding in the workings of ordinary consciousness, and this is where CN can be of greatest service. Many CN researchers have made the explanation of human consciousness their supreme goal, and we have already had several opportunities to discuss their findings and theories in this regard. Now is the time to look even more closely at CN investigations of everyday conscious awareness and a cluster of brain–mind processes directly involved in its functioning: perception, association, volition, subjectivity, and neural self-integration. Given the vast technical literature that has grown around these topics in recent years, we can do little more here than summarize what the majority of CN researchers currently believe about them. A leading representative of the mainstream CN approach to consciousness is Eric Kandel, neurobiologist at Columbia University and winner of the 1998 Nobel Prize in Medicine for his work on learning and memory in the sea snail *Aplysia*. His *Principles of Neural Science*, now in its fourth edition, is a major textbook in the field (and, at 1414 pages and almost 8 pounds, a gargantuan presence on any bookshelf). Kandel's rendering of the CN perspective is consistent with the ideas of most of the other researchers we have been discussing, and he offers an honest summary of what CN does and does not know about the nature and functioning of human consciousness.

The frontispiece of *Principles of Neural Science* is an Egyptian papyrus from the Twelfth Dynasty of the Middle Kingdom (seventeenth century B.C.E.) which provides the first physical description of the brain in recorded human history. The text describes two people who suffered skull fractures and were experiencing various sensorimotor impairments. By opening his book with the striking image of this ancient papyrus, Kandel deliberately stimulates the historical self-awareness of CN and points the field toward a specific set of future goals. CN, in his view, has the mission of moving beyond the imaginative but specious fancies of religion, the interesting but unverifiable speculations of psychoanalysis, and the rigorous but sterile experiments of behaviorism. Unlike many of his CN colleagues, Kandel says more about the deficiencies of behaviorism than of psychoanalysis or religion:

> [D]uring behaviorism's most influential period, the 1950s, many psychologists accepted the most radical behaviorist position, that observable behavior is *all* there is to mental life. As a result, the scientific concept of behavior was largely defined in terms of the limited techniques used to study it. This emphasis reduced the domain of experimental psychology to a restricted set of problems, and it excluded from study some of the most fascinating features of mental life.[4]

Kandel's criticism is worth underscoring. Behaviorism mistook the map for the territory; it succumbed to the grandiose fantasy of believing its experimental methods offered a perfectly comprehensive knowledge of reality, with the damning consequence that whatever could not be examined by those methods was dismissed as nonexistent. Kandel wants CN to resist that narcissistic temptation by drawing on a wider variety of scientific methods and concentrating more carefully on the inner workings of consciousness. By doing so, Kandel argues, CN can provide not only the most powerful explanation of normal mental activity ever devised but also a valuable new resource in the clinical treatment of people suffering from different kinds of psychopathology.

In contrast to the behaviorist emphasis on simple reflex actions, CN seeks a deeper understanding of the brain–mind processes involved in more complex forms of human behavior. Kandel follows psychoanalysis and Gestalt psychology in claiming that a vast array of mental activities, both conscious and unconscious, intervene between the input of sensory information and the output of behavioral response. "[O]ur knowledge of the world is based on our biological apparatus for perceiving the world … perception is a *constructive* process that depends not only on the information inherent in a stimulus but also on the mental structure of the perceiver."[5] CN has succeeded in identifying several discrete elements of this essentially creative process, from the unimodal perceptual pathways devoted to a single sense to the multimodal association areas involved in connecting numerous sources of sensory input with preexisting structures of expectation (memory) and ultimately to the prefrontal cortex and its executive functions of attention, planning, and goal-directed action.

Consciousness, says Kandel, is "one of the great mysteries of cognitive neural science, in fact of all science."[6] CN researchers generally agree that philosophical dualism (e.g., Descartes) is wrong and that "consciousness derives from the physical properties of the brain."[7] Kandel endorses the philosophical studies of John Searle and Thomas Nagel in their analysis of three dominant features of consciousness: subjectivity, unity, and intentionality.[8] *Subjectivity* refers to our private sense of the "realness" of our experience, the vivid immediacy of our emotions, and the personal meaningfulness of our engagement with the world. *Unity* is the quality of seamless integration of multiple perceptual processes into a stable and continuous conscious experience; somehow, all the different streams of sensory input are brought together and made into a single, ongoing state of awareness. *Intentionality* designates our capacity for selective attention (i.e., our ability to focus our awareness on one thing rather than another). Kandel admits that CN has learned very little so far about subjectivity: "[T]he brain does indeed *construct* our perception of an object, but the resulting perception is not *arbitrary* and appears to correspond to independently determined physical properties of the objects. What we do not understand is how action potentials give rise to meaning. Why is it that you see a *face* when the neurons of the inferotemporal cortex fire action potentials?"[9] Although some researchers and philosophers (e.g., Daniel Dennett, Francis Crick, Owen Flanagan) use CN findings to argue that subjectivity is an inessential, epiphenomenal byproduct of brain neurology, Kandel will at least admit that any decent theory of human consciousness must include an account of our felt experience of being, realness, and value in the world. CN cannot yet provide such an account, but Searle and Nagel have properly framed the goal: "to state the *laws of correlation* between neural phenomena and subjective experience."[10]

Little more can be said about the feature of unity. CN research on the integrated quality of consciousness is known as "the binding problem": How does the brain create a single, stable condition of awareness? The great advances that CN researchers have made on the neural localization of certain cognitive functions (e.g., speech, vision, memory) put the problem in even sharper relief — no one "place," no specific location exists in the brain where all the various types of sensory information are put together, nor can CN even rely on the simple assumption that the integration proceeds in a unidirectional fashion, from the unimodal to the multimodal to the executive. Binding does not just happen at the "end" of the perceptual process, but all along the way in back-and-forth interactions and feedback loops ("cross-talk") between each of the functional systems. Kandel makes the stunning confession that understanding the unity of consciousness is beyond the reach of current CN research: "It is in fact pointless pursuing this *grand synthesis* design. For here one comes across an important anatomical fact: There is no single cortical area to which all other cortical areas report exclusively, either in the visual or in any other system. In sum, the cortex must be using a different strategy for generating the integrated visual image."[11] The best guess at this point about such a "different strategy" is Crick's notion of unified consciousness as a product of synchronized neural firing and over-arching cortical harmonization, which we discussed earlier in connection to the wonder-provoking power of music. Whether or not that turns out to be the right path to follow, future CN research on the unity of consciousness will have to shift its emphasis from anatomical localization to broader patterns of brain–mind functioning, moving from a narrow census of the neural trees to a wider appreciation of the cortical forest.

For Kandel the most promising area of research on consciousness involves the feature of intentionality. He harkens back to another monumental textbook of brain–mind science, James' *Principles of Psychology* (1890), in which James affirms the crucial role of selective attention in human consciousness:

> Millions of items ... are present to my senses which never properly enter my experience. Why? Because they have no *interest* for me. *My experience is what I agree to attend to....* Everyone knows what attention is. It is the taking possession by the mind, in clear and vivid form, of one out of what seems several simultaneously possible objects of trains of thought. Focalization, concentration of consciousness are of its essence. It implies withdrawal from some things in order to deal effectively with others.[12]

Kandel is confident CN will soon be able to explain intentionality in precise neural terms (researchers have already made big strides in their investigation of the executive functions of the prefrontal cortex), and he advocates this effort as the best one for researchers to pursue: "Thus, rather than grapple with the broad concept of consciousness, neurobiology approaches the problem of consciousness by studying tractable, well-defined components of consciousness, such as selective attention.... Neural scientists are thus beginning to address aspects of the fundamental question of consciousness by focusing on a specific, testable problem: What neural mechanisms are responsible for focusing visual attention?"[13] This, then, is what current mainstream CN research on consciousness comes down to: A focus on focusing, concentration on concentration, the prefrontal cortex studying itself.

Ironically, pursuing that goal has led some scientists back to religion, specifically to those religious practices such as prayer and meditation that involve sustained intentionality and concentration. The earliest subject of this kind of research was transcendental meditation (TM). Since the early 1970s, hundreds of experimental studies have been performed to investigate the physiological effects of the meditation technique taught by the founder of TM, Maharishi Mahesh Yogi.[14] According to these studies, TM produces a significant drop in respiration, heartbeat, and oxygen consumption; electroencephalogram (EEG) readings show a dramatic shift from the alpha-wave activity predominant in quiet restfulness to a much slower pattern of theta-waves, and in especially deep meditatational states an overlay of faster beta-waves emerges. Most intriguingly, some studies have shown that the electrical activity of the brain tends toward synchronization and cross-brain coherence during meditation. EEG monitors tracked the new brainwave patterns (presumably initiated by the concentration of the meditator) as they gradually spread throughout the brain, to the point where the EEG readings from multiple scalp locations showed a uniformity of frequency, amplitude, and wave form.[15]

One of the pioneering researchers in the experimental study of TM and meditation more generally is Herbert Benson, who has invented a contemplative technique of his own called the "relaxation response."[16] Benson's technique involves two components: first, a focus on a repeated sound, word, phrase (either silently or aloud) or muscular activity (e.g., walking, dancing, bowing), or a fixed gaze at a special object (e.g., icon, mandala); second, a passive disregard for distracting everyday thoughts and a continual return to one's focus. Benson and his research colleagues have documented not only the physiological changes that are produced by his technique (decreased metabolism, heart rate, blood pressure, respiratory rate) but also the therapeutic effectiveness of eliciting the relaxation response in people who are suffering from stress, chronic pain, and other health problems. Benson is forthright in his conviction that the technique represents a universal core of mystical experience. In his 1975 book *The Relaxation Response*, he speaks of the connection between his research and the world's religions in these terms:

> Many authors have pointed out the similarities between Eastern and Western mysticism, and have emphasized a universality of certain impulses in the human mind. Indeed, the subjective accounts of practitioners of different meditative backgrounds are similar to many experiences depicted in religious, historical, and philosophical writings. We will attempt to show that the Relaxation Response has been experienced throughout history. We will do so by extracting methods described in various literatures, primarily religious. Some of these methods are thousands of years old. Our chief purpose is to illustrate the age-old universality of this altered state of consciousness by citing certain elements that appear to be necessary to evoke this experience, or "response." No technique can claim uniqueness.[17]

For Benson and many other researchers in this area of inquiry, a primary goal is to promote the tremendous therapeutic benefits of contemplative practice, not only within the clinical context but also among the general public. This instrumental approach connects Benson's work with that being done on two other related phenomena, intercessory prayer and the placebo effect. Dozens of studies have investigated the possibility that one person's prayer can affect another person's health.[18] Well-designed and methodologically sound studies on prayer have produced suggestive results (e.g., Randolph Byrd's finding that cardiac patients who received prayer were significantly less likely to develop additional health complications as compared to patients who received no prayer), but skeptics have not yet been persuaded that such results are statistically meaningful. Even the advocates of prayer cannot say with any exactitude how these apparent effects are generated, beyond the obvious fact that the person praying is striving to focus all his or her mental energy on positive thoughts aimed at the patient.

With the placebo effect, the situation is somewhat the reverse: Its reality is unmistakable, and most physicians today are schooled on the importance of developing a warm, reassuring, sympathetic rapport with their patients in recognition of the well-established fact that the patients' subjective beliefs and expectations about the healing process genuinely do improve their chances for actual recovery. Some researchers (Benson among them) have endorsed the active use of the placebo effect to promote positive medical outcomes. For other researchers, however, the phenomenon is a nuisance, an unpredictable variable that disrupts controlled scientific efforts to test new psychoactive drugs. In a typical drug trial, researchers will give half of the patients the experimental medication and half of the patients a sugar pill, or placebo. A significant percentage of the patients who receive the placebo show improvements in their symptomatology — they get better, even though they did not really take any medication at all. For the researchers to prove the new medication has any effectiveness, the patients who take it must improve at an even higher rate than that of the placebo group. This means that the greater the placebo effect, the heavier the burden of proof, thus the more difficult it is to bring new psychoactive drugs to market. CN now finds itself in a push-me–pull-you situation, with some investigators trying to enhance the placebo effect as a "natural" means of healing while other researchers (the ones with far more commercial and governmental funding) are trying to suppress it as an impediment to the development of better drug treatments.

Either way, the placebo effect highlights the inability of CN to explain how complex mental states can influence neurophysiological processes and heal physical and psychological suffering: "The difficulty of defining or predicting improvement in placebo controls illustrates how little we know about the natural history of most disorders and the possibility for spontaneous improvement."[19]

The Christian branch of this research has produced, in addition to the prayer studies, a small literature on the neuroscientific basis for traditional Christian conceptions of faith, the immortal soul, and God's action in the world.[20] Ashbrook and Albright's *The Humanizing Brain* is the most prominent work from this perspective, and it relies heavily on Paul MacLean's notion of the "triune brain," by which the structural evolution of the human brain is seen to consist of a "reptilian" behavioral core (the brainstem); a "mammalian" middle region for emotions, memory, and sociability (the limbic system); and the newest development — the "human" outer region (the prefrontal cortex), which allows us to concentrate, plan, and make volitional decisions.[21] At each level of neural organization, Ashbrook and Albright see correlations between brain–mind functioning and Trinitarian Christian doctrine. Thus, the role of the brainstem in basic bodily functioning and psychophysiological homeostasis is said to reflect the numerous biblical portrayals of God as "territorial, hierarchical, watchful, persistent, unchanging," with the deceptive serpent of Genesis 3 serving as an apt image of the tendency of the reptilian brain toward selfish cunning and sudden aggression. CN shows that the limbic system provides the emotional basis for social relatedness and the formation of communities, and Ashbrook and Albright take this as neurobiological evidence in support of God's benevolent action in endowing us with a divine capacity to love our neighbors. Research on the neocortex, with its capacity for complex and purposeful cognitive processing, is in their view not only compatible with but actually enhances the traditional Christian theological portrait of God: "We propose that the God of this universe is *complexifying, interactive, dynamic,* and *loving,* and that the combination of these characteristics indicates a God who is *purposeful.*"[22]

Although Ashbrook and Albright's work has attracted some interest among Christian theologians, the main thrust of research in this area has been the study of Buddhist meditational techniques, with many of the scientific investigators being active Buddhist meditators themselves. Jeffrey Schwartz is one example, a psychiatrist at UCLA whose research on obsessive–compulsive disorder (OCD) has merged with his personal practice of Buddhist meditation and led him to develop a therapeutic regime for treating OCD that centers on a concentrated effort by the patient to turn his or her thoughts away from pathological ideas and toward positive, healthful ones (his contemplative method has four basic steps: Relabel, Reattribute, Refocus, Revalue). Schwartz has found that using this approach produces tangible and enduring changes in the patients' brain–mind functioning, as shown by positron emission tomography (PET) scans in which the part of the brain that becomes hyperactivated in OCD patients (the caudate nucleus of the prefrontal cortex) significantly decreases its metabolic activity following ten weeks of his four-step technique.

In its explicit and enthusiastic allegiance with Buddhism, Schwartz's research follows the lead of James Austin, whose 1998 work *Zen and the Brain* is surely the most intimidating and weightily erudite book in this area. Although not quite of Kandelian proportions, Austin's book takes an epic approach to the whole question of how brain–mind science relates to religious and mystical experience. He is himself a long-time practitioner of Zen Buddhist meditation, and he attributes the passion of his research interests to a sudden, surprising moment of revelation in a London subway station: "*Time was not present. I had a sense of eternity. My old yearnings, loathings, fear of death and insinuations of selfhood vanished. I had been graced by a comprehension of the ultimate nature of things.*"[23] Austin took this wonderful experience as the inspiration to use his neuroscience training to investigate the neural processes underlying moments of enlightenment like his own. To summarize very briefly his very lengthy argument, Austin presents a wealth of CN evidence showing that enlightenment experiences involve diminished activity in the limbic system, particularly the fear-detection circuits of the amygdala; diminished activity in the parietal lobe areas responsible for orientation in space and self-world distinction; and diminished activity in the prefrontal systems involved in the executive functions of ordinary conscious awareness. Austin believes his findings have relevance for the general study of religious experience, but he reserves his strongest claims for Zen Buddhism. He says Zen meditation is highly effective in creating the neural context in which profound revelations are prone to emerge (Austin's subway epiphany occurred while he was traveling to a Zen retreat). "Our thesis," he writes at the outset of *Zen and the Brain*, "is that prior meditative training and daily life practice help release basic, preexisting neurophysiological functions. This thesis will lead to the following proposition: mystical experiences arise when normal functions reassemble in novel conjunctions."[24] The capacity for such experiences is an essential feature of being human, in Austin's view, and he presents his work as a new CN advance on earlier theories of religious experience: "Aldous Huxley called mankind's basic trend toward spiritual growth the 'perennial philosophy.' Herein, I take a different perspective. To me, the trend implies a dynamic, intimate perennial *psychophysiology*. It is a series of processes, slowly evolving, that culminate in defining moments of an extraordinary character."[25]

The research interests of Western scientists such as Austin, Schwartz, and Benson have been reciprocated by an increasingly active interest by some Buddhist leaders in the latest findings of CN. Most prominent in this regard is Tenzin Gyatso, the 14th Dalai Lama and religious and political leader of the Tibetan Buddhist tradition. In a series of conferences, books, and lectures, the Dalai Lama has cultivated a close familiarity with current CN research, and he has made representatives of his tradition available for experimental study. His avowed interest is in promoting the global value of mindfulness meditation as a means of fighting against what he calls "destructive emotions" and "dangerous impulses — impulses that collectively can lead to war and mass violence."[26] In an op-ed article he recently wrote for *The New York Times*, the Dalai Lama speaks with special enthusiasm about the work of Richard Davidson at the University of Wisconsin. Davidson (a Vipassana meditator since college) conscripted a group of employees from a nearby biotechnology company (Promega) and had 25 of them participate in an eight-week program to train them in mindfulness meditation. At the end of the eight weeks, he used an EEG to compare the activation patterns of the 25 meditators as compared to the other 16 Promega employees who did not receive the training. The meditators showed greater activation in the left anterior region of the prefrontal cortex, a region that CN researchers have previously found to be associated with positive emotional states. Davidson also tested the immune systems of both groups and discovered that the meditators developed significantly more antibodies in response to a shot of flu vaccine than did the control group. Furthermore, the meditators who demonstrated the greatest increase in left-side brain activation also produced the strongest immunological response.[27] The Dalai Lama takes research such as Davidson's as scientific corroboration of the ancient spiritual teachings of the Tibetan Buddhist tradition, although he does not insist that his is the only path to follow: "[T]he benefits of these practices are not just for monks who spend months at a time in meditation retreat.... You don't need a drug or an injection. You don't have to become a Buddhist, or adopt any particular religious faith. Everybody has the potential to lead a peaceful, meaningful life."[28] The Dalai Lama explicitly links his teachings to the public horrors of September 11 and its violent international aftermath, and he offers mindfulness meditation as a potent political tool in a bloody world. "We would do well to remember that the war against hatred and terror can be waged on this, the internal front, too."[29]

Andrew Newberg and Eugene d'Aquili have provided additional evidence of the measurable, observable neurological effects of contemplative practice. (Although d'Aquili died in 1998, Newberg still names him as a co-author in his 2001 book *Why God Won't Go Away: Brain Science and the Biology of Belief.*) Using the resources of the radiology laboratory at the University of Pennsylvania, Newberg and d'Aquili examined the brains of Buddhist meditators and Franciscan nuns in prayer using a single photon emission computed tomography (SPECT) camera to measure blood flow in their brains. The results of this research provide what Newberg and d'Aquili coyly suggest may be a "photograph of God." *Why God Won't Go Away* opens with Newberg describing his use of the SPECT camera on a subject named Robert, who is meditating in the laboratory: "I'm waiting for Robert's moment of mystical transcendence to arrive, because I intend to take its picture." Newberg tries to make good on his tantalizing promise by explaining how during states of intense meditation and prayer the areas of the brain responsible for sensory perception and orientation essentially shut down due to a lack of meaningful input, while the prefrontal executive regions responsible for the abilities "to concentrate, plan future behavior, and carry out complex perceptual tasks" becomes highly activated. In such a neurological condition, lacking any of the information normally used to define self and world and yet highly aroused and attentive, the brain interprets its experience as suddenly being devoid of boundaries:

> The brain would have no choice but to perceive that the self is endless and intimately interwoven with everyone and everything the mind senses. And this perception would feel utterly and unquestionably real. This is exactly how Robert and generations of Eastern mystics before him have described their peak meditative, spiritual, and mystical moments.[30]

Newberg and d'Aquili describe several other means of achieving this extraordinary brain state, including practices of hyperarousal (ritual dancing, drumming, chanting) and even relatively secular activities such as attending a musical concert or taking a warm bath. Whatever the technique, Newberg claims they all aim at the same fundamental neurological goal, the experience of what he and d'Aquili in their earlier book, *The Mystical Mind*, called "Absolute Unitary Being," or AUB:

> The transcendent state we call Absolute Unitary Being refers to states known by various names in different cultures — the Tao, Nivrana, the *Unio Mystica*, Brahman-atam — but which every persuasion describes in strikingly similar terms. It is a state of pure awareness, a clear and vivid consciousness of *no-thing*. Yet it is also a sudden, vivid consciousness of *everything* as an undifferentiated whole.[31]

These correlations between contemplative practice and brain–mind functioning are directly relevant to what Kandel and other mainstream CN researchers consider their supreme goal, namely an understanding of human consciousness. The meditation research has especially significant implications for CN investigations on selective attention, insofar as it reveals in neurological terms the paradoxical phenomenon of focusing so intently on one's capacity to focus that focus itself dissolves. Austin has the best insight here, with his argument that meditation functions to "desynchronize" habitual states of consciousness and open the brain–mind system up to the creation of new modes of awareness. The process as he describes it closely corresponds to our ongoing discussion of wonder as an experience of surprise, shock, and radical decentering that opens the way to a creative new recentering.

The gains in this area of religion-and-science research are real, the implications are important, and the future potentials for new research and discovery are bright. Unfortunately, many studies are flawed by serious conceptual and methodological problems that impede rather than facilitate further RS/CN dialogue. I will concentrate my critique on Newberg and d'Aquili, both because the major problems appear in especially egregious form in their work and because the wide public readership of *Why God Won't Go Away* indicates the unfortunately broad social appeal of its misleading claims.

To begin with, Newberg and d'Aquili privilege meditation and prayer as the preeminent representatives of religious experience, the highest and most refined forms of the spiritual life. This is a questionable assumption, and RS scholars have openly rejected such efforts to define the "essence" of religion in terms of contemplative practices that are performed by only a small minority of religious community's members.[32] One of the reasons I am coming around to the subject of contemplative practice only now, in the fourth chapter of this book, is to underscore the many different kinds of religious and spiritual experience *other* than those involving meditation and prayer. From an RS perspective it is a fundamental mistake to overemphasize the ideal-typical status of contemplative practice; however, making the assumption that attention-oriented meditation is the pinnacle of all religious experience is a natural move for CN insofar as the emphasis of the field on the powerful executive functions of the brain constitutes what can fairly be termed a cult of the prefrontal cortex. Privileging these contemplative practices has irresistible benefits for researchers such as Newberg and d'Aquili for a simple reason: Meditation and prayer are *easy* for CN to study. The practitioners are sitting still for long periods of time, making them ideal subjects for brain measurement technologies such as the EEG, SPECT, PET, and functional magnetic resonance imaging (fMRI). Seen in this regard, meditation research represents a happy conjunction of disciplinary bias, technological ability, and reliable obedience on the part of the research subjects, whose own interests, motivations, and desires to please the investigators are never questioned. To take the most obvious example, the Dalai Lama and his monks have an urgent need to enlist Western political support in their desperate fight to preserve their culture against Chinese encroachment. Tibetan Buddhists who volunteer for hi-tech scientific research projects (especially projects sponsored by prominent American universities) have a compelling self-interest to provide the CN investigators with favorable results. This does not completely invalidate the findings of such studies, but it does call into question their scientific objectivity and their applicability to the brain–mind functioning of other people in other settings. This same concern about the conveniently convergent motivations of researchers and their subjects also applies to TM meditators, Christian distance healers, and the employees of the biotechnology company Promega in Davidson's mindfulness meditation studies.

This brings us to a second problem, a problem we discussed earlier in relation to dream research: the lab effect. Simply put, the experimental attempt to replicate a certain kind of experience in a laboratory setting inevitably influences, shapes, and alters the experience in a variety of subtle but significant ways. In dream research, people who serve as subjects in sleep laboratories tend to have dreams with less fear, aggression, and sexuality than people who sleep in a home setting; the lab evidently has a homogenizing effect on people's dreams, making it less likely that they will have rare or unusual types of dreaming.[33] What is true of dreams is likely to be true in the case of highly unusual phenomena such as religious experiences. Newberg and d'Aquili evince only the slightest methodological awareness of how this problem drastically qualifies the significance of their research. Although they confess that, "because peak experiences are quite rare, the likelihood of catching one when the subject is hooked up for electrophysiological readings is slim,"[34] they never question the axiomatic (and, according to their scientific discipline, necessary) assumption that experiences in a laboratory setting can be generalized to experiences outside the lab. Do people meditating and praying in a laboratory, "hooked up for electrophysiological readings" as part of a scientific experiment, have the same kinds of experiences as people meditating and praying in other settings? Newberg and D'Aquili assume the answer is "yes," but I would argue the answer is "no." Similarities between the two conditions may well exist, but just as certainly major differences exist. *Why God Won't Go Away* takes a steamroller approach to the latter. The overriding goal of the book is to identify a *common* system of neurological activity responsible for *all* forms of religious experience. Personal differences are secondary accretions to the fundamentally identical neural process.

Here we come to the third and perhaps most serious problem, that of runaway universalism. Ironically, Newberg and d'Aquili are even less interested in culture, history, and individual differences than a hard-core "blank slate" CN researcher such as Steven Pinker. At least Pinker knows enough about postmodernism to be vexed by it; Newberg and d'Aquili seem blissfully unaware of the past half-century of critical scholarship questioning universalistic claims about human nature and experience. If they were aware of this literature, I cannot imagine them writing, even in a book aimed at nonspecialists, passages such as the following:

> Essentially, all myths can be reduced to a simple framework.... Virtually all myths can be reduced to the same consistent pattern: identify a crucial existential concern, frame it as a pair of incompatible opposites, then find a resolution that alleviates anxiety and allows us to live more happily in the world.[35]

> At the heart of all the mystics' descriptions, however, is the compelling conviction that they have risen above material existence and have spiritually united with the absolute.[36]

> Neurobiologically and philosophically, there cannot be two versions of this absolute unitary state. It may *look* different, in retrospect, according to cultural beliefs and personal interpretations — a Catholic nun, for whom God is the ultimate reality, might interpret any mystical experience as a melting into Christ, while a Buddhist, who does not believe in a personalized God, might interpret mystical union as a melting into nothingness. What's important to understand, is that these differing interpretations are unavoidably distorted by after-the-fact subjectivity.... There is only absolute unity, and there cannot be two versions of any unity that is absolute.[37]

Enough was said in Chapter 2 about Wendy Doniger and the study of myth to reject Newberg and d'Aquili's claim that all myths are but elaborations on one universal pattern. We will look more closely at their claim about what exactly lies at the "heart of all the mystics' descriptions" in the next section. Here, I want to point out that whatever its failings as an understanding of religion, the proposition that AUB is the essence of religious experience is not even firmly grounded in neuroscience.[38] The theoretical claims of Newberg and d'Aquili should be understood as artifacts of the current, very imperfect state of brain-imaging technology. At present, the resolution of the various methods of neuroimaging is so poor that no one can tell with any definitive precision whether what is happening in one person's brain is exactly the same as what is happening in another person's brain. As the technology improves (and given the amount of money being poured into this research, the progress will be rapid), we are sure to discover vast new realms of unique complexity and distinctive difference in each individual's neural circuitry. This makes it quite likely that at some point in the future we will have imaging data showing how, for example, the brain–mind processes of praying Catholic nuns and meditating Buddhists (in a lab setting, of course!) are actually quite different from one another and even different from other subjects in their own tradition. Paradoxically, the very technology that Newberg, d'Aquili, and others use to defend a universalistic view of religion will, I predict, become a valuable means of highlighting the radically irreducible plurality of human religious experience.

III. Mysticism, Reconsidered

For all these reasons, the quasi-apologetic meditation research projects described earlier do not provide an adequate basis for future progress in the RS/CN dialogue. A new conceptual foundation must be laid, one that allows us to identify recurrent phenomena and meaningful patterns while at the same time highlighting creative novelty and unique individuality. Providing such a foundation is one of the major aims of this book, and here I want to further that aim by reflecting critically on the term "mysticism." A great deal of RS scholarship in recent years has focused on a reconsideration of what exactly mysticism is and whether or not we can speak of a universal, transcultural core of all mystical experience, and the time has long since come when any CN-oriented study of contemplative practice must take this scholarship into account.

For the past century the cardinal text in the study of mysticism has been James' *The Varieties* and the passage in which he describes the "four marks" constituting his definition of mystical experience:

> *Ineffability*: "It [mystical experience] defies expression ... no adequate report of its contents can be given in words.... In this peculiarity mystical states are more like states of feeling than like states of intellect."
>
> *Noetic quality*: "Although so similar to states of feeling, mystical states seem to those who experience them to be also states of knowledge. They are states of insight into depths of truth unplumbed by the discursive intellect."

(James says these first two marks are sufficient to identify an experience as mystical; the following two qualities "are less sharply marked, but are usually found.")

> *Transiency*: "Mystical states cannot be sustained for long.... Often, when faded, their qualities can but imperfectly be reproduced in memory; but when they recur it is recognized; and from one recurrence to another it is susceptible of continuous development in what is felt as inner richness and importance."
>
> *Passivity*: "Although the oncoming of mystical states may be facilitated by preliminary voluntary operations, as by fixing the attention, or going through certain bodily performances, or in other ways which manuals of mysticism prescribe; yet when the characteristic sort of consciousness once has set in, the mystic feels as if his own will were in abeyance, and indeed sometimes as if he were grasped and held by a superior power."[39]

Several scholars (e.g., Edwin Bucke, R.C. Zaehner, W.T. Stace, Ninian Smart, Aldous Huxley, Robert Forman) have followed James in using philosophy and comparative psychology to investigate mysticism. In all their works, the common method is to strip away extraneous surface details to reveal the deeper universal elements at the core of every mystical experience. Although these scholars differ in which universal elements they emphasize, they all agree that one particular element — an overwhelming sensation of cosmic unity — is the ultimate quality of mystical experience in all times and places. Newberg and d'Aquili stand squarely within this perennialist school of thought, and their notion of "Absolute Unitary Being" is presented as both a neuroscientifically verifiable and philosophically necessary explanation for the experience of mystical transcendence. Other meditation researchers, notably Benson and

Austin, share the perennialist assumption that mysticism can be defined as a universal phenomenon without regard for personal, cultural, religious, linguistic, and/or historical influences.

Such a view has become increasingly untenable, however, in light of a rising tide of RS research on the significant variations among the contemplative practices of the world's religious traditions. Foremost in this area of inquiry is Steven Katz, whose 1978 collection *Mysticism and Philosophical Analysis* raises several pointed questions about the adequacy of perennialist approaches to mysticism. Katz's main charge against the perennialism regards its epistemological claims. He rejects the rhetoric of "pure," "unmediated," "direct" consciousness and argues that such terms obscure the multiple roots in an actual life context of any form of consciousness, mystical or not. Katz accuses the perennialists of faulty scholarship in their mistranslations of sacred writings from various traditions and periods of history, a failing that allows them to glide over the many profound differences between the extraordinary states of consciousness described in these texts. Katz says he wants nothing more than to offer "a plea for the recognition of differences," and reading his work makes it clear he has no hostility to mysticism *per se* — he is genuinely interested in reports of mystical ecstasy and transcendent vision, and he attacks the perennialist approach precisely because he sees it as an impediment to a fuller understanding of those experiences.

The starting point of his philosophical analysis is a Kantian view of perception and knowledge:

> [L]et me state the single epistemological assumption that has exercised my thinking and which has forced me to undertake the present investigation: *There are NO pure (i.e., unmediated) experiences.* Neither mystical experience nor more ordinary forms of experience give any indication, or any grounds for believing, that they are unmediated. That is to say, *all* experience is processed through, organized by, and makes itself available to us in extremely complex epistemological ways.[40]

According to Katz, the formative influence of religious education and cultural belief is not simply a matter of secondary interpretation, but rather is integral to the mystical process: "It is at work before, during, and after the experience." For example, Jewish contemplatives, who have been raised to believe that God enters into moral–personal covenants with humans but remains ontologically distinct from them, strive for an ultimate state of experience known as *devekuth*, which means "adhesion to" or "clinging to" God. This experience is emphatically described *not* as a unitive absorption into God but rather as a lovingly intimate relationship *between* humans and God. By contrast, Buddhist contemplatives, who have grown up in a tradition that teaches life is suffering, desire is the cause of that suffering, and dissolving the self is the cure, seek through meditational practice the state of *nirvana*, a clear and tranquil awareness of the impermanence of all things. *Nirvana* is not a relational state like *devekuth*, but rather a radical *absence* of relationship. These two experiences have no "common core." Next, consider Christian contemplatives, who believe in the miraculous ontological interpenetration of human and divine in the person of Jesus Christ. Their spiritual practices usually aim at an absorptive union with God (*unio mystica*), something significantly different from the God–human relationship of *devekuth* and the Godless relational void of *nirvana*. (As yet another example of difference, we will discuss the Sufi notion of *fana* later in the chapter.) In light of these fundamental variations among the religious traditions of the world, the perennialist claim of a universal core to all mystical experience must be abandoned. Katz urges a return to the careful, linguistically sensitive investigations of RS researchers who are not misled by essentialist fantasies and who can reveal to us the rich pluralism of human religiosity. These investigations can show us something much more interesting than a monolithic sameness to all contemplative practice — they enable us to see the extraordinary *creativity* and nearly infinite variety of religious states of consciousness:

> Indeed, it appears that the different states of experience which go by the names of *nirvana*, *devekuth*, *fana*, etc., are not the ground but the *outcome* of the complex epistemological activity which is set in motion by the integrating character of self-consciousness employed in the specifically mystical modality. These synthetic operations of the mind are in fact the fundamental conditions under which, and under which alone, mystical experience, as all experience, takes place. These constructive conditions of consciousness produce the grounds on which mystical experience is possible at all.... For it is in appearance only that such activities as yoga produce the desired state of "pure consciousness." Properly understood, yoga, for example, is *not* an *un*conditioning or *de*conditioning of consciousness, but rather it is a *re*conditioning of consciousness, i.e., a substituting of one form of conditioned and/or contextual consciousness for another, albeit a new, unusual, and perhaps altogether more interesting form of conditioned-contextual consciousness.[41]

Writing well before the "Decade of the Brain," Katz did not have the CN resources we now possess to bolster his constructivist argument. Nevertheless, the above quote displays a prescient awareness of the potential for future investigations into the power of contemplative practice to "recondition consciousness" by intentionally altering the "synthetic operations of the mind." The CN research we have been discussing throughout this book provides an excellent resource in the study of the wondrous states (emphasis on the plural "states") of mystical consciousness deliberately induced by the varieties of contemplative practice. Where Katz speaks in philosophical terms of the "synthetic operations of the mind," we can speak in CN terms of the neural systems involved in processing, evaluating, and storing perceptual information. Where Katz speaks of "reconditioning consciousness," we can speak of decentering and recentering the dynamic relationship between different neural systems (e.g., via dreaming, sexuality, and creativity). The Kantian view that "there is NO unmediated experience" is confirmed by CN research on the constructive powers of the brain–mind and its subtly creative role in shaping our experiences. Katz's rejection of the allegedly universal mystical achievement of "pure consciousness" is supported by a growing CN literature on the functional anatomical differences between different forms of contemplative practice. Two recent CN studies beautifully illustrate this particular point.

In 1999, Hans Lou and colleagues used a PET technique to study the brain functioning of a group of highly experienced yoga teachers during a relaxation meditation (Yoga Nidra). The meditation involved listening to an audiotape providing 45 minutes of guided imagery, with the subjects attending sequentially to their bodies, abstract joy, visualization of a beautiful nature scene, and visualization of an abstract perception of the self (as a golden egg). The PET scanning revealed heightened activation in exactly those brain systems corresponding to the guided imagery tasks: The supplementary motor area responsible for bodily planning and attention was activated during meditation on the weight of the limbs, the left hemisphere (including Wernicke's region) was activated during the abstract meditation on the word *joy*, the regions of the posterior cortex involved in voluntary visual imagery were activated during the nature visualization, and parietal lobe regions in both hemispheres responsible for bodily representation were activated during the meditation on the self. Of particular significance, Lou et al. found that the subjects' brains showed a selective deactivation of those prefrontal regions involved in the executive functions of volition, selective attention, and goal-oriented action. In this regard, the Yoga Nidra practice resembles rapid eye movement (REM) sleep in diminishing the activity of the prefrontal executive system and stimulating the activity of the posterior visual system.[42]

In 2000, a study by Sara W. Lazar et al. used the fMRI technique to study the brain activation patterns of a group of subjects who had practiced Kundalini meditation daily for at least four years. The Kundalini technique is similar to the relaxation response (Herbert Benson is one of Lazar's colleagues) insofar as it involves close attention to one's breathing, silent recitation of a mantra, and a passive attitude toward intruding thoughts and feelings. Here again, the brain imaging data revealed patterns of activation directly related to the distinctive aims of the contemplative practice. Lazar et al. found that this meditation technique "activates neural structures involved in attention (frontal and parietal cortex) and arousal/autonomic control (pregenual anterior cingulate, amygdala, midbrain, and hypothalamus)."[43] Lazar et al. further discovered that this distinctive pattern of neural activation became more pronounced the longer the meditation went on: "These findings suggest that neural activity during meditation is dynamic, slowly evolving during practice."

These two studies lead to a rather obvious conclusion: Different types of contemplative practice produce different patterns of brain–mind activation and, thus, different states of consciousness. No one supreme state of mystical awareness exists toward which all practices strive; rather, multiple modes of extraordinary consciousness are produced by a variety of techniques, each of which is deeply rooted in the unique soil of a distinct psychological, cultural, and religious context. Such a conclusion is surprising only if one holds to a perennialist assumption about the ultimate sameness of all mystical experience. But, if one holds instead to an open-minded respect for the pluralistic manifestations of human religiosity, the CN findings of Lou et al. and Lazar et al. make perfect sense. *Contemplative practices genuinely transform the brain–mind system.* Different practices change consciousness in different ways, and the more energy one puts into a contemplative practice, the greater will be its transformational effects. Once we break free from the ideological hold of the perennial approach to mysticism, we are able to begin exploring the truly novel and uniquely creative dimensions of brain–mind functioning revealed by the many different kinds of contemplative practice found in the religious traditions of the world. As Katz suggests, what religious devotees experience is not the universal "ground" of consciousness but rather the creative *outcome* of a particular kind of contemplation, practiced by a particular individual, in a particular life historical context. I believe we are at the beginning of a new research era in which the rich historical and cross-cultural resources of RS will combine with the ever-expanding application of brain imaging technologies by CN to explore these manifold mystical outcomes, discovering previously unimagined complexities and open-ended developmental potentials in the exquisitely chaotic workings of the human brain-mind system.

Religion and Psychology Interlude III: How James Fares

Drawing upon the philosophical critique of Katz and the recent findings of CN, we can turn with fresh eyes to James' theory of mysticism as presented in *The Varieties*. Perhaps even more than Freud and Jung, James has had a decisive influence on the past century of Western psychological research on religious belief, practice, and experience. Particularly in *The Varieties* but also in his writings on psychology and philosophy, James set the basic terms for using the findings of scientific psychology to investigate the diverse phenomenology of religion. Mysticism ranks at the very top of James' list of religious phenomena to be studied. He makes it clear in *The Varieties* that he regards the essential core of mysticism to be an experience of divine union, and he proposes that such experiences lie at the heart of all authentic religiosity. Here is a characteristically eloquent passage, from Lecture XVI:

> This overcoming of all the usual barriers between the individual and the Absolute is the great mystic achievement. In mystic states we both become one with the Absolute and we become aware of our oneness. This is the everlasting and triumphant mystical tradition, hardly altered by differences of clime or creed. In Hinduism, in Neoplatonism, in Sufism, in Christian mysticism, in Whitmanism, we find the same recurring note, so that there is about mystical utterances an eternal unanimity which ought to make a critic stop and think, and which brings it about that the mystical classics have, as has been said, neither birthday nor native land. Perpetually telling of the unity of man with God, their speech antedates languages, and they do not grow old.[44]

Nothing, it seems, could express the perennialist creed more plainly, and nothing could provide a riper target for the critique of Katz and other RS scholars who question such grandiose generalizations about allegedly timeless religious truths. James' historical significance notwithstanding, his continued relevance for the investigation of contemplative practice is very much in doubt. Indeed, the easiest thing would be to dismiss *The Varieties* entirely as a noble but failed experiment, well-meaning but doomed by the limitations of its essentialist rhetoric and incapable of providing contemporary researchers with meaningful guidance in the study of religion and psychology.

I will argue against the rejection of James and for a renewed appreciation of his insights into the fertile interplay of religion and brain–mind functioning. Like Jeremy Carrette and G. William Barnard, but from a different theoretical perspective, I want to call for a "return to James" and a revisioning of his theory of mysticism. While we must acknowledge the perennialist, antihistorical comments in *The Varieties*, we must also recognize that the great preponderance of James' thinking, both in *The Varieties* and in his other writings, weighs in on the side of a pluralistic respect for the irreducible multiplicity of religious experience. James remains a vital and even necessary resource for exploring potential RS/CN connections, even if his ideas require some degree of critical reworking before they can be employed in our present-day inquiries.

Born in New York City in 1842, William was the oldest of Henry and Alice James' five children. He was named for his grandfather, an immigrant from Ireland whose straight-laced Calvinist faith and relentless commercial energy enabled him both to amass a considerable fortune and secure the prosperous establishment of New York's Presbyterian church. One has the impression that Max Weber's portrait of the "Protestant ethic and the spirit of capitalism" was developed with people like the elder William James in mind. Of young William's mother Alice we hear little; his father Henry was by all accounts the dominant force in William's childhood. Henry did not follow in his father's business footsteps, but instead cultivated his increasingly idiosyncratic spiritual yearnings. Thanks to a large inheritance after his father's death, Henry devoted extraordinary energy to his children's education, doing his best to infuse them with the same intellectual curiosity, moral seriousness, and religious passion that he felt. Henry greatly admired the visionary teachings of Emmanuel Swedenborg and the Transcendentalist philosophy of Ralph Waldo Emerson, and young William learned from early on that churches and dogmas were not essential to authentic faith. True religion, Swedenborg and Emerson taught, could only come from the free and lively movement of one's own spirit.

Having been exposed to so many different ideas, people, and places (the family traveled restlessly from one city to another — New York, Boston, Newport, London, Paris, Bologna, Bonn, etc.), William entered his adolescent years with a mind full of possible vocations and careers. He also found himself with a body that was frequently ill and subject to enervating bouts of depression and malaise (his eyes, stomach, and back were particular sources of recurrent suffering). For a time he studied to be an artist with the painter William Hunt, but then he abandoned that and enrolled in premedical courses at Harvard with the new and rather ironic intention of becoming a doctor. Although his health problems repeatedly interrupted his school attendance, he read widely and voraciously, following his ever-growing passion for the study of comparative anatomy and the functioning of the human body. The inner shadow of existential despair was also growing, however, as he realized he had no interest in the actual profession of being a doctor, nor enough stamina to work as a laboratory physiologist. Not surprisingly, his mood was also darkened by the Civil War and all the hatred, horror, and strife that came with that bloodiest of American conflicts. Two of William's brothers fought on the side of the Union; William was absolved from military service because of his frail health.

By early 1870, after years of depression and physical debility, he reached the point where thoughts of suicide besieged him with increasing intensity. His diary from this time is filled with despairing ruminations on human frailty and the ultimate futility of any effort to live a meaningful, morally worthy life. James included in *The Varieties* an anonymous account of this period of his life, which he called an "excellent example" of "the worst kind of melancholy … which takes the form of panic fear":

> I went one evening into a dressing-room in the twilight to procure some article that was there; when suddenly there fell upon me without any warning, just as if it came out of the darkness, a horrible fear of my own existence. Simultaneously there arose in my mind the image of an epileptic patient whom I had seen in the asylum, a black-haired youth with greenish skin, entirely idiotic, who used to sit all day on one of the benches, or rather shelves against the wall, with his knees drawn up against his chin, and the coarse gray undershirt, which was his only garment, drawn over them inclosing his entire figure. He sat there like a sort of sculptured Egyptian cat or Peruvian mummy, moving nothing

> but his black eyes and looking absolutely non-human. This image and my fear entered into a species of combination with each other. *That shape am I*, I felt, potentially. Nothing that I possess can defend me against that fate, if the hour for it should strike for me as it struck for him. There was such a horror of him, and such a perception of my own merely momentary discrepancy from him, that it was as if something hitherto solid within my breast gave way entirely, and I became a mass of quivering fear. After this the universe was changed for me altogether. I awoke morning after morning with a horrible dread at the pit of my stomach, and with a sense of the insecurity of life that I never knew before. . . .[45]

James presents this account of his bleak mental condition in early 1870 as an illustration of what he calls the "sick soul." From the perspective we have been developing in this book, James' experience appears as an almost nihilistic moment of wonder. The abrupt collapse of existential security, combined with the perversely vivid image of the green-skinned epileptic (a shocking image of insanity), completely destroyed the young man's ordinary center of identity and understanding. What he had taken to be the reliable anchors of human life — purpose, dignity, rationality, self-awareness — were suddenly revealed to be weak, flimsy nothings, capable of disappearing at any moment.

James pulled himself out of these dark depths and recentered his orientation toward life with the help of a new philosophical insight into free will and the creative power of human action. Here is a key diary entry from April 30, 1870:

> Not in maxims, not in *Anschauungen* [contemplations], but in accumulated *acts* of thought lie salvation. *Passer outré* [Let us go beyond]. Hitherto, when I have felt like taking a free initiative, like daring to act originally, without carefully waiting for contemplation of the external world to determine all for me, suicide seemed the most manly form to put my daring into; now, I will go a step further with my will, not only act with it, but believe as well; believe in my individual reality and creative power. My belief, to be sure, *can't* be optimistic — but I will posit life (the real, the good) in the self-governing *resistance* of the ego to the world. Life shall be built in doing and suffering and creating.[46]

This diary entry contains the spiritual germ of James' later explorations into emotion, consciousness, mystical experience, moral fortitude, and the philosophical reasons for believing in truth and valuing the good. Much like Freud's mournful, illness-ridden period of despair following his father's death and Jung's nearly psychotic "confrontation with the unconscious" after his break with Freud, James' suicidal depression of 1870 became the primal font from which all his later life's creations flowed.

In 1873 he took a teaching position at Harvard in the subjects of physiology and anatomy. Suddenly he found himself with a brand new mode of creative expression. The lecture, the academic world's primary rhetorical unit, suited James perfectly. His clarity of thought, profound erudition, and intellectual humility came shining through in the lectures he gave in his classes, and soon he felt sufficiently emboldened to push his investigations more specifically into the new-fledged field of psychology. Inspired by the empirical discoveries of pioneering European psychologists such as Pierre Janet, Frederick Meyers, and Wilhelm Wundt, James created the first laboratory of experimental psychology in America in 1875. His *Principles of Psychology* was published in 1890, and it quickly became the reigning text in the early development of American academic psychology.

James was invited in 1898 to give the prestigious Gifford Lectures at the University of Edinburgh. James knew this was an opportunity to make a very powerful statement of what he had to offer as an original contribution to scientific psychology. He decided to focus his lectures on a descriptive and analytic study of religious experience, considered in light of the latest findings of psychological research. His emphasis from the start was on the *diversity* of religious phenomena. The basic message James wanted to convey in the lectures was a simple affirmation of the many irreducibly different modes of religious expression. He himself felt only the slightest connection to any of the more positive manifestations of spiritual peace and divine presence ("I have no living sense of commerce with a God"[47]), but the vibrant testimony of his father, Henry, had given James a lifelong respect for people of strong religious feeling and intimate personal relations with the Divine. To prepare for the lectures, he plunged into a reading of religious biographies, seeking in these texts the raw testimony of personal religious experiences in all their physical, emotional, and psychological complexity.

Soon after accepting the Edinburgh invitation, James had an extraordinary experience of his own that bore fateful, life-altering fruit. He was on a vacation in the Adirondack Mountains, enjoying the splendor of the wilderness (the Transcendentalist veneration of Nature ran strong in his family), and one day he hiked all the way to the top of Mt. Marcy, at 5344 feet the highest peak in New York. That night James could not sleep, and he wandered away from his campsite and back into the darkened forest. In a letter to his wife he describes feeling an acute sense of "spiritual alertness":

> The influences of Nature, the wholesomeness of the people round me ... the thought of you and the children ... the problem of the Edinburgh lectures, all fermented within me until it became a regular Walpurgis Nacht. I spent a good deal of it in the woods, where the streaming moonlight lit up things in a magical checkered play, and it seemed as if the Gods of all the nature-mythologies were holding an indescribable meeting in my breast with the moral Gods of the inner life. The two

> kinds of Gods have nothing in common — the Edinburgh lectures made quite a hitch ahead.... It was one of the happiest lonesome nights of my existence, and I understand now what a poet is. He is a person who can feel the immense complexity of influences that I felt, and make some partial tracks in them for verbal statement. In point of fact, I can't find a single word for all that significance, and don't know what it was significant of, so there it remains, a mere boulder of *impression*. Doubtless in more ways than one, though, things in the Edinburgh lectures will be traceable to it.[48]

Though its immediate effect was to stimulate his thinking about religion and mysticism, James' "Walpurgis Nacht" (the reference is to Germanic lore regarding the eve of May Day, when the Devil and the witch world hold riotous rituals on lonely mountain tops) also had a darker consequence. The next morning James joined his well-rested friends in climbing Mt. Marcy once again. Then they marched, carrying heavy packs, all the way back out of the valley, a trip totaling ten and a half hours. Combined with his previous day's hike and his night of spiritually rapturous roaming, the physical strain was too much for his frail constitution to bear. He suffered permanent damage to his heart, leaving him vulnerable to bouts of cardiovascular crisis that struck with increasing frequency and led ultimately to his death twelve years later, at the age of 68.

The Edinburgh lectures were of course a tremendous success, and *The Varieties* quickly became an authoritative touchstone for generations of researchers who have followed his lead in using psychological frameworks to explain the diverse forms of the religious life. Displaying his well-honed rhetorical abilities as a lecturer before an interested general audience, James weaves together three different themes in *The Varieties*. First is the effort to describe religious phenomena in all their colorful, multifaceted diversity. James quotes at length from the personal testimonies of people from many, many different backgrounds, and the cumulative effect of reading these narratives is to stimulate an admiration for exactly what his title says — the *varieties* of religious experience. The second theme is the explanatory effort to account for at least some of the recurrent features of religious experience in terms comprehensible to scientific psychology. While denying that religion can be explained as nothing more than a species of psychological functioning (he denounced such a philosophically unjustified bias as "medical materialism"), James does believe that the research of Pierre Janet, Frederick Meyers, and others on the "subconscious" regions of the mind can shed valuable psychological insight into those experiences that constitute the living heart of religion, which James defines as "the feelings, acts, and experiences of individual men in their solitude, so far as they apprehend themselves to stand in relation to whatever they may consider the divine." The third theme that pervades *The Varieties* is the moral evaluation of religious experience with regard to whether or not it contributes to human well-being. Here, James advances his pragmatic philosophy (which he would greatly expand in his post-*Varieties* writings) that the truth and value of a thing depends on its practical, tangibly beneficial impact on people's lives. Judged by this standard, James argues that religion has indeed proved on the whole to strengthen people's moral fortitude, expand their interpersonal generosity, and quicken their spiritual vitality.

Even the most devoted Jamesian and passionate defender of *The Varieties* could not deny the necessity, a hundred years later, of applying his pragmatic standards to his own work. What are its fruits *today*? What if anything can *The Varieties* contribute to present-day investigations of religious experience, psychological functioning, and moral development? As noted earlier, James' treatment of mysticism betrays a tendency to universalistic pronouncements of questionable legitimacy, and this is a serious problem no matter how poetically rendered the pronouncements may be. Other scholars have cataloged a number of serious flaws and failings in James' work, including an excessive reliance on narratives of Protestant conversion, an individualistic bias that obscures the social and historical dimensions of human religiosity, a patriarchal privileging of strong male experience in contrast to weak female experience, and a reliance on subjective narratives that do not provide an adequate evidentiary foundation for his sweeping theoretical claims.[49] To those charges I would add that *The Varieties* is insufficiently attentive to the creatively stimulating role of sexuality in religion, lacks familiarity with the rich historical phenomenology of spiritually transformative dreams,[50] and evades the toughest questions about the troubling connection between religious experience and violent aggression.

For all these reasons, *The Varieties* is anything but an infallible guide in the study of mysticism. It can, however, still serve as a very helpful companion if certain of its claims can be revised and updated in light of recent findings in CN. Were James alive today, he (like Freud and Jung) would no doubt be intensely interested in the findings of brain–mind research over the past few years, and I imagine he would welcome the opportunity to include those findings in a further development of the arguments he makes in *The Varieties*. Let us then revisit James' four marks of mystical experience and see how they stand up in relation to contemporary brain-mind science.

First, let us consider *ineffability*. Common to all mystical states, James says, is a superabundance of feeling that overwhelms the individual's ordinary capacity for verbal expression. Mystical experiences are difficult to talk about, as they generate a painful tension between the grandeur of divine revelation and the pathetic inadequacy of common words. Described in this way, the ineffability of mystical experience suggests a selective activation of neural systems involved in primal emotion (e.g., the limbic system) and a selective disruption of those parts of the brain responsible for producing spoken words (e.g., Broca's and Wernicke's areas). Even those types of contemplative practice that seek to extinguish emotional responsiveness and thus dampen the neural firings of the limbic system are likely to involve a profound disordering of the prefrontal regions of the left cortical hemisphere devoted in most humans to linguistic communication. To my knowledge, no CN research has been conducted on precisely this point, so future investigations are needed to understand what exactly happens to our language system when it is (1) besieged by a highly unusual patterns of neural input from (2) a radically transformed mode of conscious awareness that is (3) oriented not toward the interpersonal dynamics of human social interaction but toward the infinite horizons of creation and the cosmos itself.

With regard to the second characteristic, *noesis*, James says mystical experiences are not only a matter of feeling but also of knowledge. They provide "insight into depths of truth unplumbed by the discursive intellect." James felt the need to apologize to his Edinburgh audience for the apparent contradiction of claiming that mystical states are simultaneously emotional and intellectual. Considered today in the light of CN research by Damasio and others, James' claim appears somewhat less shocking, and perhaps even a bit prophetic in its awareness of the deep, intricate interweaving of emotional responsiveness and conscious reasoning. Still, few mainstream CN researchers are willing to follow James in granting any special cognitive power or value to mystical experiences or, indeed, to any mode of consciousness other than the ordinary waking state. The reigning CN assumption is what I call the *deficit model*, according to which any form of brain–mind functioning is measured, defined, and evaluated in terms of everyday ego consciousness. Seen from this perspective, mystical experiences involve a severe degradation of normal cognitive functioning, thus they cannot be taken as a reliable source of knowledge about the world.

This model no longer accords with the available scientific evidence. If it is true, as strongly indicated by the flawed but still useful meditation research of Benson, Austin, d'Aquili and Newberg, Lazar, Lou, and Davidson, that certain contemplative practices produce clearly discernible shifts in the neural underpinnings of conscious awareness, then a major argument of *The Varieties* has been vindicated. More than anything, James wants to persuade his listeners that one's ordinary state of consciousness is but one of many possible modes of awareness, and at least some of these alternative modes are nonpathological and actually beneficial to the individual. This is exactly the finding of recent CN research on meditation, and a new way is now open for exploring the question of mystical noesis: To what extent do the experiences that occur during such alternative states of consciousness count as knowledge? Unless one is going to define "knowledge" as only that which is gained in a normal waking state,[51] it seems necessary to grant not just the possibility but indeed the likelihood that other modes of brain–mind functioning can process information, create new neural connections, and develop a genuine knowledge of that which the individual is experiencing. This knowledge can include a new insight into the creative workings of one's own mind, a sharper perception of deep causal influences on one's personal history, and/or an expanded recognition of one's interconnections with other powers and beings in the universe. Mystical states may not be the only or even the fastest way to gain such knowledge, and the pragmatic question remains of whether this knowledge has any value for life. Still, a fair reading of contemporary CN research (i.e., a reading unburdened by the biases of the deficit model) indicates that mystical states are plausible sources of authentic knowledge. To be sure, much work needs to be done to test the specific claims of people who have experienced such extraordinary modes of consciousness, but we have progressed far enough to dismiss once and for all the misleading belief that only waking ego consciousness can provide us with real knowledge.

Several RS scholars have already helped advance our understanding of the multiple epistemological dimensions of mystical noesis. Lee Irwin's work, as we have already seen, is directly focused on these questions. G. William Barnard's philosophically refined study of James, Sandra Dixon's self-psychological reevaluation of St. Augustine, Amy Hollywood's creative application of French psychoanalysis to medieval Christian women mystics, Jeffrey Kripal's revealing investigation of the erotic spirituality of Ramakrishna, Franz Metcalf's object-relational approach to Buddhism, Dan Capper's illuminating look at guru devotion in the United States, and William B. Parsons' nuanced examination of the correspondence between Freud and the writer Romain Rolland are all important contributions to what James called for in *The Varieties* — namely, a more psychologically precise account of that which is learned in mystical states of consciousness.[52] None of these scholars, however, makes any sustained reference to the recent findings of CN. Parsons comes the closest to including the findings of scientific psychology in his work when he draws on Arthur Deikman's studies on the formation of habitual patterns of perceptual, cognitive, motor, and behavioral functioning, patterns that can be deliberately altered by certain types of contemplative practice: "[D]evelopment from infancy to adulthood is accompanied by an organization of the perceptual and cognitive world that has as its price the selection of some stimuli and stimulus qualities to the exclusion of others. If the automatization underlying that organization is reversed, or temporarily suspended, aspects of reality that were formerly unavailable might then enter awareness."[53] Parsons sees the potential of connecting Deikman's ideas with the RS investigation of mysticism: "It [Deikman's theory] suggests the possibility that deautomatization or deconditioned modes of consciousness and the operation of intuitive faculties and deep empathic states are linked, and that the latter, once awakened and cultivated, grant one access to new modes of awareness."[54]

The third and "less sharply marked" characteristic of James' definition of mysticism is *transiency.* Here, CN has little to say, because the lab effect makes it difficult if not impossible to "capture" mystical experiences with current brain imaging technology. James notes the difficulty in remembering mystical experiences after they have ended, and on this point we can confidently connect his insight with the abundant CN research literature on state-dependent learning and the difficulty of accessing in one mode of consciousness memories formed in a different mode. To the extent that some mystical modes of consciousness can be related to the neural wildfire of epileptic seizures, the CN evidence suggests that such states are indeed short lived and ephemeral. However, the fact that the meditation studies we have been discussing all produced their findings using highly trained practitioners for subjects indicates that the capacity to enter into alternative states of consciousness can be cultivated over a long period of time (according to James, "it is susceptible of continuous development"), to the point where we can plausibly speak of the development of ongoing mystical *processes* rather than discrete, temporally limited mystical *events*. Parsons once again sees the potential here as he proposes new investigations of "the process nature of mysticism," which he says is...

> ...compatible with what James calls the methodical cultivation of mysticism. Here the noetic dimension of singular mystical experience cannot be divorced from the mystical life. The transformative effects of mystical experience, seen as part of the total response of an individual to moments of intuitive contact with the divine, is prepared for and integrated into a mystical life as defined by a particular religious tradition. The term "process," then, shifts the criteria for evaluating mysticism from mystical experiences per se to the cultivation of a specific set of dispositions, capacities, virtues, states of consciousness, and patterns of behavior.[55]

The fourth and final mark of mysticism is *passivity*, and by this James means the feeling of connection with trans-human powers vastly stronger than one's ordinary sense of self. Mystics regularly report a suspension of individual will in the moment when the tidal forces of the divine come flooding in. This feeling of connection with something *more* than the individual self can be explained, James says, in a way that satisfies the empirical demands of psychological science yet remains open to the faith claims of religious believers. The key concept in his explanation is the "subconscious," and in many ways the success of *The Varieties* as a whole depends on his strategic use of this concept. Here is his summary statement in the final lecture of the series:

> The *subconscious self* is nowadays a well-accredited psychological entity; and I believe that in it we have exactly the mediating term required. Apart from all religious consideration, there is actually and literally more life in our total soul than we are at any time aware of.... Let me then propose, as a hypothesis, that whatever it may be on its *farther* side, the "more" with which in religious experience we feel ourselves connected is on its *hither* side the subconscious continuation of our conscious life. Starting thus with a recognized psychological fact as our basis, we seem to preserve a contact with "science" which the ordinary theologian lacks.

> At the same time the theologian's contention that the religious man is moved by an external power is vindicated, for it is one of the peculiarities of invasions from the subconscious region to take on objective appearances, and to suggest to the Subject an external control. In the religious life the control is felt as "higher"; but since on our hypothesis it is primarily the higher faculties of our own hidden mind which are controlling, the sense of union with the power beyond us is a sense of something, not merely apparently, but literally true.[56]

This argument is aimed at what Friedrich Schleiermacher called the "cultured despisers" of religion, those secular critics who reject the ontological pretensions of religious belief in God or any other species of supernatural being. James' psychological explanation is perfectly consistent with the idea (held by Freud, Pinker, Boyer, Pyssiainen, Wilson, and others) that religion involves a projection of human fantasies on a cosmic screen: People of religious faith may believe they are experiencing a transcendent communion with God, but in fact they are merely accessing the subconscious levels of their own brain–mind system. James grants the plausibility of this view, yet he insists that his hypothesis about the subconscious influences on religious experience does not require a rejection of beliefs in divine, transpersonal beings — that way lies the all-too common prejudice of medical materialism by which bodily conditions are confused with ultimate origins and existential values. In an earlier passage in *The Varieties*, James makes it clear he regards his psychological explanation as being equally supportive of traditional theological teachings:

> But if you, being orthodox Christians, ask me as a psychologist whether the reference of a phenomenon to a subliminal self does not exclude the notion of the direct presence of the Deity altogether, I have to say frankly that as a psychologist I do not see why it necessarily should. The lower manifestations of the Subliminal, indeed, fall within the resources of the personal subject: his ordinary sense-material, inattentively taken in and subconsciously remembered and combined, will account for all his usual automatisms. But just as our primary wide-awake consciousness throws open our senses to the touch of things material, so it is logically conceivable that *if there be* higher spiritual agencies that can directly touch us, the psychological condition of their doing so *might be* our possession of a subconscious region which alone should yield access to them. The hubbub of the waking life might close a door which in the dreamy Subliminal might remain ajar or open.[57]

So much James argued to his Edinburgh audience a little more than a hundred years ago. How does his hypothesis hold up today? On the whole, quite well. As we found in our reconsiderations of Freud and Jung, a large body of evidence has accumulated regarding the tremendous amount of brain–mind functioning that occurs outside the bounds of ordinary waking consciousness. Experiences of wonder, mystical awe, and religious revelation clearly have multiple points of contact with these nonconscious brain–mind systems, and James' hypothesis remains a fruitful way of accounting for the interaction of psychological and religious factors in such experiences. Indeed, considered in light of current CN research, the passivity and loss of volition so common to mystical states suggests a selective deactivation of the executive systems of the prefrontal cortex — precisely those systems whose ordinary functioning we have found to be disrupted in other experiences of wonder.

What is less clear is whether or not James was right in his specific conceptualization of that which lies outside the sphere of ordinary consciousness. He followed Janet (and opposed Freud) in arguing that mental processes can have no existence apart from a conscious subject. For James, the extraordinary phenomena of religion and mysticism involve thoughts and feelings experienced not by the ordinary waking self but by alternate selves with alternate centers and peripheries, hence his emphasis on *sub*conscious rather than *un*conscious experiences. As always, he wants to highlight the multiplicity of human religiosity and the psychological integrity of mystical states of consciousness. Some findings of contemporary CN support James on this point; Damasio's developmental model of core consciousness, extended consciousness, and autobiographical consciousness, for example, and Ramachandran's work on the variable dynamics of neural self-representation. Furthermore, the aim of many of the world's contemplative traditions does seem to be the cultivation of a radically shifted center of conscious awareness and brain–mind orientation. More research in both CN and RS will be needed before James' view on this specific question is fully vindicated. But, with regard to his central psychological claim in *The Varieties*, ample evidence now exists to join with him in affirming that "in religion we have a department of human nature with unusually close relations to the transmarginal or subliminal region."

IV. The Satanic Verses

This chapter will close with some reflections on religion, science, and contemplative practices in Islam. At a minimum, I want to expand the CN/RS dialogue on contemplative practice beyond the confines of Buddhism and Christianity to include a tradition that has a rich history of integrating spiritual experience and intellectual inquiry. More ambitiously, I want to consider Muhammad's revelation as the product (on its hither side) of an especially powerful reconfiguration of consciousness and brain–mind functioning. This is not to deny Muhammad's claim that the ultimate source of his revelations was God. You may or may not accept that theological claim, but either way you can still acknowledge the influence of Muhammad's mind, body, and personal life circumstances on his Prophetic mission. Because so much detailed biographical information about Muhammad's life has been preserved (in the

Qur'an, the *hadith*, and other texts), we are able to see with unusual clarity the complex interplay of forces that generated one of the world's most momentous religious revolutions.[58] Viewed in this light, the religious culture of Islam appears as a highly effective agent in reproducing vital elements of the special mode of creative self-awareness that Muhammad developed to such an extraordinary degree.

Throughout the *Qur'an*, Muhammad directs people's attention toward the natural world as unmistakable evidence of God's power and benevolence: "Behold! In the creation of the heavens and the earth, and the alternation of Night and Day, these are indeed Signs for men of understanding."[59] God is God because of this ultimate power of generativity, the ability to create life and all the wondrous bounties of this world. "To him is due the primal origin of the heavens and the earth: when He decrees a matter, He says to it: 'Be,' and it is."[60] Muhammad lays particular stress on the orderliness of nature and the beautiful, elegant regularity of its workings. To contemplate these marvelous laws of the created world leads directly toward a greater awareness of and appreciation for God's supreme potency and benevolence toward humankind. "It is Allah Who has subjected the sea to you, that ships may sail through it by His command, that you may seek of His Bounty, and that you may be grateful. And He has subjected to you, as from Him, all that is in the heavens and on earth: behold, in that are Signs indeed for those who reflect."[61]

This exhortation to reflect on the laws of nature led, in the centuries following Muhammad's death, to the development of a dynamic scientific tradition of inquiry, experimentation, and systematization. Thanks in large part to the rapid military expansion of Islam's geographic control, the Muslim community suddenly grew large and prosperous enough to devote unprecedented resources to the scientific study of nature. Building on the achievements of ancient Greek and Roman naturalists (whom the medieval Christians of Europe had for the most part piously rejected), Islamic scientists pushed human knowledge forward in several important areas: mathematics, optics, astronomy, geography, and linguistics, to name only a few. In physiology and applied medicine the progress was especially dramatic, as Muslim physicians developed increasingly sophisticated models of somatic functioning, while pharmacologists compiled an impressive store of knowledge about the curative effects of various compounds, herbal extracts, and other medicinal drugs. Surgical treatments became far more effective because of the innovative use of antiseptic alcohol for the wounds and anesthesia to minimize pain. In all these ways, Islamic scientists forged ahead of their contemporaries in Europe, inspired by the mandate given them by the Prophet Muhammad to use all their sensory and intellectual powers to investigate the laws of nature, which are nothing other than the physical manifestation of God's absolute creative power.

Along with their wonderment at the natural world, Muslims also turned within for spiritual insight and divine revelation. The contemplative practices gathered under the name "Sufism" followed Muhammad's lead in another direction, along the inner path of intensely focused devotion to God. All faithful Muslims are hopeful of meeting God in the afterlife; Sufis are seeking a personal experience of God in the *present* life. Muhammad's life and teachings provided the Sufis with a wealth of guidance for purifying the soul and making oneself more worthy of God's beneficence and love. This desire for greater spiritual intimacy with the divine grew all the stronger in the years following the unexpectedly swift rise of the Umayyad dynasty. Amid the newfound splendor and wealth of the Islamic empire, many ordinary Muslims became concerned about the irreligious temptations of worldly power. In rejection of such temptations these people returned to the simple, humble practices of Muhammad as recounted in the *Qur'an* and *hadith*. The Arabic word for Sufism, *tasawwuf*, seems to have originated in the rough clothing made of *suf*, or "wool," worn by the earliest ascetics of Islam. Sufis saw the cultivation of a greater intimacy with God as a lifelong pursuit, a methodical road (*tariqah*) that departs from the lower self of passions and desires ("the human soul [*nafs*] is certainly prone to evil"[62]) and leads toward an ever more personal and loving embrace with the divine. Most Sufi practices revolve around the rhythmic recitation of verses from the *Qur'an*. Performed both silently and aloud, these recitations (known as *dhikr*, for "remembrance") seek to fulfill God's injunction in the *Qur'an* to *remember* — "Then you remember Me; I will remember you.... [C]all your Lord to mind when you forget, and say, 'I hope that my Lord will guide me ever closer than this to the right road.'"[63] Along with the practice of *dhikr*, Sufis also used poetry (e.g., the verses of Jalal ad-din Rumi), listening to music (*sama*), and bodily movement (e.g., the turning of Mevlevis) to induce a heightened state of receptivity to God's presence.

Considering what we have discussed in this chapter about the CN research on the constructive nature of consciousness (which depends crucially on the smooth operation of both short- and long-term memory systems), these Sufi practices can be understood to be highly refined techniques of shifting an individual's center of brain–mind functioning. They enlist the executive functions of the neocortex in the cause of eliminating all ordinary, daily concerns and focusing conscious attention exclusively on Muhammad's teachings, with the deliberate intention of replicating his pure, humble faith orientation toward God. Our discussion in Chapter 3 about the wonder-provoking power of music is clearly applicable here, as is the analysis in Chapter 1 of RS and CN approaches to dreaming (dreams play a major role in Sufi life, and dreaming of Muhammad himself is considered uniquely true and meaningful). Sufism draws upon all of these potent sources of wonder as means of continually stimulating the brain–mind system with Muhammad's divine vision, training the faithful to feel, think, and perceive nothing but the enveloping presence of God. The emphasis is very much on creating a *new* center of awareness that is different from ordinary, day-to-day mental life (though it remains potentially compatible with the highest functions of reasoning, as the philosophers Ibn al-Arabi and al-Ghazzali argued).

As might be expected given what we have seen of the social conflicts generated by such transformative practices, Sufism has endured its share of controversy and condemnation for challenging the conscious *status quo*. Though their devotions are deeply rooted in the teachings of Muhammad, Sufis have nevertheless been accused of importing impure religious practices from foreign cultures, and their quest for esoteric dimensions of meaning in the sayings of Muhammad has elicited scorn from more literally minded theologians.[64] Most problematically, Sufis speak of their most intense spiritual experiences in terms that sound suspiciously like a total identification of themselves with God, something that would be in direct violation of Muhammad's clear insistence (in deliberate contrast with the incarnational theology of Christianity) that neither he nor any other human can claim such an identification. Sufi descriptions of *fana* ("annihilation") do veer dangerously close to a language of total union, but never to the point of forgetting that God is God and humans are but mortal servants of the divine. *Fana* is better understood as the ultimate extension of the Sufi process of creating a kind of trans-consciousness by which the majestic unity of the divine is allowed to swallow the whole of individual awareness. All human particularity falls away, all distracting impurity disappears, leaving nothing but an absolute openness to God.

The paradigmatic event for Sufi mysticism is mentioned briefly in *sura* 17, which mentions Muhammad's Night Journey (*isra*) to Jerusalem: "Glory to Allah Who took His Servant for a Journey by night from the Sacred Mosque to the Furthest Mosque, whose precincts We did bless — in order that We might show him some of Our Signs: for He is the One Who hears and sees all things."[65] Muhammad repeatedly referred to this amazing experience in later conversations with his followers, and several *hadiths* present colorful elaborations of what he saw and learned. According to tradition, the Night Journey occurred soon after the "Year of Sadness" (619 C.E.), so named because of the deaths of his ever-supportive wife Khadija and his protective uncle Abu Talib. One night, a mournful, troubled Muhammad went by himself to the Ka'ba to pray and to sleep. Suddenly he was awakened by Gabriel, who beckoned him to mount a heavenly creature (*buraq*). Muhammad did so, and off he went into the air and through the heavens on a spectacular voyage of revelation, during which he met other prophets (most prominently, Abraham, Moses, and Jesus), prayed at the "Furthest Mosque" of Jerusalem, and finally made the supreme ascent (*miraj*) to the Seventh Heaven, wherein resides the Throne of God.

When Muhammad returned to Mecca and told people the next morning what he had experienced, his followers were enchanted, but his enemies were scornful. How, they asked, could Muhammad have traveled so far in such a short time? Everyone knew a journey to Jerusalem would take many days, not just one night. Here, his critics said, was fresh evidence of Muhammad's delusional madness.

Islamic tradition has remained unsettled on the question of what exactly happened during Muhammad's *miraj*. Many Muslims hold to the view that this is one of God's truly miraculous interventions into the natural world. Despite its seeming impossibility, the *miraj* actually involved a physical transportation of Muhammad from Mecca to Jerusalem and back in the space of one night. (Various *hadiths* emphasize that after the *miraj* Muhammad made accurate predictions about the arrival of distant caravans he could only have seen while in flight.) Other Muslims believe the *miraj* was a spiritual experience that did not involve Muhammad's physical body. Whether or not this implies the *miraj* was a dream is still a topic of debate. Considering the facts that Muhammad's experience took place (1) at night, (2) in a sacred shrine, (3) after he had gone to sleep, and it involved (4) vivid imagery, (5) ecstatic sensations of flight, and (6) a revelatory vision of the divine, it certainly seems legitimate to consider a comparison of the *miraj* with other extraordinary dream experiences reported in other religious contexts. In many of these cases, people describe their dreams in very Jamesian terms as "more" than just regular dreams, as experiences feeling somehow *realer* than anything in waking life.[66] In this regard, RS research on unusual types of dreams finds some degree of confirmation from contemporary CN research, specifically from Mark Solms' findings on the neuropsychological phenomenon of waking/dreaming confusion. Solms attributes this vividly unsettling state of epistemological uncertainty to the disruption of the anterior limbic region of the brain. When this neural system is functioning properly, an individual can properly distinguish what is real from what is a dream; when this system is damaged or destroyed, the boundaries become unstable, the mind's capacity to inhibit dream-like experience is lost, and the individual is besieged by hyper-vivid dreams and fantasy intrusions into waking. "We may speculate," Solms says, "that seizure activity anywhere in the limbic system is apt to generalize within that system and overwhelm the frontal-limbic mechanisms that inhibit dreams and dreamlike thinking. This fits neatly with the classical observation of 'dreamy states' in temporal lobe epileptics."[67]

Based on the information provided by Muslim tradition, it seems plausible to view the *miraj* as involving on its hither side an extraordinarily intense activation of the dreaming brain–mind with (perhaps) an especially dramatic suspension of normal inhibitory mechanisms centered in the limbic region. Now, does this inevitably lead us back to the long-standing (Christian) charge against Muhammad that his revelations were nothing other than the deranged products of epileptic fits? No, absolutely not. Whatever may be said of Muhammad's religious teachings, he clearly possessed the capacity to think and behave in normal, healthy, adaptive ways. In fact, he displayed several remarkably strong and highly effective cognitive skills, including the abilities to use spoken language eloquently and persuasively, discern people's inner motivations, evaluate complex social situations, and organize heterogeneous groups of people into a cohesive community. Far from being mentally impaired, Muhammad had a sharp mind and a richly developed personality. No evidence suggests that his revelatory experiences detracted from those attributes, and efforts to pathologize his life or teachings should be rejected.

What is really at stake in this debate is whether Muhammad's prophetic mission was a pure transmission of God's word or was somehow influenced or corrupted by his personal desires and psychophysiological constitution. This goes beyond the possibly oneiric provenance of the *miraj* to a much deeper tension at the heart of Muhammad's teachings. The *Qur'an* contains numerous passages in which Muhammad insists his message is absolutely pure and unmediated. Not a single word comes other than from God, and Muhammad is merely a humble recipient, the "unlettered" (*ummi*) prophet who serves as nothing more than a conduit for the divine. And, yet, the Muslim tradition has preserved several stories that openly question this key tenet of the faith. *Sura* 58 presents contradictory rules about alms giving that seem to reflect a process of Muhammad rather than God changing his mind. In *Sura* 33, God explicitly endorses Muhammad's potentially scandalous desire to take a beautiful woman named Zaynab as a new wife, even though she was a cousin of his *and* already married to another man. (Muhammad seems to have experienced a kind of sudden sexual wonder when he saw Zaynab one day, reportedly exclaiming "Praise be to God who changes men's hearts.") The conveniently quick revelation from God approving of Muhammad's new marriage prompted Aisha, the boldest of his other wives (after Khadija's death, Muhammad took a total of eight additional spouses), to comment "truly thy Lord makes haste to do thy bidding." Also, a scribe named Abdallah ibn Sa'id made several small changes of wording while Muhammad dictated Quranic verses to him (e.g., from "Allah is knowing and hearing" to "Allah is knowing and wise"), just to see if the Prophet would notice the difference; Muhammad did not, and when he finally found out Abdallah was nearly executed for his impiety.

Of all the stories that wonder about the certainty of the Quranic revelation, the episode of the Satanic verses is perhaps the most infamous, and most revealing. The earliest source for the story is the authoritative commentary of al-Tabari (839–923 C.E.), although other biographers of the same era say nothing of it. To this day, people sharply disagree about whether or not the incident ever happened (as anyone who lived through the violent controversy surrounding the publication of Salman Rushdie's 1988 novel *The Satanic Verses* well knows), and this in itself suggests the ambivalent intensity of the questions raised by the supposed temptation. Without being able to comment one way or the other on the historical accuracy of the story, I still find it striking that Satan's alleged intrusion into the revelatory process occurs precisely *here*, at this very difficult moment in the Prophet's early mission. Muhammad was still living in Mecca, the leader of a small but passionate band of followers, acutely aware of the growing resistance among the city's most powerful clans against his radical, iconoclastic claims. The question on everyone's mind was whether his religious message could coexist with the traditional religious beliefs of other people. Whether or not Satan briefly misled him into saying otherwise, the final text of *sura* 53 marks a decisive moment when the Prophet answered *no* — God's revelation to Muhammad supersedes all other faiths, all other spiritual beliefs, all other existential insights. After the Prophet announced the new, uncompromising verses against the goddesses al-Lat, al-Uzza, and Manat, the path toward absolute monotheism was fixed. In time, and after much bloody warfare in which Muhammad both killed and was almost killed himself, that path led him to conquer Mecca with an army of 10,000 men, to enter the Kaba, to reverently touch the Black Stone with his staff, and to destroy all the sacred idols to other gods while chanting a verse from *sura* 17 (the *sura* of the Night Journey): "Truth has now arrived, and Falsehood perished; for Falsehood is by its nature bound to perish."

As *sura* 53 made clear, Muhammad's path of monotheistic purity would allow no deviations into pluralistic contemplation of the cosmos, no concessions to multiple dimensions of truth and reality, no recognition of other creative powers in the world. Wonder at the *many* was rejected, and only wonder at the *one* was allowed. The "Seal of the Prophets" (*Khatam an-Nabiyin*) thus threatened to become a seal on the wondering imagination.

Conclusion: The Evolution of Wonder

Conclusion

I sat with the other cadets in my platoon (2nd platoon, Delta Company, 15th battalion, 4th training brigade) in open wooden bleachers overlooking a half-mile stretch of hills, trees, and bushes. The high summer sun bore down on us through a steamy, grayish-blue haze. Sweat poured freely down our faces, soaking our heavy olive-drab uniforms. We were silent, excited, expectant. It was the sixth day of reserve officer training corps (ROTC) basic camp at Fort Knox, Kentucky, and we cadets were about to witness our first firepower display.

We had been at camp long enough to develop a keen curiosity about the weapons used by the regular Army soldiers stationed there. The booming artillery could be heard around the clock, and thunderous explosions of varying intensities formed a constant soundtrack to our training exercises. Fort Knox is known as the "Home of Armor," and it prided itself on having the world's largest collection of mechanized field weaponry (i.e., bigger than any single base in the Soviet Union). Ronald Reagan was President of the United States at the time, and he had recently christened the U.S.S.R. "The Evil Empire," while his linguistically creative Chief of Staff General Alexander Haig promoted a massive arms buildup to counter Soviet military superiority: "The warning message we sent the Russians was a calculated ambiguity that would be clearly understood." A renewed sense of martial urgency had risen in the country, a heightened sense of danger from and animosity toward an enemy who could, if he chose, destroy us with the press of a button, just as easily as we could destroy him with a press of our button.

The identity of this enemy was made absolutely clear to us cadets the moment we set foot on the base. Now, at last, we would get a chance to see the weapons that were firing all around us, the weapons we would soon be trained be to use ourselves.

A sergeant walked to the front of the bleachers and explained the scenario. A squad of our soldiers had taken positions in hidden trenches just ahead of us, and they were going to repel an imagined enemy assault coming from the far ridge approximately 1000 yards away. At each stage of the assault, our troops would engage their targets using a different weapon system appropriate to that tactical situation.

The sergeant stepped aside, and up rumbled an M60A1 tank. Our eyes grew wide as the huge armored vehicle, the premier weapon in the U.S. Army, pulled to a stop on our right and aimed the long barrel of its 155-mm cannon downrange. Suddenly, it fired with a flash, a deafening BOOM, and a belch of black smoke. A moment later came a dull explosion as the shell struck a bush on the far ridge, sending up a fiery cloud of dirt and debris. The tank fired again, and again. Two more smoky clouds sprouted up on the far ridge.

The sergeant, now narrating over a loudspeaker, said the enemy was advancing from the ridge, moving downhill toward the protection of a depression behind the next closest ridge. From hidden positions to our left and right, tripod-mounted M60.50-caliber machine guns opened up, their red tracer rounds spraying back and forth across the distant hillside.

The sergeant said the enemy has reached the low ground behind the ridge, and now a 70-mm mortar came into action, lobbing shells in a carefully calibrated arc over the ridge and directly on top of the enemy position. More clouds of dirt and smoke rose in front of us.

"They're about to make a final assault," the sergeant said, "Straight at us. Our troops are preparing for close combat."

And now a new sound came over the loudspeaker —

Music.

The music of dozens of piping flutes, all soaring up a scale of tense, unstable notes, darting higher and higher toward a quivering, unbearable height —

"Here they come!" the sergeant shouted.

The M60 machine guns went to work again, spewing a torrent of .50-caliber rounds back and forth, ripping up the ground 100 yards ahead of them. Soldiers from multiple positions let loose with M16 rifles on full automatic and M270 grenade launchers.

And then the warbling flutes gave way to a rousing melody that soared over the ear-splitting tumult, a melody that was familiar to us all yet perhaps had never *really* been heard until now:

"Dah-duh-duh-Dah, duh, Dah-duh-duh-DAH, duh, Dah-duh-duh-DAH, duh, Dah-duh-duh-DAH!"

The M60A1 tank let loose with several more cannon blasts at nearly point-blank targets. Every weapon in the arsenal opened up in a climactic eruption of firepower, and the air swelled with explosions, smoke, and music.

Suddenly it all stopped. Silence fell on the range.

Our ears ringing, we watched the smoke clear and our soldiers step out of their trenches, waving at us and grinning with obvious pleasure at the fun they had just been having.

We cadets rose as one to our feet, laughing and clapping and cheering.

I. War and Wonder

The Old Norse myth of the Valkyries, daughters of the heavenly king Wotan, portrays a host of fearsome goddesses who fly on mighty steeds over fields of war, choosing who will live and who will die. Those warriors blessed with the honor of dying in battle are carried by the Valkyries to a wonderful afterlife in the divine realm of Valhala. In 1856, the German composer Richard Wagner (among other things, the most influential figure in Nietzsche's intellectual life) wrote "The Ride of the Valkyries" as part of his four-opera cycle *Nibelungenleid* (*The Ring of the Niebelung*). Wagner's rousing martial music was then adopted by National Socialists in the 1930s as a fitting sonic accompaniment to the rise of the Thousand Year Reich. We may well imagine Jung listening to this music during his visits to Germany at that time.

Then, fifty years and two difficult, ambiguously concluded American wars later, "The Ride of the Valkyries" was put to a different symbolic use by Francis Ford Coppola in his film *Apocalypse Now* (1979). Set in the Vietnam war but narratively structured by Joseph Conrad's novel *The Heart of Darkness* (1902), the film portrays battle-weary Captain Benjamin Willard's journey to the ultimate savage depths of war. His mission begins with Lt. Colonel Bill Kilgore, who takes Willard on an airborne raid using U.S. army helicopter gunships to attack a Vietnamese village. As the soldiers excitedly load their weapons and the helicopters swoop down on the unsuspecting peasants, Lt. Colonel Kilgore orders the music to start. From huge speakers mounted on the underbellies of the helicopters, the warbling flutes of Wagner's opera fill the sky. Willard looks in wonder at Kilgore, who shouts over the din just before the slaughter begins, "It scares the hell out of the slopes. My boys love it!"

Coppola's stated intention in making *Apocalypse Now* was to launch a major artistic protest against America's military actions in Southeast Asia. "My film is not about Vietnam. It is Vietnam."[1] The object of intense controversy well before its release, the movie presented a wild phantasmagoria of bloody carnage, absurd suffering, violent beauty, and existential horror — a film of awful wonder and irresistible emotional power. A huge critical and commercial success, *Apocalypse Now* earned Coppola his second Academy Award for Best Director, and Lt. Colonel Kilgore's Wagnerian assault became one of the film's signature scenes.

This modern cinematic elaboration on an ancient myth of war conveys multiple meanings that mutually reinforce one another, as Wendy Doniger points out:

> When Coppola played the Valkyries music as the helicopters attacked, he was simultaneously implying that the helicopters were like Valkyries (flying and choosing the dead) and like Nazis (waging an evil war), but only the first meaning was literally there in the music; to get to the second meaning, you had to know that the Nazis had used the myth in their own way, as did Coppola in his. Clearly it behooves us to distinguish among

> the very different uses to which the basic theme has been put, but at the same time we must acknowledge that our understanding of Coppola's film is greatly enhanced by an understanding of both the *Nibelungenlied* and modern German history — two tellings, one on each side of the historic moment of Wagner.[2]

Although I knew nothing of Doniger's work at the time I trained at Fort Knox, I now realize I was picking up on what, in her terms, would constitute a third telling of the Valkyries myth, a third dimension of symbolic meaning. I clearly remember during the exhilarating mayhem of the firepower display my amazement that the Army would actually use Wagner's opera as background music for a firepower display. *Apocalypse Now* was still fresh in everyone's minds — I had seen it five times in the past two years — and like many people I viewed the film as a passionate denunciation of the monstrous evil and total wastefulness of war. How, I wondered, could the Army *possibly* think it was a good idea to remind us of Coppola's surreal anti-Vietnam manifesto?

The answer to that question was on the faces of my fellow cadets and in my own gut. We were entranced by the sheer *power* of these weapons, by the primal potency and vigorous expansion of identity we felt. Seeing the brilliant explosions, imagining our evil enemies blown to bits, feeling the rich shock waves wash over our bodies — it was horrifying, to be sure, but it also felt *good*. The Army sergeant at Fort Knox knew exactly what he was doing when he played "The Ride of the Valkyries" for us. The Valkyries were carrying us beyond Vietnam, beyond Wagner and Nazism to a vividly physical experience of the terrible daughters of Wotan riding the winds and singing into being the joyful savagery of war. This is exactly the violent spirit the Army wanted to quicken within us, decentering us from our ordinary sense of moral self-restraint and stimulating an exuberant desire to fight, kill, and destroy. Despite Coppola's antiwar political intentions, *Apocalypse Now* effectively aroused those same primal aggressive desires that helped originally give rise to the Valkyries myth.[3] Our sergeant recognized that, and he cleverly used it to his and the Army's advantage. Who cares about left-wing Hollywood directors? Who cares about moralistic hand-wringing over possible affinities with Nazism? In playing "The Ride of the Valkyries" for us at that particular moment, the Army was aiming at nothing less than our physical, psychological, and spiritual transformation. We were being initiated into the wonders of war.

Having reached these final pages of this book, and having explored the religious and scientific dimensions of wonder in relation to dreams and visions, sexual experience, creativity, and contemplative practices, I want to bring the discussion to a close by taking a fresh look at what is perhaps the preeminent political question of this or any human civilization: *What can and should we do about the wonderful impulse to war?* History provides several sharply contrasting responses to this question. For many people, the wonders of war reflect its glorious, noble, and invigorating qualities. Violently destroying one's enemies is a divinely sanctioned act and the highest expression of human strength (cf. Apache warrior culture of the North American plains, the crusades of medieval Christian knights, Leni Riefenstahl's cinematic paean to Hitler, *Triumph of the Will* [1936]). For other people, however, the wonders of war are nothing but cruelly seductive obscenities, signs of existential weakness rather than virtue or strength. This small but eloquent minority of people (including many of the world's major religious leaders, George Fox, Mohatma Gandhi, Martin Luther King, Jr., etc.) regard human violence as an evil that brings only sorrow and ruin and that we must, through our own efforts and with divine guidance, learn to overcome. Many classic sacred texts (the Hindu *Bhagavad Gita*, Homer's *The Iliad*, the Hebrew *Torah*, the Muslim *Qur'an*) portray both the marvelous glory *and* the sorrowful futility of war, giving free voice to each of these powerfully contradictory impulses. Most religious traditions have both opposed war and promoted it; they have simultaneously denounced it as bestial and sanctioned it as a sacred duty. The present historical moment gives ample evidence of this spiritual polarity.

According to leading evolutionary psychology (EP) authorities, the evolutionary roots of war are very deep in human nature. Darwin's sober dictum that "all nature is at war" has set the tone for contemporary biological science in its estimation of the human propensity to violence. War *feels* good, EP says, because war *is* good in terms of promoting the genetic propagation of our species. Each one of us today is alive because our ancestors were great warriors and killers — they defeated their enemies, destroyed the reproductive capacity of their rivals, and accumulated more resources to promote their own genetic interests. Applying the EP tool of reverse engineering to the origins of war in the early ancestral environment, Steven Pinker argues that, "In foraging societies, men go to war to get or keep women — not necessarily as a conscious goal of the warriors (though often it is exactly that), but as the ultimate payoff that allowed a willingness to fight to evolve. Access to women is the limiting factor on males' reproductive success... Warfare among Western peoples is different from primitive warfare in many ways, but it is similar in at least one way: the invaders rape or abduct women."[4] Pinker goes on to quote the codification of this evolutionary function in the Hebrew Bible:

> When you go forth to war against your enemies, and the Lord your God gives them into your hands, and you take them captive, and see among the captives a beautiful woman, and you have desire for her and would take her for yourself as wife, then you shall bring her home to your house, and she shall shave her head and pare her nails. And she shall put off her captive's garb, and shall remain in your house and bewail her father and her mother a full month; after that you may go in to her, and be her husband, and she shall be your wife.[5]

The ability of humans to form violent coalitions against other humans is, in EP perspective, actually a quite sophisticated cognitive achievement that requires the employment of elaborate mechanisms for ensuring group solidarity in the face of mortal danger. Our highly evolved minds seem specifically designed to make warfare easy for us. Just look, Pinker says, at how easy it is to evoke an "instant ethnocentrism" in otherwise normal, civilized people.[6] I can testify to that ethnocentric propensity based on my Fort Knox experiences. The sergeants watched with satisfaction as we cadets of the 2nd platoon mocked, taunted, and jeered at the (randomly assigned) cadets of the 1st, 3rd, and 4th platoons, only to forget all that whenever we found ourselves marching near Bravo or Charlie companies, at which times we instantly reconstituted our self-awareness as the united cadets of Delta company, in boisterously hostile opposition to the (randomly assigned) cadets of the other groups.

Evolutionary psychology researchers such as Pinker hasten to say that despite our bloodthirsty origins, humans are not doomed to an eternal Hobbesian war of all against all. Progress can be made; impulses can be controlled, secure institutions created, new pacifistic traditions nurtured. As evidence of this possibility, Pinker surprisingly cites the case of the Dalai Lama. The Dalai Lama, like any other human being, has violent inclinations within himself. As a child, he loved to play with guns and other war toys, and still today he remains fascinated by the military hardware used in World War II. He is a human male, an evolved biological organism with all the aggressive predispositions that have served his species so well. Yet, somehow he has managed to develop countertendencies strong enough to enable him to promote peace on an unprecedented global scale. Pinker offers no comment on the "how" of Tenzin Gyatso's extraordinary cognitive achievement, but he tacitly endorses its socially beneficial transformative power by allowing the Dalai Lama this quote: "[H]uman nature is such that when we face a tremendous critical situation, the human mind can wake up and find some other alternative. That is a human capacity."[7]

Jean-Pierre Changeux offers some insight from cognitive neuroscience (CN) on the human potential to overcome its own warring inclinations. He points to the early emergence in child development of a "theory of mind," allowing humans from a very young age to recognize other humans as autonomous, thinking, feeling agents like themselves. (Autism, sometimes called "mindblindness," results from severe damage to this capacity for attributing personhood to others). Having a theory of mind means that impulses to violence are increasingly opposed by empathetic emotions generated by the perceived suffering of other people. Sympathy, guilt, and remorse take hold in the brain–mind system very early in normal human development, suggesting the influence of evolutionary pressures to limit warfare in favor of survival strategies that enhance the felt bonds of human community.

Paul Ricoeur tries to incorporate these CN findings into a mixed discourse along the lines of what Descartes, Spinoza, and Kant attempted. He agrees with Changeux that "our deepest conviction about humanity [is] that it is better to be at peace than at war,"[8] and he praises Kant's "daring" move to create a philosophical basis for achieving real, lasting peace — the third form of the categorical imperative: "Act in such a way that the maxim of your will can always hold at the same time a principle of universal law."

In light of contemporary CN research, Kant's moral vision looks like a radical universalization of the innate human capacity for empathy, an infinite extension of our ability to identify with the feelings, desires, and perspectives of others. It also, from a RS perspective, appears fundamentally consistent with the Christian "Golden Rule," the Buddhist doctrine of compassion, and the doctrines of ethical mutuality found in many other religious traditions.[9] Ricoeur goes beyond Changeux and other CN researchers in claiming that this religious and philosophical passage into ethical reasoning marks a dramatic rupture in evolutionary history and a momentous transformation in the self-awareness of life. Kant himself seems to have felt as much, as indicated by his celebrated conclusion to *The Critique of Practical Reason* (1788):

> Two things fill the mind with ever new and increasing admiration and awe, the oftener and more steadily we reflect on them: the starry heavens above me and the moral law within me. I do not merely conjecture them and seek them as though obscured in darkness or in the transcendent region beyond my horizon: I see them before me, and I associate them directly with the consciousness of my own existence. The former begins at the place I occupy in the external world of sense, and it broadens the connection in which I stand into an unbounded magnitude of worlds beyond worlds and systems of systems and into the limitless times of their periodic motion, their beginning and their continuance. The latter begins at my invisible self, my personality, and exhibits me in a world which has true infinity but which is comprehensible only to the understanding — a world with which I recognize myself as existing in a universal and necessary (and not only, as in the first case, contingent) connection, and thereby also in connection with all those visible worlds. The former vie of a countless multitude of worlds annihilates, as it were, my importance as an animal creature, which must give back to the planet (a mere speck in the universe) the matter from which it came, that matter which is for a little time provided with vital force, we know not how. The latter, on the contrary, infinitely raises my worth as that of an intelligence by my personality, in which the moral law reveals a life independent of all animality and even of the whole world of sense — at least so far as it may be inferred from the purposive destination assigned to my existence by this law, a destination which is not restricted to the conditions and limits of this life but reaches into the infinite.
>
> But though admiration and respect can indeed excite to inquiry, they cannot supply the want of it....[10]

Kant's dual wonder at the starry skies above and the moral law within provides us with strong leverage against the wonders of war. The Job-like humility produced by a contemplation of the heavens works against the arrogant righteousness of humans at war — fighting for this patch of land or that clutch of females no longer seems so important when we achieve the cognitive state of being able to see ourselves *sub specie aeternis*. Intimately related to wonder at the infinitude of space is wonder at the transcendent clarity of moral conscience. Here, the decentered self is not reduced to insignificance but is rather recentered in a feeling of connection to and communion with the rational structure of the universe. Such a feeling is perhaps the supreme antidote to the infectious appeal of war.

To put these wondrous insights into practice requires, as Kant reminds us, more than simple enthusiasm. It requires the painstaking acquisition of empirical knowledge gained by the scientific work of observation, analysis, and experimentation. More specifically, it requires the careful, methodologically sophisticated investigation of the mental terrain wherein dwell the "moral capacities of our nature." The more we know about how these capacities develop and function, the better able we will be to stimulate their growth in ever greater numbers of people — the more we can promote peace over war.

Over the last century, Western psychological science, from the depth psychologies of James, Freud, and Jung to the brain–mind marvels of contemporary CN, has established a solid foundation of knowledge regarding what Kant calls the "invisible self" and what we have been speaking of as the "unconscious." We know, first and foremost, that ordinary consciousness is aware of only a miniscule portion of all that is happening in the brain–mind system at any given moment. A tip of an iceberg, a tiny island in a vast ocean, a candle in a great dark room — these timeworn metaphors remain accurate portrayals of this fundamental fact of human psychology. We know, furthermore, that shifting a person's state of consciousness can bring into awareness new, previously unknown portions of the unconscious (this is how our knowledge of the "invisible self" develops, by systematically correlating many different reports from many different states of consciousness). We know more now than ever before about the nonconscious workings of perception, emotion, memory, reasoning, language, and imagination. We know that the drives and desires of the unconscious can come into conflict with each other, and we know that they can also join together in surprising harmonies of creative power. We know that consciousness has some degree of freedom to guide its own drives and desires, and we know that this flexible "executive" capacity for selective attention and volitional action can be powerfully shaped by interpersonal relationships, cultural symbols, and social institutions. Humans are innately inclined to aggression, deceit, and selfishness, but we are also predisposed to cooperation, friendliness, and caregiving.

What all this hard-won psychological knowledge tells us is this: War may always be wonderful, and humans may always be wolves to each other, but *real peace*, peace in the sense of a cessation of organized, large-scale violence by one group against another group, is right there before us, eminently achievable and within our cognitive capacity to make real. A civilization that could fully stimulate the creative vitality and dynamic flourishing of its members *without recourse to war* — that would be a wonder indeed.

II. The Rainbow

After God cast Adam and Eve out of the Garden of Eden, they and the other creatures of the world multiplied and spread all across the land. The "daughters of man" mated not only with human males but also with the Nephilim, an obscure race with apparently extraordinary powers whose half-human progeny became the "mighty men that were of old, the men of renown."[11] Whatever marvelous deeds these racially mixed heroes may have performed, however, could not prevent God from sadly deciding that he must destroy all the life he had created by means of a great, world-drowning flood. The Biblical story of the flood in Genesis 6–9:20 is woven together from at least two narrative strands, one from an earlier mythological source and the other from a later priestly tradition. Here is the first strand:

> The Lord saw that the wickedness of man was great in the earth, and that every imagination of the thoughts of his heart was only evil continually. And the Lord was sorry that he had made man on the earth, and it grieved him to his heart. So the Lord said, "I will blot out man whom I have created from the face of the ground, man and beast and creeping things and birds of the air, for I am sorry that I have made them." But Noah found favor in the eyes of the Lord.

Here is the second:

> Now the earth was corrupt in God's sight, and the earth was filled with violence. And God saw the earth, and behold, it was corrupt; for all flesh had corrupted their way upon the earth. And God said to Noah, "I have determined to make an end of all flesh; for the earth is filled with violence through them; behold, I will destroy them with the earth."

The two variants share the same highly paradoxical idea that God is driven to destroy life because of life's irresistible propensity to destroy life. Human vs. human warfare provokes divine vs. human warfare. The two Biblical variants also agree that one man, Noah, was sufficiently faithful and righteous to be spared from watery death at God's hand. We never find out what exactly makes Noah appear so favorably to God or how he manages to remain blameless in a violent world; he just does. Through Noah, and through the creature-filled Ark that he is carefully instructed to build, a tiny possibility for new life survives the annihilating deluge and return to pre-creation chaos. God's violent reaction to the fact of biological violence is thus tempered by a glimmer of hope, though hope of a very peculiar kind. God does *not* expect any fundamental change in the aggressive nature of his creatures. He accepts that "the imagination of man's heart is evil from his youth,"[12] and he goes on to promise that "while the earth remains" he will preserve the life-sustaining cycles of nature and never again "curse the ground because of man."[13] Although the rainbow is commonly understood as a sign to humans of this divine promise, God's decision to "set my bow in the cloud" is chiefly meant to be a reminder to himself: "When the bow is in the clouds, I will look upon it and remember the everlasting covenant between God and every living creature of all flesh that is on the earth."[14] God certainly wants Noah to be aware of this, but his primary motivation in setting his weapon in the sky is to assist his *own* memory.

In this story (one of the most anthropomorphic portraits of the divine in the Hebrew Bible), God evidently anticipates that one day in the future he will again look with sadness upon life and its relentless wickedness, and he will feel an instinctive impulse to destroy it all. To guard against his own bursts of violence, God creates the rainbow to help himself remember this moment's humbling awareness of his creatures' inexorably violent ways. The rainbow in Genesis is only secondarily a sign to humans; it is in the first instance a divine mnemonic, a mournful cosmic affirmation of life as life.

This is the rainbow myth most familiar to Western readers, but the rainbow has also figured prominently in many other religious and mythic traditions. In the Scandinavian legends called the *Eddas*, the rainbow (*bifrost*) is a skillfully constructed bridge connecting earth to Asgard, the home of the gods. This is the bridge across which the Valkyries ride, bearing the bodies of slain war heroes. Among the Iroquois and Huron of North America, Rainbow is the wife of Hino the Thunder Spirit, while the Incans of South America worshipped the rainbow as Cuycha, one of the divine attendants on the Sun and the Moon. Similar to the Genesis version, Hindu traditions portray the rainbow as the bow of the mighty god Indra, another deity who merges warlike destructiveness with life-affirming fertility. Traditional religions of both West Africa and Australia venerate a celestial rainbow snake as a cosmogonic power that sustains the world and all its living creatures. The historical and cross-cultural prevalence of these myths speaks, at one level, to a primal human experience of wonder in response to this brilliantly colorful natural phenomenon. Rainbows are singular manifestations of geometric perfection and polychromatic harmony; more than any other atmospheric event, they immediately appeal to humankind's emergent visual capacity to appreciate form, structure, color, and perspective. Coming with the nourishing rains, rainbows connect land, water, sky, and sun. They signal the end of a storm, the renewal of clarity and light. The metaphor of a rainbow as a bridge between heaven and earth thus works at many different but related levels.

In the *Theaetetus*, Socrates makes a brief but crucial reference to the rainbow in connection with what is perhaps the most oft-quoted statement in the Western tradition about wonder. This dialogue involves Theodorus, an old friend of

Socrates, bringing a quick-witted young man (Theaetetus) to the master for an examination of his youthful intellectual qualities. Using his formidable skills of seductive, playful, critically acute conversation, Socrates leads Theaetetus to the surprising realization that all his seemingly sure knowledge in fact depends on a host of unconscious assumptions that wildly conflict with one another. Thrown into severe epistemological confusion by Socrates' baffling questions, the young man soon admits that, "It is extraordinary how they [such puzzles] set me wondering whatever they can mean. Sometimes I get quite dizzy with thinking of them." This is exactly what Socrates has been hoping for: "That shows Theodorus was not wrong in his estimate of your nature. This sense of wonder is the mark of the philosopher. Philosophy indeed has no other origin, and he was a good genealogist who made Iris the daughter of Thaumas."[15]

Thaumas, whose name is the Greek word for wonder and who is born of the gods of earth and water, joined with Ocean's daughter Electra to produce the Harpies, a horde of frightful winged females, and Iris, the rainbow. In Greek myth, Iris serves as the messenger of Zeus, transmitting information, guidance, and warning from the heavens to the earth and back again — another cultural variant on the theme of the rainbow as a sacred bridge. When Socrates links Theaetetus' distressing experience of radical unknowing to the mythic genesis of the rainbow, he gives the whole enterprise of philosophy a startlingly simple purpose and justification: *Philosophy is the cultivation of wonder as an ongoing state of mind.* Philosophers wonder at *everything* — at the natural world, human bodies, mathematical truths, the mythic tales of old, and the fathomless mysteries of the soul. Conversely, a moment of wonder is an invitation to philosophical inquiry. The decentering of old knowledge stimulates the impulse to seek a new center of awareness. The process of enacting this impulse is, in Socrates' view, the life of the philosopher.

The Biblical story of the flood and Socrates' comment to Theaetetus provide the necessary context in which to understand Rene Descartes' treatment of the rainbow. As an attachment to his *Discourse on Method*, Descartes wrote three scientific treatises to illustrate the practical application of his new philosophical method. The three essays were titled *The Dioptics*, *The Meteors*, and *The Geometry*, and the middle text took as its task the scientific explanation of celestial marvels. Starting with the words, "We naturally feel more wonder for those things above us than for things at our own level," Descartes devotes *The Meteors* to a methodical study of meteors, thunder, and the rainbow.[16] Although previous Western writings on the rainbow had always used the term "Iris," Descartes deliberately breaks with that mythic tradition and writes instead "*l'arc-en-ciel*" (the arc in the sky). Taking this phenomenon as an ideal case in which to apply his new philosophical method of pure mathematical reasoning, Descartes explains that the rainbow always occurs at an angle of 41.5 degrees between the sun, the rainbow, and the observer (see figure). He concludes the treatise by describing how easy it is for anyone to reproduce a rainbow effect with the spray of a fountain.

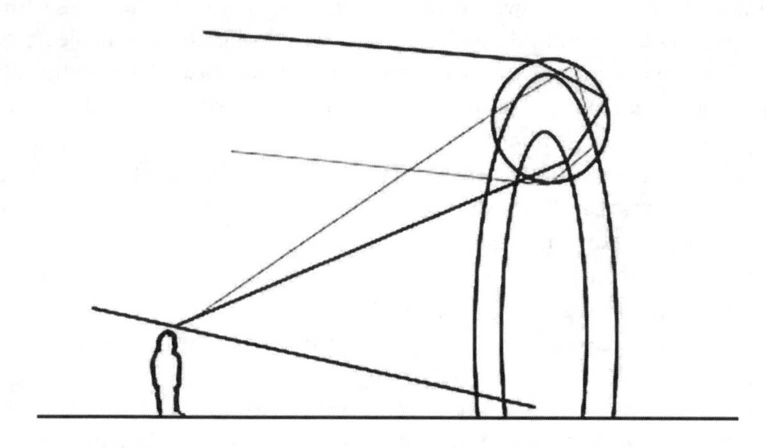

Geometry of the rainbow.

No longer an expression of God's promise to care for life nor a mythic trace of open-ended philosophical awareness, the rainbow in Descartes' hands is reduced to a trick of the eye and an amusing means of startling the credulous.[17] Although he starts with wonder as his primary emotion, Descartes' vision of philosophy ultimately leads to the elimination of wonder, not its cultivation. He evidently feels some sadness at this, some sense of loss and mourning, but he nevertheless believes the progress of human civilization depends on increasing our rational control over our experiences of wonder:

> And although this passion seems to diminish with use, because the more we meet with rare things which we wonder at, the more we accustom ourselves to cease to wonder at them and to think that all those which may afterwards present themselves are common, still, when it is excessive, and causes us to arrest our attention solely on the first of the objects which are presented, without acquiring any other knowledge of them, it leaves behind a custom which disposes the soul in the same way to pause over all the other objects which present themselves, provided that they appear to it to be ever so little new. And this is what causes the continuance of the malady of those who suffer from a blind curiosity — that is, who seek out things that are rarely solely to wonder at them, and not for the purpose of really knowing them: for little by little they become so given over to wonder, that things of no importance are no less capable of arresting their attention than those whose investigation is more useful.[18]

Descartes agrees with Socrates that philosophical investigation begins with wonder, but the young Frenchman is determined to show that the *end* of philosophy is to *destroy* wonder. Human maturation and scientific progress depend on rational domination over the passion of wonder. He urges strenuous public efforts to protect people from the "malady of blind curiosity" and to prevent the development of a habitual disposition toward idle wonder, steering people's energies instead toward those areas from which useful knowledge can be gained.

This, I suggest to you, is Descartes' real error. It is not, as Antonio Damasio and other CN researchers have supposed, the abyssal separation of mind and body. Descartes' most lamentable error was his bellicose use of science as a weapon against wonder. His inability to envision the possibility that wonder can *survive* scientific explanation reflects a failure of imagination and a fatally wounded capacity for change, growth, and hope. Whether because of the meager family warmth and multiple illnesses of his childhood, or the mind-stunting Scholastic education of his youth, or the painful loss of his friendship with Isaac Beekman, or the horrific warfare and religious fanaticism sweeping through seventeenth-century Europe, young Descartes decided he needed a foundation of identity that would *not* change and could *not* be decentered by anyone or anything. Having made such an existential commitment, his prime enemy became the experience of wonder, which is nothing if not a forced decentering of selfhood. Achieving his new ideal of the *cogito* became, in practice, an effort to annihilate wonder. Descartes hid away his Olympian journal, never again mentioned his three revelatory dreams, and devoted himself to persuading others to adopt his philosophical crusade against "blind curiosity."

What Descartes did not appreciate was the way in which new knowledge can give rise to new experiences of wonder. Yes, rational explanations of phenomena such as the rainbow undermine narrow, literalistic belief in mythic and religious stories, but such explanations do not necessarily diminish or eliminate feelings of wonder when encountering such phenomena. Now that you know Descartes' mathematical explanation, I predict the next time you find yourself suddenly confronted by a rainbow you will feel no less startled than before, no less pleased by the brilliant colors, no less engaged by the smoothly arcing trajectory. What I suspect will happen is that *in addition* to those reactions, you will also find yourself observing more closely the relative positions of yourself, the rainbow, and the sun, trying to get a feel for that 41.5-degree angle of visual opportunity. (And, if you really want to have fun, you can also follow Isaac Newton's lead and look for the secondary rainbow between 51 and 54 degrees.)

The ultimate point is this: Whatever feelings of wonder may be lost in the process of analysis, explanation, and knowledge formation, the potential always exists for a renewed and expanded capacity for surprise, amazement, and curiosity. Socrates understood this better than Descartes, and this is why he located wonder at the very heart of the philosophical life. For Socrates, wonder is not simply the disposable starting point of philosophy nor merely a temporary quality of youthful naivety. Wonder is the philosophical state of mind itself, a mode of consciousness that draws upon new knowledge as a continuing stimulus to engage in ever deeper explorations of the world around us.[19]

The best illustration of this mutually inspiring relationship between wonder and knowledge is the very material we have been considering in this book. Can anyone honestly say, after the tremendous expansion of scientific knowledge following the "Decade of the Brain," that we now have any *less* cause for wonder at the human brain–mind system? The more we have learned, the more we realize we do not know, and the more amazed we become at the mysterious complexities that simultaneously stand before us and lie within us.

In that spirit, let me summarize what can confidently be said, at this moment in the religious studies/cognitive science dialogue, about the evolution of a capacity wonder. The following points should be understood as provisional integrations and directions for future investigation, certainly not as a final merger of all we have been covering. *This is not the time for grand theories — this is a time for radical openness to new discoveries, insights, and multidisciplinary understandings.*

Wonder springs from many different sources. The stars, nature, human creations, and our bodies can provoke wonder, and so can phenomena that do not depend on external sensory input such as dreams, visions, and contemplative practices. The fact that wonder can be experienced in both waking and dreaming immediately indicates that its neural substrate can be activated in radically different brain–mind states. It can also be stimulated by different sensory modalities. Vision plays a special role in wonder as it does in all of human life, but auditory and tactile-kinesthetic sensations also figure prominently, and most wonder experiences involve a lively combination of all of these perceptual systems.

Wonder may be a purely spontaneous occurrence or it may be the culmination of elaborate ritual preparation. Either way it is characterized in the first instance by a sharp sense of surprise and disorientation. The executive functions of the prefrontal cortex are momentarily stunned; attention has been seized, volition suspended, ordinary expectations overwhelmed. Likewise, the language centers of the brain (Wernicke's and Broca's areas) are temporarily disrupted as conventional language is incapable of grasping and communicating the magnitude of the experience. The vivid immediacy and viscerally felt intensity of wonder suggest a sudden shift in the reality monitoring system of the frontal-limbic region, an unusually strong physiological arousal comparable to the startle response mediated by the amygdala, and an upsurge in seizure-like ponto-geniculo-occipital (PGO) spikes. The large expanses of association cortex that distinguish the human brain are hyperactivated as radically new input must be processed, upsetting established neural systems and forcing the creation of new ones. In terms of the range and complexity of neural connections, I would propose as a testable hypothesis that *wonder makes the brain grow.*

The emotional dimension of wonder often has an element of fear to it, as a consequence of our evolutionarily programmed tendency to feel alarm whenever we become lost, vulnerable, and/or exposed. Just as often, though, wonder involves feelings of delight, pleasure, and aesthetic appreciation. The capacity to experience wonder is itself a developmental achievement, requiring a sufficient degree of safety and security (a good enough transitional space, in Winnicottian language) so that the natural fear of being decentered does not smother the pleasurable creative response in seeking a new center.

This creative response brings the executive functions of the brain–mind system back into action. Wonder as existential surprise becomes wonder as knowledge-seeking curiosity. The meaning-making impulse that is so powerful in our species drinks deeply from the springs of wonder, and any account of evolved human nature must acknowledge the stimulating effects of wonder on our noetic investigations of ourselves and the world around us. If humans occupy a "cognitive niche" in the biological environment of Earth, experiences of wonder continually push the boundaries of that niche and provoke an expansion of our self-awareness within the environment as a whole.

It would be difficult to argue that wonder qualifies as an evolutionary adaptation in the strict sense of that term, but wonder is positively associated with the basic adaptive behaviors of *Homo sapiens* (e.g., sexuality, sociability, exploration, creative problem solving, warfare), thus it can be understood as providing selective advantage to those individuals who have a well-developed capacity to experience it. The traditional association of wonder with childhood is further evidence of its developmental significance in the growth and flourishing of the brain–mind system, and recent research indicates that a surprising degree of neural mutability remains (at least potentially) throughout the lifespan. In light of this, future investigations will have to discard homeostatic models and recognize, with Heraclitus, that all life is flux.

We are no closer to finding a consensus answer about the ultimate extension of experiences of wonder. Do feelings of revelation and mystical ecstasy derive entirely from chemical and electrical activities inside the brain, or do such feelings connect people *through* their brains and bodies to transcendent powers and cosmic patterns of relatedness? In this, we come to essentially the same position as James did when he reached the end of the *Varieties*, and like him I leave the question open, while strongly endorsing efforts to explore the latter possibility.[20]

Wonder depends on individual perspective. My wonder is not necessarily your wonder. I may see a glorious *arc-en-ciel* while you, from a slightly different angle, may see nothing. A grove of redwood trees may provoke pantheistic rapture in some people, while others quickly calculate board feet and lumber prices. Miranda, the wonder-struck maiden in Shakespeare's *The Tempest*, may exclaim "O brave new world!" when she first beholds a group of shipwrecked sailors, but the same sight prompts her jaded magician father Prospero to mutter, "'Tis new to thee." A massive display of military firepower may elicit shock and awe in some but only sadness and despair in others. Our different perspectives mean that wonder will always be a source of discord in human life, always a cause of tension and conflict. A richer appreciation of the endlessly various manifestations of wonder should never blind us to the fact that a pluralistic universe is a universe always on the brink of war.

Endnotes

Introduction

1. My usage derives from *The Oxford English Dictionary*, which gives as the first major definition of wonder "something that causes astonishment" and the second as "the emotion excited by the perception of something novel and unexpected, or inexplicable; astonishment mingled with perplexity or bewildered curiosity. Also, the state of mind in which this emotion exists." According to John Ayto's *Dictionary of Word Origins* (Ayto 1990), "*Wonder* is something of a mystery word. It is widespread in the Germanic languages (German *wunder*, Dutch *wonder*, Swedish *undran*, and Danish *undren*), but its ultimate ancestry is unknown." See also Keen (1969), Fisher (1998), and Emmons (2002).
2. Damasio (1999, 83).
3. The question of how many people share both views (i.e., how many people are both conservative Christians and professional neuroscientists) is an interesting one. I know of no direct evidence on this point, but according to social scientific data presented and summarized by Benjamin Beit-Hallahmi and Michael Argyle (Beit-Hallahmi and Argyle 1997), approximately half of all scientists in America have no religious affiliation (in contrast to the 98% of all Americans who identify themselves as Protestants, Catholics, Jews, or members of some other faith tradition). Research also suggests that "physical scientists are (relatively) more religious, social scientists less so" (181), with psychologists being the least religious of all (one study found that in a sample of American Psychological Association members, 34% were atheists, compared to 2% of the general U.S. population). For an argument against the inherent antagonism of religion and science, see Watts (2002).

Chapter 1

1. I have made several small changes to the text in order to hide the identity of the young man until the end of the chapter.
2. Jedrej and Shaw (1992), Tedlock (1987), Young (1999a), Irwin (1994), Von Grunebaum and Callois (1966), Bulkeley (1995, 1999, 2001).
3. Thompson (2000, 24).
4. Damasio (1994, 15).
5. Thompson (2000, 23).
6. Kandel et al. (2000, 349).
7. Controversy exists over this issue among cognitive neuroscientists; see LeDoux (1996, 98–103).
8. Thompson (2000, 18).
9. Kandel et al. (2000, 350).
10. Kandel et al. (2000, 992).
11. Thompson (2000, 17).
12. Springer and Deutsch (1998, 40).
13. Quoted in Springer and Deutsch (1998, 52).
14. Ashbrook and Albright (1997, 124–127). Lee Irwin also speaks to the relative cultural influences on left and right hemispheric functioning, but in a much more cautious fashion (Irwin 1994).
15. Ramachandran and Blakeslee (1998, 279–280).

16. Thompson (2000, 25); see also Kandel et al. (2000).
17. It should be noted that the "axon sends, dendrites receive" model is not absolute; see Kandel et al. (2000) and Thompson (2000, 43–44).
18. Thompson (2000, 3).
19. Ramachandran and Blakeslee (1998, 8).
20. Changeux and Ricoeur (2000, 78–79).
21. Damasio (1994, xvi).
22. Damasio (1994, 11).
23. See Changeux and Ricoeur (2000, 160–161), where Changeux approvingly quotes the Russian neurologist Alexander Luria, who called the frontal lobe the "organ of civilization."
24. Damasio (1994, 33).
25. Damasio (1994, 19).
26. Damasio (1999, 122–125); emphasis in original.
27. Damasio (1999, 280).
28. Damasio (1999, 56).
29. Certainly in the following texts: Crick (1994), Kandel et al. (2000), Pinker (1997), Thompson (2000), Wilson (1998).
30. Damasio (1999, 130).
31. Damasio (1999, 315).
32. Damasio (1999, 94).
33. Aserinsky and Kleitman (1953, 1955) and Dement (1972).
34. Smith (1993), Greenberg et al. (1972), Cartwright (1991), Hartmann (1995, 1998), Revonsuo (2000).
35. Hobson (1988).
36. Hobson (1999, 135).
37. It has been criticized for various failings by researchers from various disciplines (Hunt 1989, LaBerge 1985, Domhoff 2001, Taylor 1992, Van de Castle 1994).
38. Solms (2000, 42).
39. Solms (2000, 47–48).
40. Solms (2000, 161). Solms does, however, acknowledge that deeper semantic systems related to language may be crucial to normal dreaming.
41. Solms (1997, 153, 241–242); emphasis in original. For his criticism of REM-dreaming isomorphism, see also Solms (1997, 2, 54–55, 126, 132, 152, 157, 173, 213). Unfortunately, the alternative offered by Solms to replace Activation–Synthesis turns out to be a pale restatement of Freud's sleep-protection theory (Freud 1965). Solms, unlike Freud, takes no interest whatsoever in the study of dream content (Solms 1997); however, he fully endorses Freud's sleep-protection model of dream formation (Solms 1997, 135, 165, 169, 174, 213, 241), and the ultimate, though modestly stated, intention of Solms' 1997 book is to promote a neuropsychological revival of psychoanalytic theorizing.
42. A further point of interest in Solms' work is the syndrome of "excessive dreaming," or *anoneirognosis*. This syndrome involves people experiencing intensely emotional and hyperrealistic dreams, often with unusual characters and other content features. Although Solms takes no interest in content, his clinical descriptions of the ten patients who had this syndrome include dream reports of meeting deceased loved ones (Solms 1997, 185–186), visiting the "pearly gates" (178), visiting a very beautiful place (183), and having a black snake crawl into the dreamer's vagina (192). Although Solms' patients would probably be happy to give up their hyper-vivid dreams if they could just regain normal brain–mind functioning again, the experiential similarities of their dreams to the types of dreams frequently reported in the religions of the world are highly suggestive. If Solms is right that frontal limbic lesions are the cause of this syndrome (197–200), this may be a key region of the brain to study in connection with highly memorable dreams. Also of interest is Solms' account of the syndrome of recurrent nightmares. Patients who have damage to the temporal–limbic areas of the brain are especially prone to an increase in nightmares, Solms says, because that particular kind of damage often produces intense neural discharges and seizure activities that overwhelm the ordinary functioning of the brain and inject the patients' dreams with a relentless sense of anxiety. Solms speculates that seizure activity anywhere in the brain can set the dreaming process in motion (211). This suggests that a potentially fruitful way to study dreams, some of which are terribly frightening and nightmarish, is to investigate their connection to states of heightened temporal–limbic activation, such as occurs in epilepsy and perhaps other kinds of religious experience. Many common features of dreams (e.g., the number and frequency of emotions, the activation of instinctive behavior patterns such

as fight-or-flight, the strong physiological arousal that periodically occurs upon awakening) may well be attributable to the extraordinary activation of certain neural processes in the temporal–limbic regions of the brain.
43. http://www.aarweb.org.
44. This fact and all following demographic statistics come from the database of adherents.com.
45. http://www. adherents.com.
46. For example, if adherence to a religion were defined not simply by self-identification but by some measure of orthodox practice, it is possible that Islam would have a higher total membership than Christianity. Likewise, if membership in a religion were defined by some measure of commitment to an orthodox set of beliefs, Hinduism might dissolve as an "official" religion and thus be left off lists of major world traditions.
47. Irwin (1996, 28).
48. Irwin (1996, 29).
49. Irwin (1996, 30, 31).
50. Irwin (1996, 26).
51. Irwin (1996, 25).
52. Irwin (1996, 32).
53. Irwin (1996, 175).
54. Irwin (1996, 67–68).
55. Irwin (1996, 79).
56. Irwin (1996, 19).
57. Irwin (1996, 192).
58. See also Patton (2004).
59. Benedict (1922), Hallowell (1966), Radin (1936).
60. Irwin (1994, 79–80).
61. Irwin (1994, 170).
62. Freud (1963, 1974).
63. Freud (1974, 204).
64. Von Franz (1991, 108); emphasis in original.
65. Cole (1992).
66. Descartes (1960, 8).
67. The actual journal has been lost to history. The version of Descartes' dreams we have comes by way of his first biographer, Adrien Baillet, and the philosopher Gottfried von Leibniz, both of whom had the opportunity to read the original journal. For the reliability of Baillet's transcription, which I have been quoting, see Cole (1992, 19–58).
68. Cole (1992, 33).
69. Tedlock (1987), Jedrej and Shaw (1992), Irwin (1994), Von Grunebaum and Callois (1966).
70. Descartes emphasized the importance of these dreams and their connection to his philosophical insights by marking in the margins of the *Olympica* exactly a year later (November 11): "I began to understand the foundation of the wonderful discovery" (Cole 1992, 22).
71. Damasio (1994, 249–250).
72. Ricoeur does point in this direction near the beginning of his discussion with Jean-Pierre Changeux (Changeux and Ricoeur 2000, 40), but he never develops the notion nor makes any reference to his work on energetics and hermeneutics in *Freud and Philosophy.*
73. Descartes (1989, 40).
74. Descartes (1989, 56).
75. Descartes (1989, 58).
76. Descartes (1989, 59).

Chapter 2

1. 2000, directed by Sam Mendes, screenplay by Alan Ball. The film won Academy Awards for Best Picture, Best Director, Best Actor, Best Original Screenplay, and Best Cinematography (Conrad Hall).
2. All quotes from Ball (1999).
3. Mallanga (2002, 42, 59).
4. This is Donald Symons' definition of EP: "Psychological research that is explicitly informed by the knowledge that human psychological adaptations were shaped over vast periods of time to solve the recurrent behavioral problems that our ancestors faced." Quoted in Abramson and Pinkerton (2002, 229).

5. Pinker (1997, 21, 22). Here, as elsewhere, Pinker draws heavily on the work of John Tooby and Leah Cosmides, and readers interested in the primary texts of EP should consult their work, particularly their contribution to Barkow et al. (1992).
6. Pinker (1997, 21).
7. Wilson (2000, 315). Here is the earlier insight of Darwin: "Why is life short and sexual reproduction so important? Because sexual mixing produces variants and a fast turnover spreads them through the population. Sex causes variety, which is necessary to enable species to meet new conditions. If climates alter, species can respond quickly, generating new adaptations automatically." Quoted in Desmond and Moore (1991, 229).
8. Wilson (2000, 157). Wilson goes on to note the practical benefits of this for working scientists: "Entomologists have used the principle to force matings of butterflies and ants in the laboratory. The female is lightly anesthetized to keep her calm, the male is beheaded, and the abdominal tips are touched together until the rhythmically moving male genitalia achieve copulation."
9. Pinker (1997, 464). The original author of the theory of parental investment was Robert Trivers; see Trivers (1985).
10. Pinker (1997, 468).
11. Hamann et al. (2004) and Holstege et al. (2003).
12. Zuk (2002, 147).
13. See Ramachandran's lampoon of fanciful EP theorizing in Ramachandran and Blakeslee (1998, 289).
14. Zuk (2002, 142). Gould's ideas shed new light on the ancient and widespread practice of female genital mutilation (especially cliterodectomy) in certain African, Middle Eastern, South Asian, and Australian Aboriginal cultures. This practice seeks to impose culturally what evolution has made possible — namely, the ability of females to reproduce without any sexual pleasure.
15. Quoted in Zuk (2002, 144).
16. Freud (2000, 86–97).
17. Abramson and Pinkerton (2002, 129–130).
18. Michael et al. (1994, 130).
19. Mallanga (2002, 31, n. 14).
20. Zuk (2002, 152).
21. Zuk (2002, 150).
22. Zuk (2002, 151).
23. Zuk (2002, 152).
24. To anticipate the next section, Doniger says this is precisely the significance of the *Kamasutra*: "The *Kamasutra* can be viewed as an account of a psychological war of independence that took place in India some two thousand years ago. The first aim of this struggle was the rescue of erotic pleasure from the crude purposefulness of sexual desire, from its biological function of reproduction alone." (Mallanga 2002, xxxix).
25. Runzo and Martin (2000, 3).
26. Lavine (1999, 890).
27. Wade (1999, 149).
28. Lavine (1999, 889).
29. Lavine (1999, 888).
30. *The Koran* (1974, 2.222–2.223).
31. Young (2001, 14); see also Young (1999b).
32. Crapanzano (1975).
33. Wade (1999, 147).
34. Runzo and Martin (2000, 24).
35. Quoted in Runzo and Martin (2000, 27).
36. Young (1999b, 958). Young finishes her point: "In other words, ritually speaking, actual women are frequently passive, secondary, or absent, whereas symbolic women (e.g., goddesses), although they may be tempermentally active, will ultimately be absorbed back into the Absolute. Tantra is essentially a theoretical valorization of the feminine, and as such has had very little impact on the lives of the vast majority of Buddhist and Hindu women."
37. Doniger (1998, 2). An earlier account of her view of myth comes in *Other People's Myths: The Cave of Echoes* (O'Flaherty 1988): "A myth is a story that is sacred to and shared by a group of people who find their most important meanings in it" (27) … "The best short definition of a myth is that it is a true story" (31).

38. *The Implied Spider: Politics and Theology in Myth* was written, Doniger says, as a retrospective justification for the method she was using in her studies of myth and sexuality (Doniger 1998, 5). It is also worth noting that her scholarly career has been "doubled" — writing first as Wendy Doniger O'Flaherty and then, beginning in 1991, as Wendy Doniger.
39. Doniger (1999b, 1).
40. Doniger (1999b, 305).
41. Doniger (1999a, 3); emphasis in original.
42. Doniger (1999a, 3, 9).
43. Doniger (1999a, 137).
44. Doniger (1998, 139).
45. Doniger (1998, 76).
46. Crick (1994, 21).
47. Crick (1994, 245); emphasis in the original.
48. Abramson and Pinkerton (2002, 121) and Reinisch and Beasley (1990).
49. Mulvey (1989).
50. Harris (2004). "In one early clinical trial, researchers gave six women Viagra and six others a placebo, sat them in front of erotic videos and used a pelvic probe to measure any change in genital blood flow. The sex organs of women given Viagra were more engorged than those given placebo. The program seemed to be succeeding.... But a larger trial that included a questionnaire found that although Viagra was associated with greater pelvic blood flow, the women experiencing this effect did not feel any more aroused."
51. Doniger (1999b, 106).
52. Doniger (1999b, 108).
53. Doniger (1999b, 293). The story comes from Ovid, *Metamorphoses*, 3.316–340.
54. Doniger (1999b, 101).
55. Mallanga (2002, 33, n. 19).
56. Ramachandran and Blakeslee (1998). Ramachandran was raised in India, as a Hindu. Although he does not dwell on his religious upbringing, it seems at least partly responsible for his vastly more respectful and open-minded attitude toward religion than is found in the work of many other CN researchers. For example, Francis Crick would never speak, as Ramachandran does, of "the divine spark that exists in all of us" (188), nor would he quote the Upanishads and rhapsodize about the liberating realization that "you're really part of the great cosmic dance of Shiva, rather than a mere spectator, [and] your inevitable death should be seen as a joyous reunion with nature rather than as a tragedy" (157).
57. Ramachandran and Blakeslee (1998, 36).
58. Ramachandran and Blakeslee (1998, 36).
59. Ramachandran and Blakeslee (1998, 36).
60. Quoted in Doniger (1998, 141).
61. Crews (1995, 4).
62. Crews (1998, xxvii).
63. Crews (1998, xxiii).
64. Damasio (1999, 228).
65. Ramachandran and Blakeslee (1998, 131).
66. Ramachandran and Blakeslee (1998, 134).
67. Ramachandran and Blakeslee (1998, 152).
68. Crews admits that Freud's account of defense mechanisms may in fact be true (Crews 1998, xxv), but then complains that Freud left us no reliable method of determining when these mechanisms are operating and when they are not. While the complaint is justified, Crews does not appreciate the magnitude of his initial concession to the legitimacy of this much of the psychoanalytic model of the mind.
69. Quoted in Ashbrook and Albright (1997, 11).
70. Springer and Deutsch (1998, 36).
71. Springer and Deutsch (1998, 39). LeDoux, along with many other CN researchers, sees these findings as decisive evidence against the reliable use of introspection in CN.
72. Pinker (1997, 421).
73. The subtitle of Wright's book is telling: *Evolutionary Psychology and Everyday Life*. The focus on what is normal, average, and everyday excludes as a matter of methodological principle that which is rare and extraordinary.
74. Wright (1994, 321).
75. Wright (1994, 314).
76. Wright (1994, 320–321).

77. Domhoff (2003, 140).
78. Freud (1966, 314).
79. I thank Bill Parsons for this insight.
80. Later in the film we see this scene again, and now we recognize that it is only within the context of her new relationship with Ricky that she can open up this much about the anger, hurt, and raging darkness within her. This time the scene continues beyond Jane saying she wants to kill her father. Ricky asks Jane if she would rather have her dad paying sexual attention to her, and this incisively therapeutic question breaks the spell of her parricidal fantasy, enabling her to laugh and restate her feelings in a more moderate and realistic fashion.
81. This is a good time to note that Pinker's claim that male homosexuality showcases a "pure" form of male sexuality rests on two questionable assumptions: (1) all male homosexuals are the same in their sexuality (i.e., Jim and Jim are the same as Col. Fitts), and (2) all male sexuality can be measured on a single scale of greater or lesser purity.
82. It remains possible that Angela is lying when she says she is a virgin, and that she only says this as a last-ditch effort to defend herself against what she may be experiencing as a rape.

Chapter 3

1. Cross (2001, 339). Much of the information on Cobain's life comes from Charles R. Cross' biography, *Heavier Than Heaven: A Biography of Kurt Cobain*.
2. Thompson (2000, 319).
3. Thompson (2000, 320).
4. Schwartz and Begley (2002, 112).
5. Kandel et al. (2000, 1123).
6. Schwartz and Begley (2002, 99).
7. Schwartz and Begley (2002, 127–129). They go on to say, "The wiring up of the brain during gestation, infancy, and childhood — and, we now know, adolescence — is almost as wondrous as the formation of a living, breathing, sensing, moving, behaving organism from a single fertilized ovum."
8. Schwartz and Begley (2002, 129).
9. Changeux and Ricoeur (2000, 175). This view of the nature and value of art marks another unacknowledged agreement between Freud and CN.
10. Changeux and Ricoeur (2000, 240); see also 87, 112, and 183.
11. Changeux and Ricoeur (2000, 176, 305).
12. Changeux and Ricoeur (2000, 303).
13. Wilson (1998, 216).
14. Wilson (1998, 213).
15. Wilson (1998, 224).
16. Wilson (1998, 225).
17. Wilson (1998, 226).
18. Thompson (2000, 153).
19. This is not to deny the value of using psychoactive medications to help mentally ill people become stable enough that they can participate in and benefit from other types of psychotherapy, a point made to me by Kathleen Greider.
20. For example, Schwartz grudgingly admits that Freudian psychoanalysis may have some value in discerning the personal life basis for the specific behavioral manifestations of OCD but will not go so far as to allow psychotherapy any curative power in treating the disease (Schwartz and Begley 2002, 56).
21. O'Flaherty (1975, 25 ff.).
22. Scarre (1989).
23. Sullivan (1997).
24. In Roman times the Muses became associated with particular types of art: Clio, history; Euterpe, flute; Thalia, comedy; Melpomene, tragedy; Terpischore, choral dancing; Erato, lyre; Polyhymnia, sacred hymns; Urania, astronomy; and Calliope, epic poetry (Green 1999).
25. Beck (1993).
26. Sullivan (1997, 2).
27. Gleick (2003).
28. Quoted in Sullivan (1997, 6).
29. James (1958, 322).
30. Becker (1997, 49–50).

31. Becker (2001, 145–146).
32. Becker (2001, 149–150).
33. "We can say that the believer is not deceived when he believes in the existence of a moral power upon which he depends and from which he receives all that is best in himself: this power exists, it is society" (Durkheim 1965, 257).
34. *Republic,* III.411 (Plato 1961a, 655). The phrase "feeble warrior" is a quote from the *Iliad*, 17.588.
35. Nasr (1997, 227).
36. Nasr (1997, 233).
37. Greeley's 1975 demographic survey of religious experience found that "listening to music" was the most often cited trigger of religious experience, with 49% of his respondents reporting it. The other triggers cited were prayer (48%); beauties of nature, such as a sunset (45%); moments of quiet reflection (42%); attending services (41%); listening to a sermon (40%); watching little children (34%); reading the Bible (31%); being alone in church (30%); reading a poem or novel (21%); childbirth (20%); sexual activity (18%); your own creative work (17%); looking at a painting (15%); physical exercise (1%); and drugs (0%) (Greeley 1975).
38. Pinker (1997, 528).
39. Pinker (1997, 534).
40. Darwin (1998, 593–594).
41. Wierzbicki (1989).
42. Fernald (1992, 410–411). Fernald does not directly quarrel with Pinker on the question of music being an adaptation; she prefers to call music an "exaptation" (i.e., a feature that first appeared as the accidental byproduct of a real adaptation and that subsequently developed beneficial, survival, and procreation-promoting powers) (395). Peretz, however, argues that music is indeed an adaptation in the true EP sense of the term: "In support of the contention that music has an adaptive value, particularly for the group, is the fact that music possesses two design features that reflect an intrinsic role in communion (as opposed to communication, which is the key function in speech). Pitch intervals allow harmonious voice blending when sounding together, and temporal regularity facilitates motor synchronicity. These two musical features are highly effective in promoting simultaneous singing and dancing.... These special features fit with the important criterion, discussed by Buss and collaborators, that for a system to qualify as 'adaptive' it must offer effective solutions to a problem. The system must have a 'special design.' The bonding problem in the case of music is to override 'selfish genes' for the benefit of the group" (Peretz 2001, 115).
43. The following research findings are drawn from Juslin and Sloboda (2001), Jensen (2000), and Jourdain (2002).
44. Rauscher et al. (1993).
45. Juslin and Sloboda (2001, 5).
46. Gabrielsson (2001, 433, 437). Gabrielsson connects his work with that of Abraham Maslow on "peak experiences" and M. Csikszentmihalyi on "flow."
47. Crick (1994).
48. This line of thinking reaches a point very close to that of Claude Levi-Strauss in *The Raw and the Cooked*, where he uses musical structures as hermeneutic guides in the analysis of myth: "If, of all human products, music strikes me as being the best suited to throw light on the essence of mythology, the reason is to be found in its perfection.... [T]he musical creator is a being comparable to the gods, and music itself the supreme mystery of the science of man, a mystery that all the various disciplines come up against and which hold the key to their progress" (Levi-Strauss 1969, 18, 27).
49. Qureshi (1997, 279).
50. Homans (1989, 307).
51. Eberwein (1984).
52. Homans (1989, 311). He acknowledges that people are increasingly engaged with a multiplicity of "screens," so that "today one cannot simply refer to the film screen; one must also include the television screen, the pictorial magazine screen, the photographic screen, and so forth" (310).
53. The psychological impact of films, it should be noted, is not simply a matter of visual imagery — music plays a major role in the emotional impact of cinema, as shown by Annabel J. Cohen (Cohen 2001).
54. Hobson (1988, 12, 65–68).
55. Wulff (1997, 414).

56. Domhoff (2003, 144–147) and Wulff (1997, 461–471).
57. Crews and Bulkeley (2001, 367).
58. Domhoff (2003, 144).
59. Jung (1974a, 101).
60. Crews and Bulkeley (2001, 367).
61. See, for example, O'Flaherty (1988, 33–37, 163–164), Doniger (1998, 143), and especially Doniger (1999b, 191): "How unimaginative can it get? Jungian, that's how."
62. Jung (1989, 22–23); emphasis in original.
63. Noll (1997, 275).
64. Jung (1974b, 40).
65. Homans (1989, 263, 276).
66. Wilson calls this "reductive synthesis," moving from the culturally complex to the biologically simple. He admits that this is much easier than "prospective synthesis," starting with the biological and accurately predicting the cultural. This is why it is so difficult to predict accurately future events in cultural life.
67. Wilson (1998, 78). See also Darwin (1998, 73–74), where his observation of the primate predisposition to fear snakes is offered as the main piece of evidence in support of his claim that "all animals feel *Wonder*, and many exhibit *Curiosity*."
68. Wilson (1998, 80).
69. This reformulation avoids the charge of circularity by emphasizing the extraordinarily heightened sensitivity that people feel toward certain recurrent situations of human life, *more* than can be accounted for by the ordinary learning that comes with either individual experience or group socialization.
70. Jung (1980, 50).
71. Meier (2001, 64).
72. Meier (2001, 69). It should be noted that the Pauli–Jung letters are permeated with transference and counter-transference energies, with the younger Pauli writing long and mostly adoring missives to his analyst and the older Jung writing shorter, cooler replies to his famous patient.
73. Kahn and Hobson (1993), Kahn et al. (2000), Freeman (2000).
74. Cobain (2002, 18).
75. Cross (2001, 41).
76. Cobain (2002, 56–57).
77. Cross (2001, 60).
78. Cross (2001, 63). Crisafulli's earlier book says even less about the depth or significance of Cobain's piety, claiming that he stayed only a month with the Reeds (Crisafulli 1996, 43).
79. Cross (2001, 60).
80. Cobain (2002, 111).
81. Cobain (2002, 2).
82. Cross (2001, 114).
83. Cross (2001, 90, 95). (The original text has "conscience" for "conscious" and "merely" for "nearly.")
84. Cross (2001, 144).
85. Cobain (2002, 164, 262) ("has consciously" for "have consciously").
86. Cross (2001, 271).
87. Cross (2001, 318).
88. Sandford (1996, 336–337); the letter writer's name was Katie Hess.
89. *The Rush Limbaugh Show*, April 11, 1994.
90. Sandford (1996, 337).
91. Rooney (1994) and Sandford (1996, 337).

Chapter 4

1. *Sura* 96.1 (*The Koran* 1974).
2. Commentators on Islam continue to debate the question of whether Muhammad experienced one or the other or both of these visionary events.
3. *Sura* 53:19–26 (*The Koran* 1974).
4. Kandel et al. (2000, 382); emphasis in original.
5. Kandel et al. (2000, 383); emphasis in original.
6. Kandel et al. (2000, 396).
7. Kandel et al. (2000, 396).

8. Kandel et al. (2000, 396).
9. Kandel et al. (2000, 398).
10. Kandel et al. (2000, 400); emphasis in original.
11. Kandel et al. (2000, 505); emphasis in original.
12. Quoted in Kandel et al. (2000, 400).
13. Kandel et al. (2000, 400, 402).
14. The findings of this research are usefully summarized by Jonathon Shear and David Wulff (Shear 2001, Wulff 1997).
15. Wulff (1997, 183).
16. Benson and Klipper (1975) and Benson and Stark (1996); Shear offers experimental evidence that questions whether the relaxation response has physiological effects equal to those produced by TM.
17. Benson and Klipper (1975, 127).
18. The most enthusiastic recent summary of research supporting intercessory prayer is Dossey (1993).
19. Hart (1999, 39).
20. Included here, in addition to Ashbrook and Albright's work, is Russell et al. (1999), Hogue (2003), and Watts (2002).
21. See MacLean (1990). For a critique of MacLean's tripartite model, particularly its overly generalized portrait of the limbic system as the source of human emotions, see LeDoux (1996).
22. Ashbrook and Albright (1997, 148).
23. Quoted in Begley (2001); emphasis added.
24. Austin (1998, 18).
25. Austin (1998, xix); emphasis in original.
26. Gyatso (2003).
27. Davidson et al. (2003).
28. Gyatso (2003).
29. Gyatso (2003).
30. Newberg et al. (2001, 6).
31. Newberg et al. (2001, 147).
32. See Wulff (1997) and Beit-Hallahmi and Argyle (1997).
33. Domhoff (2003) argues that the lab effect is not as great as I am suggesting, but his claims take insufficient account of the phenomena of unusually impactful, highly memorable dreams, which appear to be far less frequent in lab dreams than in home dreams.
34. Newberg et al. (2001, 31).
35. Newberg et al. (2001, 62).
36. Newberg et al. (2001, 101–102).
37. Newberg et al. (2001, 122–123).
38. Austin is somewhat more cautious on this point. He distinguishes his view from that which sees all mystical experience as essentially the same. For him, "all mystical experience falls into a relatively small class of *subtypes*. These cut across all cultural boundaries. Whereas the several subtypes are not culture-bound, the language used to describe them *is* culture bound. I hold this interpretation" (Austin 1998, 22; emphasis in original). Although I applaud his emphasis on the multiplicity of religious experience, Austin's "perennial psychophysiology" still fails to address the essentialist questions I want to raise with Newberg and d'Aquili.
39. James (1958, 292–293); emphasis in original.
40. Katz (1978, 26); emphasis in original.
41. Katz (1978, 57, 63); emphasis in original.
42. Pace-Schott, however, points out that the Yoga Nidra meditation also involves a deactivation of the anterior cingulate and other brain regions related to emotional arousal; these regions are selectively activated in dreaming (Pace-Schott 2002, 342).
43. Lazar et al. (2000, 1582). I am adding the qualification about "this meditational practice." Lazar, following the perennialism of Benson, speaks of "meditation" as a generic, timeless practice.
44. James (1958, 321).
45. James (1958, 135); emphasis in original.
46. Quoted in John McDermott's Introduction to *The Writings of William James* (James 1977, xxviii; emphasis in original). McDermott notes that the phrase "be built in" in the last sentence is doubtful in the original manuscript.

47. Quoted in Barnard (1997, 19).
48. Quoted in Barnard (1997, 20).
49. See Taves (1999), Carrette (2002), Barnard (1997), Wulff (1997).
50. James, however, does mention one of his dreams as having a special impact on him (James 1978, 161); see also Bulkeley (1999, 1–6).
51. This prejudice is plainly stated by Wilson: "Nothing else ever worked [to know the world], no exercise from myth, revelation, art, trance, or any other conceivable means; and notwithstanding the emotional satisfaction it gives, mysticism, the strongest prescientific probe into the unknown, has yielded zero" (Wilson 1998, 46). Likewise from Richard Dawkins: "If we come back in a thousand years, we would have our minds blown away by what science has discovered in the meantime, whereas religion or spirituality or mysticism will have discovered nothing more. They never have discovered anything" (quoted in *The New York Times*, November 9, 2003, Section 4, page 2; from an interview in *Seed Magazine*).
52. Metcalf (2002); Kripal (1995), Dixon (1999), Barnard (1997), Hollywood (2002), Parsons (1999).
53. Quoted in Parsons (1999, 160–161).
54. Parsons (1999, 161). At the end of this sentence, Parsons adds a lengthy discursive footnote in which he (justly) critiques other aspects of Deikman's theory and endorses Barnard's retrieval of the pluralist approach of William James. In a way, the present work is a book-length reply to that footnote.
55. Parons (1999, 122).
56. James (1958, 386–387); emphasis in original.
57. James (1958, 194–195); emphasis in original.
58. It should be noted, however, that some contemporary scholars are calling many of the traditional biographical reports into question; see Brown (2003).
59. *Sura* 3:190 (Ali 2002).
60. *Sura* 2:117 (Ali 2002).
61. *Sura* 45:12–13 (Ali 2002).
62. *Sura* 12:53 (Ali 2002).
63. *Suras* 2.152, 18.24 (Ali 2002).
64. Fazlur Rahman is a contemporary voice of criticism against Sufism. He calls its later development "a veritable spiritual jugglery through auto-hypnotic transports and visions, just as at the level of doctrine it was being transmuted into a half-delirious theosophy.... [With the rise of Sufism] Islam was at the mercy of spiritual delinquents" (Rahman 1979, 153).
65. *Sura* 17.1 (Ali 2002).
66. See Young (1999a), Irwin (1994, 1996), Jedrej and Shaw (1992), Kelsey (1991), Bulkeley (1995, 2000).
67. Solms (1997, 211).

Conclusion

1. Hunter (1992, 18).
2. Doniger (1998, 104).
3. Disturbing testimony to this effect comes from Anthony Swofford's memoir *Jarhead: A Marine's Chronicle of the Gulf War and Other Battles* (Swofford 2003, 5–6): "After hearing the news of imminent war in the Middle East [in August of 1990, under command of the first President Bush], we march in a platoon formation to the base barber and get fresh high-and-tight haircuts. And no wonder we call ourselves jarheads — our heads look just like jars. Then we send a few guys downtown to rent all of the war movies they can get their hands on. They also buy a hell of a lot of beer. For three days we sit in our rec room and drink all of the beer and watch all of those damn movies, and we yell *Semper fi* and we head-butt and beat the crap out of each other and we get off on the various visions of carnage and violence and deceit, the raping and killing and pillaging. We concentrate on the Vietnam films because it's the most recent war, and the successes and failures of that war helped write our training manuals. We rewind and review famous scenes, such as Robert Duvall and his helicopter gunships during *Apocalypse Now*.... Vietnam war films are all pro-war, no matter what the supposed message, what Kubrick or Coppola or Stone intended."
4. Pinker (1997, 510, 511).

5. Deut. 21:10–13; cf. also Deut. 20 for more on holy war ideology. Note that the allotted period of time (one month) provides not only a humane space for mourning but also an opportunity for the captive woman to menstruate and thus prove she is not surreptitiously carrying the child of a slain enemy. The passage goes on to limit the warrior's treatment of the woman: "Then, if you have no delight in her, you shall let her go where she will; but you shall not sell her for money, you shall not treat her as a slave, since you have humiliated her" (Deut. 21:14–15).
6. Pinker (1997, 513): "In numerous experiments by Henri Taijfel and other social psychologists, people are divided into two groups, actually at random but ostensibly by some trivial criterion such as whether they underestimate or overestimate the number of dots on a screen or whether they prefer the paintings of Klee or Kandinsky. The people in each group instantly dislike and think worse of the people in the other group, and act to withhold rewards from them even if doing so is costly to their own group."
7. Pinker (1997, 520).
8. Changeux and Ricoeur (2000, 220).
9. Browning (1987).
10. Kant (1956, 166).
11. Gen. 6:4.
12. Gen. 8:21.
13. Gen. 8:21–22.
14. Gen. 9:16. I do not agree with Fisher (1998, 38–39) in his intemperate denunciation of religion in connection with the Genesis story of the flood, even though I am sympathetic to his broader point that premature explanations from religion, science, or any other source can "preempt the possibility of wonder."
15. Plato (1961b, 860). Soon after, Socrates raises the question with Theaetetus of how we can tell the difference whether we are awake or dreaming (862–863).
16. Quoted in Fisher (1998, 44).
17. Descartes' explanation does have this affinity with the Genesis story, that the rainbow displays the fundamentally mathematical structure of world. The rainbow thus serves as a different kind of divine sign, and Descartes' invitation to people to try making rainbows themselves is in effect an invitation to wield the powers of God — a daring thing to do in the era of the Catholic Church's persecution of Bruno, Galileo, and other scientific freethinkers.
18. Quoted in Fisher (1998, 56).
19. Richard Dawkins has given contemporary voice to this sentiment (Dawkins 2000, 27): "It is my thesis that the spirit of wonder which led Blake to Christian mysticism, Keats to Arcadian myth, and Yeats to Fenians and fairies is the very same spirit that moves great scientists, a spirit which, if fed back to poets in scientific guise, might inspire still greater poetry." Although I agree with Dawkins here, the overall tone of his work is (like Steven Pinker's) so bitterly combative that he can be of only limited help in creating new interdisciplinary frameworks for future knowledge.
20. Likewise, I follow James Jones in rejecting hasty efforts to unite religion and science and affirming the need for multiple models of consciousness: "[T]he drive for a unitary world view obscures the inherent incompleteness in all human theorizing, especially concerning as paradoxical a phenomenon as self-awareness" (Jones 1992, 201).

Bibliography

Abramson, Paul R., and Steven D. Pinkerton. 2002. *With pleasure: Thoughts on the nature of human sexuality*. Revised ed. New York: Oxford University Press.

Ali, Abdullah Yusuf. 2002. *The Qur'an Translation*. Elmhurst: Tahrike Tarsile Qur'an.

Andrae, Tor. 1960. *Mohammed: The man and his faith*. Translated by T. Menzel. New York: Harper Torchbooks. Original edition, 1936.

Armstrong, Karen. 1992. *Muhammad: A biography of the prophet*. New York: HarperCollins.

Aserinsky, Eugene, and Nathaniel Kleitman. 1953. Regularly occurring periods of eye motility and concomitant phenomena during sleep. *Science* 118:273–274.

———. 1955. Two types of ocular motility occurring in sleep. *Journal of Applied Physiology* 8:1–10.

Ashbrook, James B., and Carol Rausch Albright. 1997. *The humanizing brain: Where religion and neuroscience meet*. Cleveland: The Pilgrim Press.

Austin, James H. 1998. *Zen and the brain*. Cambridge, MA: MIT Press.

Ayto, John. 1990. *Dictionary of word origins*. New York: Arcade.

Ball, Alan. 1999. *American Beauty: The shooting script*. New York: Newmarket Press.

Barkow, J.H., L. Cosmides, and J. Tooby, eds. 1992. *The adapted mind: Evolutionary psychology and the evolution of culture*. New York: Oxford University Press.

Barnard, G. William. 1997. *Exploring unseen worlds: William James and the philosophy of mysticism*. Albany: State University of New York Press.

Beck, Guy L. 1993. *Sonic theology: Hinduism and sacred sound*. Columbia: University of South Carolina Press.

Becker, Judith. 1997. Tantrism, Rasa, and Javanese gamelan music. In *Enchanting powers: Music in the world's religions*, ed. L.E. Sullivan. Cambridge, MA: Harvard University Press.

———. 2001. Anthropological perspectives on music and emotion. In *Music and emotion: Theory and research*, ed. J.A. Sloboda. Oxford: Oxford University Press.

Begley, Sharon. 2001. Religion and the brain: In the new field of "neurotheology," scientists seek the biological basis of spirituality. Is God all in our heads? *Newsweek*, May 7, p. 50.

Beit-Hallahmi, Benjamin, and Michael Argyle. 1997. *The psychology of religious behavior, belief, and experience*. London: Routledge.

Benedict, Ruth. 1922. The vision in plains culture. *American Anthropologist* 24 (1):1–23.

Benson, Herbert, and Miriam Klipper. 1975. *The relaxation response*. New York: Harpertorch.

———, and Marg Stark. 1996. *Timeless healing: The power and biology of belief*. New York: Fireside.

Boyer, Pascal. 2001. *Religion explained: The evolutionary origins of religious thought*. New York: Basic Books.

Brown, Daniel W. 2003. *A New Introduction to Islam*. Oxford: Blackwell.

Browning, Don S. 1987. *Religious thought and the modern psychologies: A critical conversation in the theology of culture*. Philadelphia: Fortress Press.

Bulkeley, Kelly. 1995. *Spiritual dreaming: A cross-cultural and historical journey*. Mahwah: Paulist Press.

———. 1999. *Visions of the night: Dreams, religion, and psychology*. Albany: State University of New York Press.

———. 2000. *Transforming dreams: Learning spiritual lessons from the dreams you never forget*. New York: John Wiley & Sons.

———, ed. 2001. *Dreams: A reader on the religious, cultural, and psychological dimensions of dreaming*. New York: Palgrave.
Carrette, Jeremy R. 2002. The return to James: Psychology, religion and the amnesia of neuroscience. In *The varieties of religious experience: Centenary edition*, ed. J.R. Carrette. New York: Routledge.
Cartwright, Rosalind. 1991. Dreams that work: The relation of dream incorporation to adaptation to stressful events. *Dreaming* 1(1):3–10.
Changeux, Jean-Pierre, and Paul Ricoeur. 2000. *What makes us think? A neuroscientist and a philosopher argue about ethics, human nature, and the brain*. Translated by M.B. DeBoise. Princeton: Princeton University Press.
Cobain, Kurt. 2002. *Journals*. New York: Riverhead Books.
Cohen, Annabel J. 2001. Music as a source of emotion in film. In *Music and Emotion: Theory and Research*, eds. P.N. Juslin and J.A. Sloboda. Oxford: Oxford University Press.
Cole, John R. 1992. *The olympian dreams and youthful rebellion of Rene Descartes*. Urbana: University of Illinois Press.
Crapanzano, Victor. 1975. Saints, jnun, and demons: An essay in Moroccan ethnopsychology. *Psychiatry* 38:145–159.
———, ed. 1998. *Unauthorized Freud: Doubters confront a legend*. New York: Penguin Books.
Crews, Frederick. 1995. *The memory wars: Freud's legacy in dispute*. New York: New York Review of Books.
———, and Kelly Bulkeley. 2001. Dialogue with a skeptic. In *Dreams: A reader on the religious, cultural, and psychological dimensions of dreaming*, ed. K. Bulkeley. New York: Palgrave.
Crick, Francis. 1994. *The astonishing hypothesis: The scientific search for the soul*. New York: Touchstone.
Crisafulli, Chuck. 1996. *Teen spirit: The stories behind every Nirvana song*. New York: Fireside.
Cross, Charles R. 2001. *Heavier than heaven: A biography of Kurt Cobain*. New York: Hyperion.
Damasio, Antonio. 1994. *Descartes' error: Emotion, reason, and the human brain*. New York: Quill.
———. 1999. *The feeling of what happens: Body and emotion in the making of consciousness*. San Diego: Harcourt.
Darwin, Charles. 1998. *The descent of man*. New York: Prometheus. Original edition, 1871.
Davidson, Richard J. et al. 2003. Alterations in brain and immune function produced by mindfulness meditation. *Psychosomatic Medicine* 65:564–570.
Dawkins, Richard. 2000. *Unweaving the rainbow: Science, delusion, and the appetite for wonder*. New York: Houghton Mifflin.
Dement, William. 1972. *Some must watch while some must sleep: Exploring the world of sleep*. New York: W.W. Norton.
Descartes, Rene. 1960. *Discourse on method and meditations*. Translated by L.J. Lafleur. Indianapolis: Bobbs-Merrill.
———. 1989. *The passions of the soul*. Translated by S. Voss. Indianapolis: Hackett Publishing. Original edition, 1649.
Desmond, Adrian, and James Moore. 1991. *Darwin: The life of a tormented evolutionist*. New York: W.W. Norton.
Dixon, Sandra Lee. 1999. *Augustine: The scattered and gathered self*. St. Louis: Chalice Press.
Domhoff, G. William. 2001. *A new neurocognitive theory of dreams*. Dreaming 11 (1):13–33.
———. 2003. *The scientific study of dreams: Neural networks, cognitive development, and content analysis*. Washington, D.C.: American Psychological Association.
Doniger, Wendy. 1998. *The implied spider: Politics and theology in myth*. New York: Columbia University Press.
———. 1999a. *The bed trick: Tales of sex and masquerade*. Chicago: University of Chicago Press.
———. 1999b. *Splitting the difference: Gender and myth in ancient Greece and India*. Chicago: University of Chicago Press.
Dossey, Larry. 1993. *Healing Words*. New York: Harper.
Durkheim, Emile. 1965. *The elementary forms of the religious life*. Translated by J.W. Swain. New York: The Free Press. Original edition, 1915.
Eberwein, R. 1984. *Film and the dream screen: A sleep and a forgetting*. Princeton: Princeton University Press.
Emmons, Robert A. 2002. *Awe and wonder as the basis for gratitude in G.K. Chesterton*. Paper read at American Psychological Association, Chicago.
Fernald, Anne. 1992. Human maternal vocalizations to infants as biologically relevant signals: An evolutionary perspective. In *The adapted mind: Evolutionary psychology and the generation of culture*, eds. J.H. Barkow, L. Cosmides, and J. Tooby. Oxford: Oxford University Press.

Fisher, Philip. 1998. *Wonder, the rainbow, and the aesthetics of rare experiences*. Cambridge, MA: Harvard University Press.
Freeman, Walter J. 2000. *How brains make up their minds*. New York: Columbia University Press.
Freud, Sigmund. 1963. Remarks upon the theory and practice of dream-interpretation. In *Therapy and technique*, ed. P. Rieff. New York: Collier Books. Original edition, 1923.
———. 1965. *The interpretation of dreams*. Translated by J. Strachey. New York: Avon Books.
———. 1966. *Introductory lectures on psychoanalysis*. Translated by J. Strachey. New York: Liveright. Original edition, 1916/1917.
———. 1974. Some dreams of Descartes': A letter to Maxime Leroy. In *The standard edition of the complete psychological works of Sigmund Freud*, ed. J. Strachey. London: The Hogarth Press. Original edition, 1929.
———. 2000. *Three essays on the theory of sexuality*. Translated by James Strachey. New York: Basic Books, pp. 86–87.
Gabrielsson, Alf. 2001. Emotions in strong experiences with music. In *Music and emotion: Theory and research*, ed. J.A. Sloboda. Oxford: Oxford University Press.
Gleick, James. 2003. *Isaac Newton*. New York: Pantheon.
Greeley, Andrew M. 1975. *The sociology of the paranormal*. London: Sage.
Green, Tamara M. 1999. Muses. In *Encyclopedia of women and world religion*, ed. S. Young. New York: Macmillan.
Greenberg, Ramone, R. Pillard, and C. Pearlman. 1972. The effect of dream (REM) deprivation on adaptation to stress. *Psychosomatic Medicine* 34:257–262.
Gyatso, Tenzin. 2003. The monk in the lab. *The New York Times*, April 26, p. 29.
Hallowell, Irving. 1966. The role of dreams in Ojibwa culture. In *The dream and human societies*, eds. G.E. Von Grunebaum and R. Callois. Berkeley: University of California Press.
Hamann, Stephan, Rebecca A. Herman, Carla L. Nolan, and Kim Wallen. 2004. Men and women differ in amygdala response to visual sexual stimuli. *Nature Neuroscience* 7(4):411–416.
Harris, Gardiner. 2004. Pfizer gives up testing Viagra on women. *The New York Times*, February 28, 1–2.
Hart, Carol. 1999. The mysterious placebo effect. *Modern Drug Discovery* 2(4):30–40.
Hartmann, Ernest. 1995. Making connections in a safe place: Is dreaming psychotherapy? *Dreaming* 5(4):213–228.
———. 1998. *Dreams and nightmares: The new theory on the origin and meaning of dreams*. New York: Plenum.
Hobson, J. Allan. 1988. *The dreaming brain*. New York: Basic Books.
———. 1999. *Dreaming as delirium: How the brain goes out of its mind*. Cambridge, MA: MIT Press.
Hogue, David. 2003. *Remembering the future, imagining the past: Story, ritual, and the human brain*. Cleveland: Pilgrim Press.
Hollywood, Amy. 2002. *Sensible ecstasy: Mysticism, sexual difference, and the demands of history*. Chicago: University of Chicago Press.
Holstege, Gert, Janniko R. Georgiadis, Anne M.J. Paans, Linda C. Meiners, Ferdinand H.C.E. van der Graaf, and A.A.T. Simone Reinders. 2003. Brain activation during human male ejaculation. *The Journal of Neuroscience* 23(27):9185–9193.
Homans, Peter. 1989. *The ability to mourn: Disillusionment and the social origins of psychoanalysis*. Chicago: University of Chicago Press.
Hunt, Harry. 1989. *The multiplicity of dreams: Memory, imagination, and consciousness*. New Haven: Yale University Press.
Hunter, Allan. 1992. *Movie classics*. Edinburgh: Chambers.
Irwin, Lee. 1994. *The dream seekers: Native American visionary traditions of the Great Plains*. Norman: University of Oklahoma Press.
———. 1996. *Visionary worlds: The making and unmaking of reality*. Albany: State University of New York Press.
James, William. 1958. *The varieties of religious experience*. New York: Mentor.
———. 1977. *The writings of William James*. Chicago: University of Chicago Press.
———. 1978. *Essays in philosophy*. Cambridge, MA: Harvard University Press.
Jedrej, M.C., and Rosalind Shaw, eds. 1992. *Dreaming, religion, and society in Africa*. Leiden: Brill.
Jensen, Eric. 2000. *Music with the brain in mind*. San Diego: The Brain Store.
Jones, James. 1992. Can neuroscience provide a complete account of human nature? A reply to Roger Sperry. *Zygon* 27(2):187–202.
Jourdain, Robert. 2002. *Music, the brain, and ecstasy: How music captures our imagination*. New York: Quill.

Jung, C.G. 1974a. General aspects of dream psychology. In *Dreams*. Princeton: Princeton University Press. Original edition, 1934.

———. 1974b. The practical use of dream analysis. In *Dreams*. Princeton: Princeton University Press. Original edition, 1934.

———. 1980. *The archetypes and the collective unconscious*. Translated by R.F.C. Hull. Princeton: Princeton University Press.

———. 1989. Wotan. In *C.G. Jung: Essays on current events*, ed. A. Samuels. Princeton: Princeton University Press.

Juslin, Patrik N., and John A. Sloboda, eds. 2001. *Music and emotion: Theory and research*. Oxford: Oxford University Press.

Kahn, David, and J. Allan Hobson. 1993. Self-organization theory and dreaming. *Dreaming* 3(3):151–178.

———, Stanley Krippner, and Allen Combs. 2000. Dreaming and the self-organizing brain. *Journal of Consciousness Studies* 7(7):4–11.

Kandel, Eric R., James H. Schwartz, and Thomas M. Jessel, eds. 2000. *Principles of neural science*. 4th ed. New York: McGraw-Hill.

Kant, Immanuel. 1956. *Critique of practical reason*. Translated by L.W. Beck. Indianapolis: Bobbs-Merrill. Original edition, 1788.

Katz, Steven T., ed. 1978. *Mysticism and philosophical analysis*. Oxford: Oxford University Press.

Keen, Sam. 1969. *Apology for wonder*. New York: Harper & Row.

Kelsey, Morton. 1991. *God, dreams, and revelation: A Christian interpretation of dreams*. Minneapolis: Augsburg Publishing.

Koran, The. 1974. Translated by N.J. Dawood. London: Penguin Books.

Kripal, Jeffrey J. 1995. *Kali's child: The mystical and the erotic in the life and teachings of Ramakrishna*. Chicago: University of Chicago Press.

LaBerge, Stephen. 1985. *Lucid dreaming: The power of being awake and aware in your dreams*. Los Angeles: Jeremy Tarcher.

Lavine, Amy. 1999. Sexuality. In *The encyclopedia of women and religion*, ed. S. Young. New York: Macmillan.

Lazar, Sara W., George Bush, Randy L. Gollub, Gregory L. Fricchione, Gurucharan Khalsa, and Herbert Benson. 2000. Functional brain mapping of the relaxation response and meditation. *NeuroReport* 11(7):1581–1585.

LeDoux, Joseph. 1996. *The emotional brain: The mysterious underpinnings of emotional life*. New York: Touchstone.

Levi-Strauss, Claude. 1969. *The raw and the cooked: Introduction to a science of mythology*. Vol. 1. Translated by J.A.D. Weightman. New York: Harper & Row.

MacLean, Paul D. 1990. *The triune brain in evolution: Role in paleocerebral functions*. New York: Plenum.

Mallanga, Vatsyayana. 2002. *Kamasutra*. Translated by S. Kakar. Oxford: Oxford University Press.

Meier, C.A., ed. 2001. *Atom and archetype: The Pauli–Jung letters, 1932–1958*. Princeton: Princeton University Press.

Metcalf, Franz. 2002. *What would Buddha do?: 101 answers to life's daily dilemmas*: Berkeley, CA: Ulysses Press.

Michael, Robert T., John H. Gagnon, Edward O. Laumann, and Gina Kolata. 1994. *Sex in America: A definitive survey*. New York: Warner Books.

Mulvey, Laura. 1989. *Visual and other pleasures (theories of representation and difference)*. Indianapolis: Indiana University Press.

Nasr, Seyyed Hossein. 1997. Islam and music: The legal and the spiritual dimensions. In *Enchanting powers: Music in the world's religions*, ed. L.E. Sullivan. Cambridge, MA: Harvard University Press.

Newberg, Andrew, Eugene D'Aquili, and Vince Rause. 2001. *Why God won't go away: Brain science and the biology of belief*. New York: Ballantine.

Noll, Richard. 1997. *The Aryan Christ: The secret life of Carl Jung*. New York: Random House.

O'Flaherty, Wendy Doniger. 1975. *Hindu myths*. New York: Penguin Books.

———. 1988. *Other people's myths*. New York: Macmillan.

Pace-Schott, Edward F. 2002. Postscript: Recent findings on the neurobiology of sleep and dreaming. In *Sleep and Dreaming*, ed. E.F. Pace-Schott. Oxford: Oxford University Press.

Parsons, William B. 1999. *The enigma of the oceanic feeling: Revisioning the psychoanalytic theory of mysticism*. Oxford: Oxford University Press.

Patton, Kimberley. 2004. "A great and strange correction": Intentionality, locality, and epiphany in the category of dream incubation. *History of Religions* 44(3):194–223.

Peretz, Isabelle. 2001. Listen to the brain: A biological perspective on musical emotions. In *Music and emotion: Theory and research*, eds. P.N. Juslin and J.A. Sloboda. Oxford: Oxford University Press.

Pinker, Steven. 1997. *How the mind works*. New York: W. W. Norton.

Plato. 1961a. The Republic. In *Plato: Collected dialogues*, eds. E. Hamilton and H. Cairns. Princeton: Princeton University Press.

———. 1961b. Theaetetus. In *Plato: Collected dialogues*, eds. E. Hamilton and H. Cairns. Princeton: Princeton University Press.

Pyysiainen, Ilkka. 2001. *How religion works: Towards a new cognitive science of religion*. Leiden: Brill.

Qureshi, Regula Burckhardt. 1997. Sounding the word: Music in the life of Islam. In *Enchanting powers: Music in the world's religions*, ed. L.E. Sullivan. Cambridge, MA: Harvard University Press.

Radin, Paul. 1936. Ojibwa and Ottawa puberty dreams. In *Essays in anthropology presented to A.L. Kroeber*. Berkeley: University of California Press.

Rahman, Fazlur. 1979. *Islam*. 2nd ed. Chicago: University of Chicago Press.

Ramachandran, V.S., and Sandra Blakeslee. 1998. *Phantoms in the brain: Probing the mysteries of the mind*. New York: Quill.

Rauscher, F., G. Shaw, and K. Ky. 1993. Music and spatial task performance. *Nature* (365):611.

Reinisch, June M., and Ruth Beasley. 1990. *The Kinsey Institute new report on sex*. New York: St. Martins Press.

Revonsuo, Antti. 2000. The reinterpretation of dreams: An evolutionary hypothesis of the function of dreaming. *Behavioral and Brain Sciences* 23(6):877–901.

Rooney, Andy. 1994. *A Few Minutes with Andy Rooney* [television broadcast], April 17.

Runzo, Joseph, and Nancy M. Martin, eds. 2000. *Love, sex and gender in the world religions*. Oxford: Oneworld.

Russell, Robert John, Nancey Murphy, Theo C. Meyering, and Michael A. Arbib, eds. 1999. *Neuroscience and the person: Scientific perspectives on divine action*. Notre Dame: The Vatican Observatory and the Center for Theology and the Natural Sciences.

Sandford, Christopher. 1996. *Kurt Cobain*. New York: Carroll & Graff.

Scarre, Chris. 1989. Painting by resonance. *Nature* 338:382.

Schwartz, Jeffrey M., and Sharon Begley. 2002. *The mind and the brain: Neuroplasticity and the power of mental force*. New York: Regan Books.

Shear, Jonathon. 2001. Experimental studies of meditation. In *Religion and psychology: Mapping the terrain*, ed. W.B. Parsons. London: Routledge.

Smith, Carlyle. 1993. REM sleep and learning: Some recent findings. In *The functions of dreaming*, eds. A. Moffitt, M. Kramer, and R. Hoffmann. Albany: State University of New York Press.

Solms, Mark. 1997. *The neuropsychology of dreams: A clinico-anatomical study*. Mahway, NJ: Lawrence Erlbaum.

———. 2000. Dreaming and REM sleep are controlled by different brain mechanisms. *Behavioral and Brain Sciences* 23(6):843–850.

Springer, Sally P., and Georg Deutsch. 1998. *Left brain, right brain: Perspectives from cognitive neuroscience*. 5th ed. New York: W.H. Freeman.

Sullivan, Lawrence E. 1997. Enchanting powers: An introduction. In *Enchanting powers: Music in the world's religions*, ed. L.E. Sullivan. Cambridge, MA: Harvard University Press.

Swofford, Anthony. 2003. *Jarhead: A Marine's chronicle of the Gulf War and other battles*. New York: Scribner.

Taves, Ann. 1999. *Fits, trances, and visions: Experiencing religion and explaining experience from Wesley to James*. Princeton: Princeton University Press.

Taylor, Jeremy. 1992. *Where people fly and water runs uphill*. New York: Warner Books.

Tedlock, Barbara, ed. 1987. *Dreaming: Anthropological and psychological interpretations*. New York: Cambridge University Press.

Thompson, Richard F. 2000. *The brain: A neuroscience primer*. New York: Worth.

Trivers, Robert. 1985. *Social evolution*. Reading: Benjamin/Cummings.

Van de Castle, Robert. 1994. *Our dreaming mind*. New York: Ballantine Books.

Von Franz, Marie Louis. 1991. *Dreams*. Boston: Shambhala.

Von Grunebaum, G.E., and Roger Callois, eds. 1966. *The dream and human societies*. Berkeley: University of California Press.

Wade, Trevor M. 1999. Chastity. In *Encyclopedia of women and religion*, ed. S. Young. New York: Macmillan.

Watts, Fraser. 2002. *Theology and psychology*. Burlington: Ashgate.

Wierzbicki, James. 1989. Saint Cecilia. *St. Louis Post-Dispatch*, November 19, p. 23.

Wilson, Edward O. 1998. *Consilience: The unity of knowledge.* New York: Alfred A. Knopf.
———. 2000. *Sociobiology: The new synthesis.* 25th anniversary ed. Cambridge, MA: Belknap Press.
Wright, Robert. 1994. *The moral animal: Evolutionary psychology and everyday life.* New York: Vintage Books.
Wulff, David. 1997. *Psychology of religion: Classic and contemporary.* New York: John Wiley & Sons.
Young, Serinity. 1999a. *Dreaming in the lotus: Buddhist dream narrative, imagery, and practice.* Boston: Wisdom Publications.
———. 1999b. Tantra. In *Encyclopedia of women and religion*, ed. S. Young. New York: Macmillan.
———. 2001. Buddhist dream experience: The role of interpretation, ritual, and gender. In *Dreams: A reader on the religious, cultural, and psychological dimensions of dreaming*, ed. K. Bulkeley. New York: Palgrave.
Zuk, Marlene. 2002. *Sexual selections: What we can and can't learn about sex from animals.* Berkeley: University of California Press.

Index

C

D

E

F

G

H

I

J

K

L

M

T

U

V

W

Y

Z